PAYING FOR INEQUALITY

D1484159

IPPR/Rivers Oram Press

Already published

The Welfare of Citizens
Developing new social rights
Edited by Anna Coote

About Time
The revolution in work and family life
Patricia Hewitt

Strangers & Citizens
A positive approach to migrants and refugees
Edited by Sarah Spencer

PAYING FOR INEQUALITY

The Economic Cost of Social Injustice

Edited by
Andrew Glyn and David Miliband

IPPR/Rivers Oram Press
London

First published in 1994 by
Rivers Oram Press
144 Hemingford Road, London N1 1DE

Published in the USA by
Paul and Company
Post Office Box 442, Concord, MA 01742

Set in 10/12 Sabon by Except*detail* Ltd, Southport
and printed in Great Britain
by T.J. Press (Padstow) Ltd, Padstow, Cornwall

Designed by Lesley Stewart

British Library Cataloguing in Publication Data
A catalogue record for this book is available from the British
Library

ISBN 1-85489-058-1
ISBN 1-85489-059-X pbk

CONTENTS

v

Contents

TABLES AND FIGURES

Tables

Figures

ACKNOWLEDGEMENTS

This book is the product of a project instigated soon after the 1992 General Election, and organised under the auspices of the Institute for Public Policy Research. John Eatwell first suggested to Andrew Glyn that the relationship between equality and efficiency would provide the ideal focus for an IPPR project. James Cornford and Patricia Hewitt, IPPR's Director and Deputy Director respectively, gave the project intellectual, organisational and financial support. Lois and James Sparling were patient and expert in the preparation of the graphs, tables and text for publication. Finally, the editors are grateful for the patience and enthusiasm of the contributors, to whom credit for the book's strengths is due.

LIST OF CONTRIBUTORS

The editors

Andrew Glyn is Fellow and Tutor in Economics at Corpus Christi College, Oxford.

David Miliband is Research Fellow at the Institute for Public Policy Research and Secretary of the Commission on Social Justice.

The contributors

Dan Corry is Senior Economist at IPPR, and editor of *New Economy*.

Tony Edwards is Professor of Education and Dean of the Education Faculty at the University of Newcastle Upon Tyne. Geoff Whitty is Karl Mannheim Professor of the Sociology of Education at the University of London Institute of Education.

Francis Green is Reader in Economics and a member of the Centre for Labour Market Studies at the University of Leicester.

Paul Gregg is Senior Research Officer at the National Institute of Economic and Social Research. Stephen Machin is Reader in the Department of Economics, University College London, and is currently Visiting Professor at Harvard University, USA. Both are Associates of the Centre for Economic Performance, London School of Economics. Alan Manning is Reader in the Department of Economics and Fellow of the Centre for Economic Performance.

John Hagan is Professor of Sociology and Law at the University of Toronto, Canada.

Paul Johnson is an economist at the Institute for Fiscal Studies in London.

Eithne McLaughlin is Lecturer in Social Policy at the Queen's University of Belfast, and a member of the Commission on Social Justice.

John Philpott is Director of the Employment Policy Institute.

Paul Ryan is Lecturer in the Faculty of Economics and Politics at the University of Cambridge and a Fellow of King's College.

John Schmitt (currently at the University of Central America) and **Jonathan Wadsworth** are researchers on the UK labour market at the Centre for Economic Performance at the London School of Economics.

Richard Wilkinson is a Senior Research Fellow at the Trafford Centre for Medical Rseearch at the University of Sussex, and Associate Director of the Centre for Health and Society in the Department of Epidemiology and Public Health at University College, London.

LIST OF ABBREVIATIONS

A Level	Advanced Level
BS	British Standard
CBI	Confederation of British Industry
CGT	Capital Gains Tax
CSE	Certificate of Secondary Education
CTT	Capital Transfer Tax
DoE/DOE	Department of the Environment
DOH	Department of Health
DSS	Department of Social Security
EC	European Community
FIS	Family Income Supplement
FTSE	Financial Times Stock Exchange
GCE	General Certificate of Education
GCSE	General Certificate of Secondary Education
GDP	Gross Domestic Product
GHS	General Household Survey
GNP	Gross National Product
HMSO	Her Majesty's Stationary Office
LEA	Local Education Authority
LEC	Local Enterprise Company
LFS	Labour Force Survey
NES	New Earnings Survey
NHS	National Health Service
NIC	National Insurance Contribution
NIESR	National Institute for Economic and Social Research
OPCS	Office of Population, Census and Surveys
TECs	Training and Enterprise Councils
TUC	Trades Union Congress
TVEI	Technical and Vocational Education Initiative
UB	Unemployment Benefit
YT	Youth Training
YTS	Youth Training Scheme

INTRODUCTION

Andrew Glyn and David Miliband

Inequality in the UK today is striking, and shocking. But is it necessary? Since 1979, the rise in inequality has been in significant measure the product of deliberate Government policy, but it also reflects fundamental changes in the operation of all advanced industrialised economies. The purpose of this book is to examine one explanation for the increase in inequality, namely that it has been necessary to spur prosperity.

The facts about inequality are not in dispute. Whatever field one examines—income, employment, education, housing, or tax—the gap between top and bottom in British society is enormous, and in many respects increasing:

- the gap between the highest and lowest paid is greater than at any time since 1886: in the five years to 1992, the pay of the top directors of the FTSE 100 companies rose by 133 per cent, to reach an average of £535,000 (CSJ, 1993); over the same period the wages of the lowest paid 10 per cent of workers grew by 38 per cent (Department of Employment, 1992);
- the richest one per cent of the population own 129 times as much marketable wealth (deposits with banks, shares etc.) per head as the fifty per cent least wealthy (CSO, 1993b);
- 31 per cent of children now live in households where income (after housing costs) is less than half the average, compared with 10 per cent in 1978-9 (DSS, 1993);
- while the bottom 10 per cent of the population pay 43 per cent of their income in tax, the figure for the top 10 per cent is 32 per cent (CSO, 1993a) and of the £31 billion tax cuts implemented between 1979 and 1992, the top one per cent of income earners received 93 times as much per head as the bottom 50 per cent (Oppenheim, 1993 and Davis et al., 1992);
- a child born into a household of professional, administrative

1

or managerial occupation is seven times more likely to get a professional job than a working class child (Marshall and Swift, 1993).

Successive Conservative governments since 1979 have helped to bring about an extension of the gap between rich and poor, and the consequent extension of incentives for the poor to become rich. Yet the reality is that far from spurring entrepreneurship and prosperity, Britain's laissez-faire regime of cuts in direct tax, deregulation and privatisation has been accompanied of by a growth rate lower than that achieved under the Labour government of the 1970s (1.6 per cent against 1.9 per cent). The temporary boom of the late 1980s has left a legacy of debt and bankruptcy that will dog the country for some time to come. In the other crucible of neo-liberal politics, the United States, the picture is similar.

The starting point of this book is therefore a conundrum: while it has become conventional wisdom since the late 1970s to assert that advanced industrialised societies face a severe 'trade-off' between equality and efficiency, the empirical research suggests that the assumption is at best unproven, and at worst wrong. The economies with the most unequal income distribution at the beginning of the 1980s, like the USA and Switzerland, showed slower productivity growth during the subsequent decade than did countries like Japan, Belgium and Sweden, where incomes are apparently least unevenly distributed. Figure 0.1 is the product of a cross-national comparison of data, and shows that the aggregate evidence does not support the claim for a positive relationship between inequality and efficiency. Whilst free market theory leads to the conclusion that 'it is impossible in practice to redistribute income without compromising efficiency' (Snower, 1993) the picture is far more complex.

This book looks behind the aggregate data, and examines the relationship between equality and economic efficiency in a wide range of policy areas to try and assess the evidence for the much-touted trade-off between the two. It therefore goes to the core of free market ideology, and asks whether one of its founding premises—that inequality generates economic success—can be justified. The book brings together the work of experts in health and labour economics, education and social policy, and taxation and criminology, but we begin with the politics of the debate.

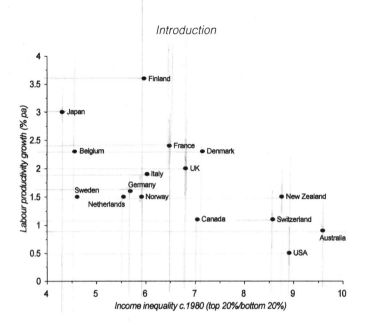

Figure 0.1   Inequality and labour productivity, 1979–90

Source: World Bank; OECD

Political context

The European post-war settlement—above all full employment for men, universal public services funded by progressive taxation, and a gradual diminution of inequality—has over the last fifteen years been abandoned. Since the mid-1970s, parties of the European Right, most notably the Conservative Party in the UK, have launched a frontal assault on the central tenets of that settlement, and capitalised to great electoral effect on its limitations. The neo-liberal project inaugurated by the election of Mrs Thatcher in 1979 has been repeated across Northern Europe. Even Labour parties in Australia and New Zealand have been heavily influenced by free market prescription; French and Spanish social democrats have been disciplined by international market forces; and elsewhere parties of the Left have been swept from office by an increasingly self-confident Right, armed with a credo of tax cuts, deregulation and privatisation. The most successful and durable bastion of the social democratic model, Sweden, has been under sustained assault since 1991.

3

The paradox is that notwithstanding the evident turn of the political tide, not least in Britain, public support for diminished inequality—and especially its props, above all the welfare state and full employment—continues to be strong. The results of the British Social Attitudes survey suggest that since 1983 support for higher taxes to pay for more social spending has actually doubled amongst both the better and the less well off; fully 66 per cent of people in both the top two and bottom two social classes now say they support higher taxes to pay for more social spending (SCPR, 1992). The recently established British Social Justice Project, bringing together political theorists and opinion pollsters, has reached a consistent conclusion:

> Most interestingly...our findings suggest that what divides Labour from Tory voters is not so much their different conceptions of what social justice requires, as their different perceptions of the extent to which contemporary Britain meets its demands...it is remarkable that the gap between the two groups of respondents is much larger over questions of what *is* than what *ought* to be (Swift, Marshall and Burgoyne, 1992).

Thus, while 84 per cent of Conservative supporters and 80 per cent of Labour supporters agree strongly or somewhat that 'it is just that disadvantaged groups are given extra help so that they can have equal opportunities in life', only 34 per cent of Labour voters compared to 58 per cent of Conservative supporters agree (again strongly or somewhat) that 'In Britain, people have equal opportunities to get ahead' (Swift et al., 1992).

For Samuel Brittan, a free marketeer of long standing, these findings are damning. A week after the election of the fourth consecutive Conservative government, on 16 April 1992, his column in the *Financial Times* was headlined 'The moral victory that is still to be won'. His article argued that 'the anti-collectivists won the general election, but have yet to win the moral argument'. Citing the contrast between opinion polls and electoral votes, he continued:

> A significant margin of people evidently thought that in some sense Labour policies for increasing the role of the state were right and respectable and the thing to tell others they supported....The forces of freedom will not have won the moral battle so long as they wince when accused of being in favour of 'two-tier' health or 'two-tier' education.

For politicians of the Right, it is clearly risky to cede the egalitarian ground. In fact, Conservative politicians now notably insist that they are egalitarians—of a sort—after all. A review of the manifestos published for the 1992 General Election concluded:

> All three (manifestos) endorse a society in which there is equality of opportunity, and all citizens enjoy certain rights. The differences between them tend to be differences of degree rather than kind....The values of a meritocratic, achievement—oriented society appear universally accepted....The achievement of full equality of opportunity for all citizens is the horizon of the political imagination as revealed in these manifestos (Gamble, 1993).

Our concern here is with what this says about Conservative politics, rather than Labour's agenda. Sir Ian Gilmour says concern with equality is nothing new: 'In the first three-quarters of the twentieth century (Conservative governments) either accepted (eventually), or themselves took, measures to diminish inequality' (Gilmour, 1992:105). But it was precisely this 'no last ditch' brand of Toryism, bending to the seemingly inexorable egalitarian tide, that Mrs Thatcher sought to reverse. As she put it in a speech to the University of Korea in 1992:

> By the time the Conservatives left office in February 1974, it was clear that there was a lot that was fundamentally wrong in Britain. The policies our party had followed had contributed to those problems rather than solved them. We Conservatives had been guilty of upholding socialist consensus politics when we should have been challenging it (quoted by Bevins, 1992).

Today, almost all Conservative politicians are at pains to denounce egalitarian measures—the EC Social Charter, minimum wage legislation, full rights for part-time workers—yet at the same time all but a few insist on their own meritocratic and egalitarian purpose: in Prime Minister John Major's words, 'a truly open society...a country in which people from all backgrounds can rise to the top in their chosen professions' (Major: 1992a), and a country in which 'more private wealth means more public wealth too' (Major, 1992b). John Major was at pains during the last election campaign to stress his own egalitarian credentials. In addition to his (in)famous pledge to create a 'classless society', he tackled head-on criticism of the Thatcherite balance of priorities between tax cuts, presumed to be of most help to the wealthy, and public services, assumed to be primarily directed at the poor. Presumably out of deference to public attitudes, he insisted on *Frost on Sunday* on 5 April 1992 :

> Look at the relationship between tax cuts and expenditure. This year in his budget Norman Lamont cut taxes by £1.8 billion and where did it go? To the low paid, to the people who have modest incomes....And what happened on public expenditure in health, and education, and social security, and pensions? Those increases in expenditure were far greater than the tax cuts by a multiple many times over. That is the right way to divide the cake.

However cosmetic the pre-election shifts in policy, and hypocritical the sentiments after a decade of grossly inegalitarian policies, this is still a far cry from the essence of Thatcherite dogma, that public expenditure beyond that needed for a nightwatchman state is evil, that tax cuts for the rich create a flourishing enterprise economy, and that wealth 'trickles down' from the wealthiest to help the poorest.

The equality/efficiency 'trade-off'

While parties of the Right have traditionally defended inequality and hierarchy in the name of tradition and order, the neo-liberal analysis and prescription of the 1970s and 1980s provided a revived economic and ethical justification for increased inequality. The famous 'trickle-down' effect was adduced to support the idea that by making the rich richer, the poor would be made richer too. Further, free marketeers argued either (following Hayek) that the only just distribution was that produced by the market, or (following Friedman) that the pursuit of egalitarianism compromised liberty. The ethical case is not our concern here, but the economic case very much is. The assertion was simple, and its implications were analyzed by Arthur Okun in a seminal text (Okun, 1975).

Okun's starting point was unambiguous: that there exists in capitalist societies a fundamental disjunction, what he called a 'double standard', between the principle of equality central to politics and that of efficiency at the heart of market operations. He argued that 'any insistence on carving the pie into equal slices would shrink the size of the pie' (Okun, 1975:48). He did, though, strongly support a degree of income redistribution to 'put some rationality into

6

equality and some humanity into efficiency' (Okun, 1975:120).

Okun's argument is simply stated on the first page of his book: inequalities in living standard and material wealth, he argued, 'reflect a system of rewards and penalties that is intended to encourage efficiency and channel it into socially productive activity. To the extent that the system succeeds, it generates an efficient economy. But that pursuit of efficiency necessarily creates inequalities. And hence society faces a trade-off between equality and efficiency.'

Okun's thesis has been widely reproduced. Professor Benjamin Higgins, an eminent development economist, states the argument as fact:

> And so we come to the basic 'contradiction' in the mixed-and-managed economy. Given the normal tendency to risk-aversion and the reluctance to venture into the unknown, in both the private and the public sector, the redistributive aspects of equity measures are likely to dilute incentives, diminish risk-taking, retard innovation, and slow down growth until the rate of development is reduced, possibly to the point where even the very level of welfare of the underdog, which the equity measures are designed to help, is lowered instead (Higgins, 1992:38).

In his book, Okun deployed at least two of the three arguments traditionally used against greater reform—be it for civil rights, extended suffrage, or the welfare state—labelled by Albert Hirschman the futility, perversity, and jeopardy theses (Hirschman, 1991). Each has been used in Britain by the Right against the post-war welfare settlement, and the greater equality it attempted to engender. The so-called 'futility' thesis takes various forms but is based on the view that 'attempts at social transformation will be unavailing...they will simply fail to "make a dent"' (Hirschman, 1991:45). It is often argued, for example, that even if one could share out the resources of a country equally, society would soon be divided between millionaires and paupers (Minogue, 1989).

The perversity thesis states that any attempt to improve some feature of the political, social or economic order will produce, 'via a chain of unintended consequences, the *exact contrary* of the object being proclaimed and pursued' (Hirschman, 1991:11). The general case has been most sharply honed with respect to welfare benefits, and their alleged deleterious effects on the fortunes of the poor, by the American social scientist Charles Murray. By trying to provide more for the poor, he argues, the welfare state—whether the

'War on Poverty' in the US, housing, social security and unemployment benefits in the UK—creates more poor (Murray, 1984 and 1989).

The third argument used against reform is what Hirschman calls the 'jeopardy thesis'—the view that the 'cost of the proposed change or reform is too high as it endangers some previous, precious accomplishments' (Hirschman, 1991:7); liberty is usually cited as the first casualty of the search for equality. This is epitomised in the Conservative canon by what John Major in a speech to the Carlton Club on 3 February 1993 called 'wariness of over-government'. 'We know the danger', he argued in a neat link with the perversity thesis, 'that unless it is reined back by constant and vigorous effort, it will grow inexorably. It is a parasite that can destroy its host.'

These arguments about the effects of attempts to create greater equality, which in various ways dominate the political and policy debate today, are above all instrumental and prudential, concerned with the effect of different policies, first on equality and second on efficiency. Interestingly enough, the faith and zeal of the early Thatcher years seems to have disappeared. The purpose of this book is to engage in the instrumental and prudential debate. In a wide range of policy areas, ranging from health to the labour market to crime, we examine the argument that greater equality makes for economic inefficiency. We are concerned not simply with the redistribution of income via taxation but also with how the expenditures of the state (education and training for example) can enhance people's position in the labour market and thus be a powerful force both for increased equality and enhanced economic contribution. In this way, we hope to overcome the limitation of the static and generally unhelpful distinction between equality of opportunity and equality of outcome: after all, one person's outcome is a major determinant of their child's opportunity.

We will be making two different claims: first, that in a number of policy areas the case for the efficiency of inequality is wrong, and that greater equality and greater efficiency can go hand in hand; second, that in various other areas the extent to which greater equality causes inefficiency has been greatly exaggerated. Chapters 1 to 6 show that the most obvious manifestations of inequality—poverty, exclusion and disadvantage—are in various ways extremely expensive for society at large, above all in their waste of human potential, and that greater equality (of both opportunity and outcome) would contribute to greater prosperity. Chapters 7 and 8 show that the case for inequality, in terms of the disincentive effects of high taxation (required to fund social programmes) and generous social security benefits, are much overstated. Finally, in order to reflect the overall impact within economies of all these factors, Chapter 9 demonstrates that the alleged trade-off between equality and economic performance is not reflected in the cross-national macroeconomic data.

Before summarising the main arguments of these chapters, the next section seeks to clarify the conceptual underpinnings of the argument about the relationship between equality and efficiency.

Concepts

There are, of course, a host of detailed technical issues surrounding the measurement of economic inequality (see Atkinson, 1983). What is involved is the extent of disparities in standards of living. Widely used measures, such as ratios of the incomes of the top 10 per cent to the bottom 10 per cent of households, reflect the distance between the best-off and the worst off, though people may attach different importance to the extent of disparities between the two ends of the distribution and the middle.

There is a wide-ranging debate about the meaning of equality, as well as its desirability. One important issue neglected in this book concerns the relationship between equality and diversity. The Right have made hay by arguing that egalitarians want everybody to be the same, or have the same education or the same health care. This is a travesty of the egalitarian case, but it has struck a chord. In reality, however, while every inequality implies difference, not every difference implies inequality: egalitarians insist that they want to relate treatment to need, for example. However, in part as a result of the challenge from the Right, a school of egalitarian thought has tried to come to terms with the need to link equality to diversity. Most comprehensively Michael Walzer has argued for a new 'complex equality', in which principles of distribution are varied between spheres of life (income, health, education etc), and crucially, in which dominance in one sphere does not give advantage in another (Walzer, 1983).

As we suggested earlier, the conventional distinction between equality of opportunity and equality of result is not altogether satisfactory: Amartya Sen's concept of 'equality of capabilities', in the sense of a person's capacity to function in society, is more convincing (see Sen, 1992 for a comprehensive treatment of the whole issue). However, notwithstanding its limiting properties, when we use the term 'greater equality' in this volume, we are generally referring either to a snapshot of income, or to a description of opportunities. If equality is not to imply uniformity, its political and theoretical bases need to be further clarified, but this volume is not the place to do that job.

We do not prescribe, either in this Introduction or in the rest of the book, a degree of equality (for example ratio of top incomes to bottom incomes) that is desirable. Our purpose is to show that the economic justification for current levels of inequality is spurious. This is not to say that all policy interventions to reduce inequality will boost efficiency; rather, that there are important ones which do. Neither is it to say that there is necessarily a continuously positive relationship (within a given policy field) between greater equality and greater efficiency: the relationship may well become negative beyond a certain point. Nor are we arguing that reducing inequality is only justified in areas where there are resulting improvements in efficiency. Many egalitarians would accept substantial efficiency costs, but obviously policies which have the double benefit of increasing both efficiency and equality can gather wider support.

The concept of economic efficiency might appear more straightforward, but there are serious problems with the obvious candidates for measuring it—total production (GDP) and productivity. Economic efficiency, understood as a concept applying to society, rather than to particular groups, firms or sectors, cannot be automatically identified with GDP or labour productivity. To take GDP first, not all increases in GDP are necessarily advantageous. Even if GDP is accepted as an adequate measure of the aggregate benefits from productive activity, the costs, above all in terms of human effort, must be brought into account. Suppose additional GDP resulted from an increase in the length of the working week (for example as a result of a cut in hourly wages). In this case the costs might well be taken to outweigh the benefits. Only those increases in GDP which flow from investment in more effective machinery, a more skilled labour force, better organisation of production or from increased opportunities for work for a previously excluded section of the population unambiguously imply increased efficiency from a social point of view.

Equally, increases in efficiency could be taken in the form of shorter hours of work or less intense working conditions, in which case they would not cause a rise in GDP. Thus greater efficiency need not entail opting for growth to the detriment of the environment. Pressure on the environment need not be raised if increased efficiency is used to increase leisure rather than production, or taken in the form of expanded welfare services where use of material inputs and generation of pollution is slight. If the term greater efficiency is to be reserved for beneficial changes, which may have to be traded off against greater equality, then changes in efficiency cannot be simply read off from what happens to GDP.

Labour productivity, or output per hour worked, seems at first sight more like an accurate measure of efficiency than GDP since output is measured against the input of effort. But labour productivity also is both too restrictive and too broad a measure. As subsequent chapters argue, economic inequality frequently takes the form of the denial to sections of the population of the opportunity to undertake paid productive activity. Whilst some of their activities when unemployed have value (such as caring for relatives) such structural exclusion must be regarded as inefficient. The potential contribution to production of those excluded is wasted. If they were employed, either consumption on average would be higher or all those employed could work shorter hours. One way or the other people are better off.

An increase in average productivity does represent an increase in efficiency from society's point of view if it results in greater output or shorter working hours. But if output does not increase, and hours of work do not fall, then the higher productivity is simply reflected in reduced employment. If the workers who lose their jobs do not find alternative work then they are effectively excluded from making a productive contribution. The increase in efficiency at the level of the firm or sector has been dissipated as far as society is concerned. Rather than increasing average living standards such a rise in productivity leads rather to an inegalitarian redistribution of what is already being produced.

No handy aggregate measure of economic efficiency flows from this discussion. Indeed the more vigorously the concept of efficiency is pursued the harder it is to stop short of an all-encompassing concept of total social welfare. Social welfare, however, inevitably incorporates considerations of how costs and benefits are distributed and not just the balance between the two totals. But once the concept of efficiency involves distribution it is no longer very helpful to pose the trade-offs facing society as a trade-off between equality and efficiency (see Dobb, 1969; Le Grand, 1990). What is really involved is the

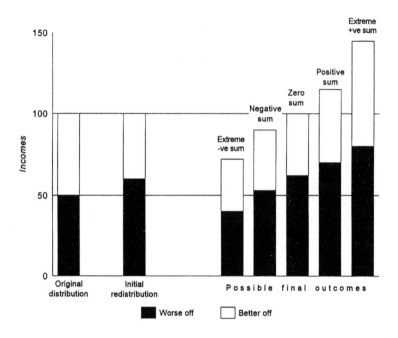

Figure 0.2 Possible outcomes after a redistribution

trade-off between one group's welfare and another's. Larger costs in terms of reduced efficiency means that those financing a given amount of redistribution lose more than if efficiency was maintained. It seems clearer, therefore, to visualise the trade-off directly in these terms rather than through the intermediary of efficiency (with its connotations of an objectively measurable national interest).

Despite these reservations, in the rest of the book we will continue to refer to the terms of the trade-off between the immediate beneficiaries from egalitarian policies and those who directly finance them as the trade-off between equality and efficiency.

The argument

As a framework for the discussion of the trade-off between equality and efficiency in the chapters which follow it may be helpful to think of the possible range of outcomes as shown in Figure 0.2. The starting point is an original distribution of income, with for simplicity a small number of 'better-off' receiving the same total income as a large number of 'worse-off' (in the UK the best off 25 per cent of the population receive about the same total income as the worst off 75 per cent). The figure envisages some policy (typically comprising additional taxation of the better off and public expenditure to the benefit of the worse off) which redistributes income and is shown as the initial redistribution. If there were no effects on economic efficiency (which will be assumed to be reflected in changes in total income) that would be the end of the matter. This is the 'zero sum' outcome, the middle possibility in the right hand side of the diagram, when redistribution has no effect on efficiency and so leaves the 'cake' to be distributed unaffected. The initial redistribution is then the final outcome.

Those who argue for the pervasiveness of the trade-off between efficiency and equality believe that redistribution reduces total income so that the outcome is negative sum. The standard negative sum case is where the reduction in incomes applies to both rich and poor, who have lower incomes than after the initial redistribution. This would be the case, for example, if extra taxation reduced the work effort of the better off (reducing their incomes), with the poor suffering as a result of consequent fall in tax revenue and thus government expenditure. Some of the tax revenue would also be dissipated in costs of collection and administration. In this case redistribution is a 'leaky bucket', in Okun's phrase, in that the poor end up with less extra income than after the initial redistribution, but better off than originally. The extreme form of the leaky bucket, or in Figure 0.2 the 'extreme negative sum outcome', occurs when the reduction in incomes is so great that the poor actually end up worse off in absolute terms than in the original distribution. An alleged example of this is the notorious Laffer Curve which asserts that raising tax rates has such strong disincentive effects that total tax revenue (and thus implicitly the welfare of the poor) is reduced.

This extreme negative sum argument has little credibility. Even one of the most prominent Chicago-school, free market economists admitted some years ago: 'most beginning graduate students could in one afternoon invent a hundred ways of bringing about major transfers at an efficiency cost of less than 20 per cent of the amounts involved' (Harberger, 1978). So whilst some redistributive policies may have some disincentive effects, the effect on efficiency is only a small percentage of the sum redistributed, as Paul Johnson in particular argues. It is perfectly sensible to try to frame redistributive policies so as to minimise such effects, but it cannot possibly be argued that *a priori* they undermine egalitarian policies.

In reality, as the chapters in this book demonstrate, there are a number of policy areas in which positive sum outcomes can result from a redistribution of the resources of society. In these cases, the impact of the redistribution on the productive contributions of the poor leads to greater economic efficiency. This benefits not only those who can now find work, or work more productively: there are external effects in this case too as tax revenues rise and benefit expenditures fall, allowing lower tax rates (or better public services) for all. This would be the case where additional public expenditure (on child care, or education, or training, or health for example) reduces the economic exclusion of worse-off groups in society. The standard positive sum case would be where the benefits which flow from this greater economic participation (in tax revenue for example) mean that the rich do not lose out as much (in absolute terms) as appears from the initial redistribution (see Van Parijs, 1992).

The extreme positive sum outcome—standing Laffer on his head—occurs where the incomes of the rich actually increase after the redistribution so that they end up better off than in the original situation. This could happen because redistribution facilitates such an expansion of incomes of the poor that the initially higher tax rates for the rich could be more than reversed. This may appear rather an extreme case when attention is limited to incomes. But welfare, it has been forcefully argued (Townsend, 1979), depends on relative material circumstances as well as absolute levels of consumption. A sense of inferiority and social exclusion, which relative material deprivation engenders, clearly imposes huge burdens on those affected. But their responses, which may include mental and physical illness and anti-social forms of behaviour, can in turn impose heavy costs on the rest of society in the form of health care costs, crime prevention and so forth (see John Hagan's chapter). If redistribution can release society from some of these costs of exclusion, as well as liberating the economic potential of the excluded, then so much the greater is the likelihood of enhanced living standards for the better off. But the financial costs of coping with the results of social deprivation do not tell the whole story, since they only mitigate rather than eliminate the impact on the rest of society, leaving greater feelings of insecurity for example. Richard Wilkinson's chapter suggests that more egalitarian societies may be less stressful and more conducive to psycho-social

14

well-being. The more important these factors are the more they enhance aggregate welfare and the more likely that those who immediately pay for the egalitarian measures will also ultimately benefit from them.

The overall outcome from redistributive packages depends on the balance between positive and negative effects. These will vary with the method of financing of the package and the content of the expenditure measures. There is no simple way of quantifying the various effects discussed in the individual chapters and thus of predicting exactly what the overall outcome of any particular package will be. Certainly the international or cross-national evidence, reviewed in this volume by Corry and Glyn (Chapter 9) does not support the notion that more egalitarian countries pay a price in terms of worse economic performance. In any case it is the contention of this book that the current structure of inequality in the UK creates many opportunities for positive sum interventions which both increase economic efficiency and reduce inequality. Richard Wilkinson begins our detailed analysis in Chapter 1. His contribution, 'Health, redistribution and growth', provides compelling and provocative reading, even for those convinced of or sympathetic to the general argument of the book. It is by now a commonplace first that ill-health is expensive, both because of the rising cost of treatment (amounting to 14 per cent of GDP in the United States) and the opportunity cost of lost production, and second that ill-health is inversely correlated with income—in other words, the poor are more ill more often than the rich. Richard Wilkinson goes further, however, and using time-series and cross-national data shows, first, that good health as measured by life expectancy is influenced by relative and not absolute standards of living, and second that differences in income distribution are the most important explanation of differences in average life-span between countries. Rather than explaining mortality rates for countries by differences in growth rates, levels of GDP, or numbers of people living below an absolute level of poverty, Wilkinson shows that for the OECD countries, it is the distribution of income that is the most powerful explanatory variable.

In other words, greater equality in the distribution of income holds out the promise of reduced economic costs of ill-health and premature death to society as a whole. The UK's slippage in terms of income distribution over the last twenty years correlates with its slippage in terms of mortality rates, and were our income distribution to approximate to the more egalitarian levels of our continental neighbours, we could expect to see a two year improvement in the average life-span. Crucially, this is not simply a question of improved life-chances for the poorest minority of citizens. The widening of the UK income distribution in the late 1980s correlates with a rise in death rates for men and women aged 15 to 44; a narrower distribution of income would *improve* the 'dependency ratio' of workers to non-workers by reducing the premature loss of young people. Over and above these direct economic costs, Wilkinson suggests that the relation between equality and health reflects a more fundamental relationship between equality and psycho-social well being. Wilkinson therefore raises a central issue concerning the effect on total welfare of the distribution of income, irrespective of its effects on economic efficiency.

Chapters 2 and 3 document the inefficiency of inequality in what almost everyone now agrees is the central economic resource of any country, namely human capital. In an age of relatively cheap international transportation and worldwide capital mobility, it is the potential skills of a nation's workforce that are its most precious economic resource. It is therefore incomprehensible that conservative governments, most notably in the UK, insist on highly stratified systems of education and training.

Tony Edwards and Geoff Whitty examine the central claim of the Right in education policy over the last twenty years, that standards have declined as the system has become more equal. What he finds, in fact, is that not only is the British education system (particularly the English and Welsh, but in international terms the Scottish as well) designed for an élite and to exclude the majority, but the elitism is not meritocratic: privilege is reproduced, generation after generation, as is disadvantage. Although there has been a more or less secular increase in standards of achievement by British schoolchildren in the post-war period, by international standards low attainment is widespread among all but the ablest twenty per cent of them. This is wasteful in and of itself, but there is a 'double waste': success at the top continues to be warped by the impact of class, race and sex.

Taking today's labour force as a whole, children of unskilled manual workers are one tenth as likely to have been to university as those of professional parents, and eight times as likely to have achieved no educational qualifications whatsoever. 'Selective rescue operations' like the Assisted Places Scheme, designed to sponsor the mobility of working class children, cannot make up for barriers—for example in the funding of schools—put in the way of the majority of children. Edwards and Whitty argue that the market or 'quasi-market' recently instituted in the schooling system—above all the commitments to a deregulation of enrolment and a funding regime based on pupil numbers—will exacerbate the inequalities, and accentuate British education's 'double inefficiency'. A system whose economic inefficiency derives above all from its social inequality is set to become less efficient as a result of increased inequality.

In Chapter 3, Francis Green documents the inequalities that exist in access to training, and the resulting economic inefficiency that afflicts the economy as a whole. Some of these inefficiencies result from the organisation of the workplace and the structure of industry, others from Government policy. Green extends the argument that Britain is trapped in a 'low skills equilibrium' where historically low supply of skills is matched by low demand from employers. Training is most readily available to those with the most education, and disadvantaged groups are left with little in the way of access or provision. The result is great waste of economic potential. In training, the problem is not simply a low average level, but also unequal access, which reproduces and intensifies the inequalities derived from the education system. Francis Green documents how, to use Richard Titmuss's famous phrase, 'services for the poor are poor services'. The Youth Training Scheme has not equipped young school-leavers with the skills necessary to make their way in the labour market; in fact, one study found that such was YTS' reputation, it actually reduced participants' chances of finding a job.

In Chapter 4, John Hagan continues the examination of the interaction between economic and social factors and documents in compelling detail the criminality that is generated by processes of social inequality and above all what he calls capital disinvestment. Drawing on extensive North American material, invaluable because it provides a test case of the effect of stark inequalities, Hagan describes three interconnected processes that structure the lives of people in deprived neighbourhoods in the United States: residential segregation, racial inequality, and the concentration of poverty. In other words, geographical, racial and labour market segregation are combined in a vicious circle that makes crime pay, and makes the legal economy distant and irrelevant. The costs are now monumental. There are now over 880,000 inmates in US prisons, one third of them drug offenders, and the federal bill for the war on drugs reached $12 billion in fiscal year 1993: over 4 years the Bush administration spent over $40 billion to suppress illegal drug use (Horgan, 1993) While the time spent in prison per violent crime tripled in the US between 1975 and 1989, violent crime did not decline.

Among young people, a vicious circle of economic failure, family breakdown and community insecurity blocks the development of social and cultural capital that is crucial for economic development. In communities that suffer from capital disinvestment and families with little social capital to invest in their children, young people are drawn to the short term benefit of crime whatever the longer term dangers. To move to the legal economy entails a sharp cut in living standards; inequality makes for illegality as well as inefficiency.

Chapters 5 and 6 provide detailed analysis of one of the most contentious areas in the debate about the relationship between equality and efficiency, namely the labour market. It is here that those in trade unions and the voluntary sector arguing against exploitation and inequality are attacked by free marketeers for demanding too much in pay and conditions, and thereby sacrificing jobs. It is here that egalitarian measures are described as 'a job destruction machine'. In Chapter 5, Paul Gregg, Stephen Machin and Alan Manning look in detail at wage inequality, and show that it cannot be justified by efficiency considerations. While orthodox labour market theory, and laissez-faire labour market policy, remains based on the notion of unproblematic matching of supply and demand to reward capability, the reality is of a market dogged by endemic failure, rooted in highly stratified power relations. Gregg, Machin and Manning examine labour market practice at the bottom and top ends of the hierarchy— the bottom where the abolition of Wages Councils, the weakening of trade unions and mass unemployment have undermined the bargaining power of workers, and the top where pay rises for top directors have far outstripped the national average in recent years.

The reality unearthed in Chapter 5 is of employers with monopsony power over the bottom end of the labour market underpaying employees by around 15 per cent of their productive value, thereby generating a double inefficiency: fewer workers are willing to work than would otherwise be the case, and those that do work have less incentive for increased productivity because they receive so little of the proceeds. They conclude that just as the 10 per cent increase in women's pay relative to that of men after the passage of the provisions of the Equal Pay Act in the 1970s did not prevent a rise in women's employment, a minimum wage could actually *increase* efficiency by raising the incentive to work and acquire skills. At the top end of the market, Gregg, Machin and Manning find monopoly power and supra-competitive wages being exacted by top managers, with no justification in terms of their economic contribution. Pay is of course just one dimension of how workplace relations can affect productivity. A recent comprehensive analysis of this issue (Blinder, 1990) found that changing the way workers are treated, involving for example substantive participation in shopfloor decisions, may boost productivity more than incentive pay schemes such as profit-sharing.

Chapter 6 brings together three contributions that probe the relationship between employment, unemployment and non-employment, and the inequalities and inefficiencies hidden in that relationship. It is commonly assumed that if someone is not employed they are classified as unemployed. John Schmitt and Jonathan Wadsworth explain, to the contrary, that since 1986 a third category, the number of economically inactive men (those unemployed but no longer in the labour market) between the ages of 16 and 64, has exceeded the number officially unemployed, and now totals over two million (compared to 1.7 million unemployed). So, 60 per cent of the fall in male employment over the period can be accounted for by an increase in the number leaving the workforce altogether and is therefore missed by the traditional unemployment count which now seriously understates the extent of male joblessness. Schmitt and Wadsworth trace the rise in inactivity among men to discouragement as a result of the decline in traditional employment opportunities. The rise in women's employment has not in general benefited households with non-employed men, since it has been concentrated among women with employed partners. The decline in relative wages and the limited employment opportunities for low skilled men prevents many job losers from rejoining the labour market; combined with the increasingly tight criteria for eligibility for unemployment benefit, the result is mass emigration to sickness-related benefits. These men have been driven out of the labour force, and are effectively written off for the purposes of labour market policy. This is a complete waste of economic potential, and generates structural dependence on benefits.

John Philpott looks at the situation of those closer to the labour market than the economically inactive, the registered unemployed. Unemployment is a symptom of the unequal distribution of work between individuals, as well as inadequate demand and a failure of supply, but the distribution of unemployment is not random. Philpott shows that the burden of unemployment is inequitably distributed by age, sex, skill, region, and race, and that the one million long term unemployed are effectively outside the labour force altogether. Not counting the social costs of unemployment in ill-health, crime etc, Philpott estimates that the direct annual average cost to the exchequer—including benefits and lost income tax—is over £8,000 per year. The greatest hardship is suffered by the long term unemployed, the victims of an economic policy designed to bear down on inflation but whose cumulative effect is to leave them with little chance of re-entering the labour force. The scarring effect of long term unemployment has costs in terms of lost production, benefit dependence and social alienation, but it also means that competition for jobs is lop-sided. While all unemployment is wasteful, the structure of unemployment in the UK, with its high proportion of long term unemployed, is particularly inegalitarian and inefficient.

Eithne McLaughlin looks at both the theoretical and practical links between the labour market and the social security system. She finds that orthodox economic theory is little help in explaining the interdependence of work and welfare. Above all, she finds that the central plank of anti-egalitarian social security policy—namely the argument that benefits must be driven down to increase incentives for people to enter the labour market—is based on fundamental misconceptions of human motivation and circumstance. It produces effects which are sometimes the opposite of those intended and which are certainly inefficient for the economy as well as punitive for the individuals involved.

McLaughlin finds, paradoxically, cases where the cutting of benefits makes escape from dependence on state support more difficult. This is above all because the levels, structure and administration of benefit leave individuals no room for manoeuvre in applying for and accepting employment, especially where employment opportunities do not carry the immediate prospect of a wage large enough to meet basic needs or where job security is limited. The result is that people are locked into unemployment by the mismatch between a rigid social security system and an increasingly flexible (including part-time) labour market. Furthermore, the assumption of female dependency (on their husbands) at the heart of the social security system produces disincentives for women to take work if their husbands are not working—their income, if it is more than £15 per week, is removed from their partners' income support. The result is a labour market structured to produce large pools of economic inactivity, with high barriers to entry; the effect could hardly be more inefficient and more unequal.

Chapter 7 by Paul Johnson looks at the efficiency implications of egalitarian tax and benefit policies—in other words higher benefits and more progressive personal tax schedules. This has been an important arena of political debate in the last fifteen years. Johnson finds that in the UK the tax system—direct and indirect taxes combined—is actually regressive: it widens the income distribution, from a ratio of 7:1 between the top and bottom quintiles for gross incomes (ie: including benefits), to 7.7:1 after tax. Johnson reports that the effect of benefit levels on the work effort of men is small, but like Eithne McLaughlin in Chapter 6 he finds that the structure of the benefits system traps married women with unemployed husbands, as well as lone mothers, in unemployment. On the tax side, Johnson finds equally scant evidence for the argument that tax cuts spur efficiency gains. Conversely, Johnson argues that moderate increases in redistributive effect, and structural reforms of the systems, could reduce inequality without harming efficiency.

Paul Ryan examines the neglected question of inheritance, its taxation, and its redistribution in Chapter 8. Inheritance of wealth and opportunity has the potential to contravene the most basic assumptions of a meritocratic society, and it is above all for this reason that the bequest of a job is generally considered unacceptable (except, it seems, in the Upper House of Parliament), and why bequests have been the subject of taxation for many years. Paul Ryan discovers however that the taxation of inheritance is indeed a twilight zone of political rhetoric and financial illusion.

Most starkly, Ryan shows that at the height of the redistributive attack on inheritance in the 1970s, revenues from inheritance taxes declined more rapidly than ever before because the avoidance industry was so effective. Equally, the inegalitarian thrust of policy in the 1980s coincided with stable (though very low) inheritance tax revenues. Efficiency arguments used by the Right against the taxation of inheritance fall by the wayside because the alleged negative effects of inheritance taxation on business performance and bequest-motivated saving do not stand up to scrutiny. Available evidence of inherited family businesses undermines the case for tax concessions, and the argument that taxation damages efficiency by deterring household saving, intuitively an attractive case ('why save when the tax man gets your money?'), is not supported by the data.

Finally, following the efforts of Chapters 1 to 8 to examine the relationship between equality and efficiency from school to grave, Dan Corry and Andrew Glyn return in Chapter 9 to the macroeconomic data on equality and economic performance within and between nations. Greater equality seems to be associated with better economic performance. This can partly be seen by dividing the post-war period into two roughly equal phases, the twenty or so years until 1974, the so-called 'golden age of capitalism' when growth soared to a (stable) average of 5 per cent per year and inequality was lower than before and diminishing, and the period since, marked by slower growth and a trend to increased inequality. Nor do unequal countries have better economic performance; if anything the reverse is true and this has been confirmed in a number of statistically sophisticated studies. The direction of causality between equality and efficiency in different policy areas and within different nations may be a matter of dispute; what cannot be claimed is a simple relationship leading from inequality to prosperity.

Claims and admissions

Before we proceed to the policy chapters which follow, the deliberately limited nature of what we have attempted should be underlined. First, although there is considerable use of international comparisons in this and other chapters, our focus is entirely on issues of economic equality within advanced capitalist nations, with emphasis on the UK experience. We make no attempt to discuss the similar issues which arise in the dissimilar context of the Less Developed Countries, nor do we touch on the question of international inequality, most notably between North and South, brought into focus again by debates over the global environment. In other words, we do not enter in this book into the debate about the relationship between equality and community; the community within which we have examined equality and efficiency is the nation state. The most extreme inequalities in the world today exist between countries, and groups of countries; a radical politics that claims to be egalitarian cannot limit itself to a single country, but in this book our focus is more narrow. Even in relation to the countries of advanced capitalism, the analysis should be extended to other issues, such as the organisation of work.

Second, we do not deal in detail with the policy measures best suited to reducing the various dimensions of inequality. Apart from anything else, they are the subject of numerous IPPR reports. Policy debates must, however, rest on a clear understanding of the underlying issues involved and that is our purpose here. We aim to nail a lie, namely that for the good of economic efficiency we must abandon attempts to achieve greater equality; inequality should not be allowed to stand on the basis of unproven assertions about its economic efficiency.

Finally, none of what we say in this book should be taken to imply that egalitarian policies provide a simple solution to the economic problems of the industrialised world. High employment and tight labour markets in the golden age generated demands for improvements in real wages, working conditions and welfare services which frequently exceeded the capacities of the economies concerned. Capitalist economies contain basic inequalities of power, for example between capital and labour, and production and investment are organised around them. The drive against equality in the 1980s expressed a wish to return to a more liberalised form for these relations, while the post-war period showed that, on the contrary, space can be secured for egalitarian policies. The chapters which follow spell out how such policies can preserve and in various ways enhance the performance of the economy, but they are not a cure-all.

We do not, of course, believe that undermining the efficiency argument for inequality will eliminate opposition to egalitarian policies. Such measures will by definition not be of direct benefit to everybody, and many who oppose redistribution do so because they do not wish to pay taxes to fund it. People do not need an economist or politician to claim that a progressive tax is 'inefficient' to know that they do not want to see their short term living standards reduced. Nevertheless, efficiency arguments have been and are important in the case against a more egalitarian distribution of resources within advanced capitalist countries like the UK. By undermining them, and by showing that the benefits of egalitarian policies are much broader than is commonly conceived, we hope to contribute to the positive case for social and economic reforms that so many people in Britain so badly need.

1 HEALTH, REDISTRIBUTION AND GROWTH

Richard Wilkinson

The disruption of productive capacity and the wastage of human skill and labour power which result from sickness and premature death are enormous. Each year premature death removes almost 100,000 men and women from the population of working age in England and Wales (DOH, 1992). At any point in time about eight times that number are rendered inactive by permanent or temporary sickness (OPCS, 1981) and, of those in work, inactive sickness absence affects about one in twenty for a day or more in an average week (CSO, 1992).

The National Audit Office estimated that sickness absence among the 66,000 staff working for the Inland Revenue cost £37 million in 1991-2 in wages, national insurance and superannuation alone (Henke, 1993). If their sickness absence rates could be reduced to the average Japanese level some £28 million of this would have been saved. Sickness absence was estimated by the Confederation of British Industry to have cost industry at least £5 billion in 1986 (CBI, 1987). Although sickness absence rates in different countries cannot be compared accurately, Britain appears to have very much higher rates than many of its competitors (Prins and De Graaf, 1986 and Henke, 1993).

What have these problems got to do with income distribution? It is often assumed that the state of the nation's health depends primarily on the standard of medical care available to the population. But the vast majority of deaths are from causes which modern medicine can neither prevent nor usually cure. It is now well-established that variations in death rates in modern societies are related not so much to levels of medical provision but to people's socioeconomic circumstances (Mackenbach et al., 1990). The impact of expenditure on medical care on population mortality rates seems to be small. It appears that the contribution of medical care is overshadowed by the power of factors affecting the initial incidence of cancers, cardiovascular diseases and infections in the population at large. The same goes for most of the common illnesses. Whether the problem is back-ache, coughs, colds, 'flu and other viral infections, or rheumatism and arthritis, treatment is often only palliative. Deaths from particular diseases or conditions 'where it is generally recognised that timely and appropriate health service intervention can (reliably) prevent the death of the patient' account for only just over two per cent of all deaths—or 12 per cent of all deaths before age 65 (DOH, 1992, p.13). While recognising that this is as it should be (there would be something wrong if a large proportion of deaths were from curable diseases), we also need to recognise that most of the modern causes of death are only marginally amenable to treatment.

In drawing attention to the growing social class differences in health, the Black Report (Townsend and Davidson, 1992) served to remind us of the continued sensitivity of health to socioeconomic circumstances. Indeed, rather than economic growth and the increasing affluence of the post-war decades having diminished health's sensitivity to differences in people's social and economic circumstances, health differences—as measured by death rates—have widened continuously.

The precise nature of the socio-economic determinants of health have now been the subject of a great deal of painstaking research throughout the developed world. The picture which is beginning to emerge suggests that health in the affluent societies is now influenced less by people's absolute standard of living than by their standard relative to others in society. Once the vast majority of the population is above some basic level of subsistence, then increasing standards of material comfort make less and less difference to health. What affects health most is the distribution of resources within each society.

The issue is not simply that smaller income differences would produce smaller health differences. It is more surprising than that: the scale of income differences affects overall mortality rates. National average death rates are so strongly influenced by the size of the gap between rich and poor in each society that differences in income distribution seem to be the most important explanation of why average life expectancy differs from one developed country to another.

Before describing the evidence, a word is necessary about its implications. Beyond the likelihood that a more equitable distribution of income would improve health and reduce the economic costs of ill health, there is another issue. When thinking about the statistical relationship between income distribution and health, it is hard to escape the conclusion that income distribution is one of the fundamental determinants of the quality of a society's social fabric. There are, as we shall see, good reasons for thinking that it is primarily through psychological rather than material processes that income differences affect health. The most likely pathways are through feelings of failure, insecurity, depression, anxiety, low self-esteem and the like.

If health is as strongly affected by income distribution as it appears to be, then it is hard to escape two conclusions. First, that inequality affects people more fundamentally than is usually recognised, and second, that such powerful psychosocial implications of inequality are unlikely to confine their effects to health. It would be surprising if they did not extend into many other areas of human functioning, perhaps particularly into social behaviour. If so, then the evidence which follows may lend support to the longstanding socialist view that income distribution has a fundamental impact on the quality of the social fabric itself.

The evidence

What are the main features of the relationship between socioeconomic factors and health? First, differences in health arising from differences in socioeconomic status are found in the large majority of diseases. Illness, disability, most cancers and the vast majority of causes of death, are more common among those lowest down the social hierarchy. Second, differences in health occur at almost all ages and give rise to death rates two or even three times as high in lower as in upper social groups. Third, although a small part of these health differences appears to be a result of the increased chances of downward social mobility among the least healthy (so that the unhealthy tend to end up in poorer circumstances), most of the relationship has to be explained as an effect of differing circumstances on health. Fourth, the differences are not explained in terms of behavioural risk factors—or for that matter by any other known risk factors. The mortality gradient is as steep among non-smokers as it is among smokers, and as steep among diseases not related to smoking as it is among those which are related to smoking. With heart disease, where health related behaviour is often thought to be particularly important, the major known risk factors (including non-behavioural ones) explain no more than about 20 per cent of the social gradient in death rates (Marmot et al., 1984 and Pocock et al., 1987). Known behavioural factors are probably more important in only lung cancer and AIDS. With heart disease, even if you heed all the behavioural do's and don'ts, it remains your most likely cause of death.

Almost all measures of socio-economic status are associated with differences in health (Whitehead, 1992 and Goldblatt, 1990). Among the plethora of socio-economic factors associated with health differences, income occupies a central position. Serving as a measure and determinant of our standard of living, affecting housing, heating, clothing, diet, leisure time activities, self-esteem, social position etc., it is strongly related to health. Not only does it appear that there is a powerful cross-sectional association between income and health, but studies attempting to establish whether the relationship is causal, have confirmed that it is. Indeed, death rates appear to be responsive to changes in income (Wilkinson, 1990 and 1986).

What is rather more surprising is that although there is a very clear gradient of falling mortality rates with increasing income within the developed countries, there appears to be no such gradient related to differences in income between them. Differences in GDP per capita among the developed countries are large: using purchasing power parities to convert national currencies to reflect differences in what people can buy with their incomes, GDP per capita is twice as high in the richer as in the poorer OECD countries (even excluding Turkey). Yet these large differences seem to have little effect on average life expectancy in each country. Across the 23 OECD countries the correlation coefficient between GDP per capita and life expectancy in 1990 was an insignificant 0.3. Looking at changes in life expectancy in relation to changes in GDP per capita over the 20 year period 1970–90 showed no relationship whatsoever (see Figure 1.1): the coefficient was 0.02 and negative.

What can be made of this apparent inconsistency? If differences in the standard of living within countries have such a pronounced effect on mortality rates, why do the differences between countries appear to have little or no effect? The answer involves the distinction between the relative and absolute standard of living. If each person's health was determined directly by their own absolute material standards of consumption and comfort, then income levels would matter regardless of the context. If, on the other hand, health is influenced by more sociological processes than that, then what would matter is each person's income or standard of living relative to others in their society. That income differences are important within, but not between,

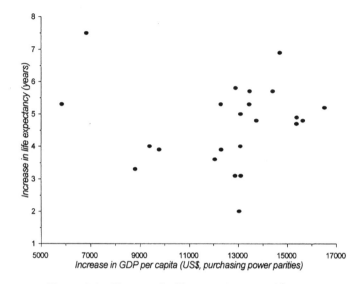

Figure 1.1 Changes in life expectancy and income,
OECD countries, 1979–90

Sources: OECD *National Accounts*, World Bank *World Tables*

societies implies that it is relative income which matters. Although among poorer countries there is obviously a stronger relationship between the absolute standard of living and health, among the richer nations this appears to have been replaced by a more sociologically based relationship between income and health.

Fortunately the validity of this picture does not rest simply on its ability to resolve an apparent inconsistency in the evidence. It finds direct confirmation in the relationship between national life expectancy and the distribution of income. In the developed countries, where absolute poverty and deprivation are suffered by sufficiently small minorities not to have much impact on national mortality data, widespread relative poverty and relative deprivation is nevertheless created by large income differences within societies. Indeed, measures of income distribution are good indicators of the extent of relative poverty and deprivation in each society.

There is a very clear tendency for the developed countries with the highest life expectancy to be those where income differences are smallest. The income distribution data shown in Figures 1.2, 1.3, 1.4 and 1.5 comes, directly or indirectly, from the Luxembourg Income

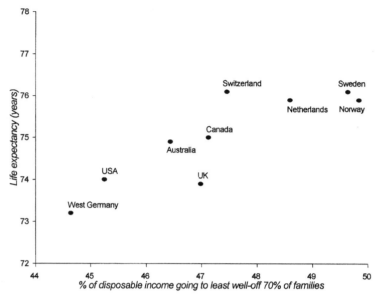

Figure 1.2 Life expectancy and income distribution, c1981

Source: Luxembourg Income Study, *working paper* 26,
World Bank *World Tables*

Note: Pearson correlation coefficient is 0.83 (significant at 1% level)

Study. Although data is available for rather few countries on the same basis, Figure 1.2 shows a statistically significant relationship between the proportion of total disposable income received by the least well off 70 per cent of families and the population's longevity. The responsiveness of life expectancy to changes in income distribution are shown in Figures 1.3 and 1.4. Figure 1.3 shows the relationship between the annual rate of change in the proportion of people in relative poverty in each of the 12 member countries of the European Community and the rate of change of life expectancy—again it is a statistically significant relationship. Figure 1.4 shows changes in the proportion of disposable income received by the least well-off half of the population (in contrast to the proportion of 'families' shown in Figure 1.2) in relation to the annual increase in average life expectancy. This figure excludes comparable data from countries where it is not possible to measure changes over periods of at least five years.

Lastly, Figure 1.5 is an attempt to include all countries for which any comparable income distribution data is available. As life

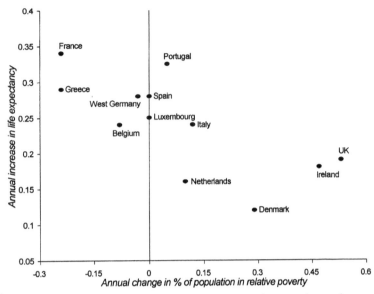

Figure 1.3 Changes in life expectancy and percentage of population in relative poverty, EC, 1975–85

Note: Pearson correlation coefficient is –0.73 (significant at 1% level)

Source: O'Higgins and Jenkins (1990)

expectancy tends to increase with time—regardless of what is happening to income distribution and economic growth—it has been necessary to adjust it to allow for the fact that some figures are much more recent than others. Without that, life expectancy would tend to be longest in the countries with the most recent data. Thus the vertical axis in Figure 1.5 shows how much each country's life expectancy is above or below what would be expected for its date (i.e. it is a residual after regressing life expectancy on the date). Again it is clear that the countries with the highest life expectancy are those with the most egalitarian income distributions. It is particularly interesting to note that the slippage in the relative position of the UK between 1969 and 1986 is very much in line with what would be predicted from its widening income distribution.

This evidence on the relationship between income distribution and national mortality rates confirms that relative income is an important determinant of health. It is also resolves the apparently inconsistent findings that health is influenced by income differences within, but not between, countries.

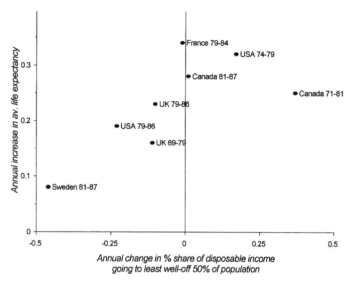

Figure 1.4 Changes in life expectancy and change in income distribution

Note: Pearson correlation coefficient is 0.72 (significant at 2.5% level)

Source: Luxembourg Income Study

A spurious relationship?

This relationship is unlikely to be an expression of the power of some underlying variable. Controlling for expenditure on medical care or for total government expenditure does not remove it. Such a close relationship is particularly unlikely to be spurious given the lack of underlying factors which may, plausibly, be even more powerfully related to both health and income distribution.

To interpret the relationship as reverse causality would mean assuming that income distribution was largely determined by health—a view which conflicts with the role of taxes and benefits, of profits and unemployment, which have played such an important role in widening income differentials during the 1980s. In addition, the relationship between class and health has been thoroughly examined for evidence of reverse causality. The effects of health on social class position appear to be only a small part of the relationship between class and health even though analyses are usually confined to people of working age when such effects would be at their maximum. In

31

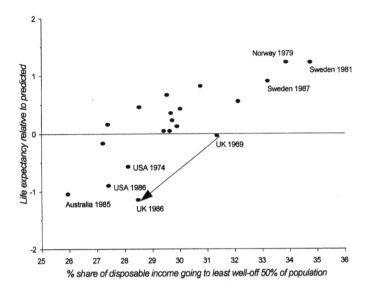

Figure 1.5 Life expectancy and income distribution

Note: Life expectancy is calculated relative to that predicted for year in question. Pearson correlation coefficient is 0.82 (significant at 1% level)

Source: Luxembourg Income Study

contrast, the evidence shown here uses life expectancy at birth which is dominated by deaths in infancy and in retirement when ill-health would not normally affect income.

It is sometimes suggested that income distribution might be related to health only because it serves as a measure of the proportion of the population still below some threshold of absolute income below which the absolute standard of living does still affect health. But if this were true, then economic growth would usually benefit national standards of health by reducing the proportion of the population remaining below that threshold level of income. Such a conclusion could only be avoided if the beneficial effects of economic growth were always offset by a widening income distribution. However, there is no sign of a tendency for richer countries to have wider income distributions. Nor, for reasons discussed below, can the relationship be interpreted as something affecting only a small minority of the population.

Apart from the direct associations which we have seen between income distribution and national life expectancy, there is considerable circumstantial evidence that health is related to relative income.

Periods when relative poverty has increased or decreased in Britain have seen the size of the class differences in mortality increasing or decreasing in parallel (Wilkinson, 1989). Since 1950 relative poverty has increased decade by decade. Using the same measures relative to the contemporary average income shows that the proportion of the families living in relative poverty increased from about 12 per cent in 1953 to 32 per cent in 1988-9 (Piachaud, 1988 and DSS, 1992). (Different proportions of the national average disposable income are used to define relative poverty for each family size. These proportions are however held constant over the whole period.) Social class differences in the rate of premature adult mortality appear to have widened during every decade over this period.

International comparisons tell the same story. In Sweden, where income differentials are much smaller than in Britain, class differences in both adult and infant mortality are also much smaller (Vagero and Lundberg, 1989 and Wilkinson, 1992). In Japan, where income differentials have narrowed substantially, class differences in mortality have—in contrast to the British experience—also narrowed (Marmot and Davey Smith, 1989). Lest it be thought that this is no more than a relationship between income inequality and health inequality, it is worth pointing out that in 1970 life expectancy and income distribution were quite similar in Japan and Britain; since then however while Japanese income distribution and life expectancy have become the best in the world, Britain has slipped on both counts relative to other countries.

Mortality and income distribution

One of the interesting features of the relationship between income distribution and health is the proportion of the population it seems to involve. There are three pieces of evidence bearing on this. The first is simply that the two-year improvement in average life expectancy which would be expected to result from Britain adopting an income distribution similar to the more egalitarian countries of Europe is too great to be accounted for in terms of improvements in the health of a small minority of the population alone. For instance, even if the high mortality rates in social classes IV and V were reduced to the average, they are too small a proportion of the population for that to account for the improvement in average life expectancy. More widespread improvements must therefore be involved.

Table 1.1 The effect on relative income of changing shares of total income

	% shares of total income to:		*Ratio of bottom to top incomes*
	Bottom 50%	*Top 50%*	
Example 1 more inequality	27	73	0.37:1
Example 2 less inequality	34	66	0.52:1
% increase in *relative income* of bottom 50%			40.5

The second indication is that correlations between life expectancy and the proportion of a country's total disposable income received by the poorest 20, 30, 40 per cent of the population show that the strongest relationship is with the poorest 50 per cent of the population (Wilkinson, 1992a) (or 60–70 per cent of 'families'). This is perhaps the best guide we have to the proportion of the population involved in this relationship.

The third indication that the proportion is more than a small minority comes from the comparisons between social class mortality differences in Sweden and in England and Wales. These comparisons are unusually accurate because researchers have, for the sake of comparison, gone to the trouble of classifying a large number of Swedish deaths according to the British social class classification of occupations. The results show not only that there are smaller social class differences in mortality in Sweden, but also that mortality among Swedish social class IV and V (semi and unskilled manual workers) is lower than among social classes I and II (professional and intermediate occupations) in England and Wales. This is true for both infant mortality and mortality of men between 15 and 64 years of age. One might surmise that while Sweden's narrower income distribution would reduce mortality rates most in lower classes, it might also be expected to produce a smaller improvement, as observed, in upper classes. This follows from the fact that even social class I will contain a few poorly paid or unemployed solicitors and company directors.

While the proportion of the population affected by this relationship seems to be large, at first sight the size of the differences in relative income associated with such big differences in life expectancy seem implausibly small. In Figure 1.5 the share of income going to the poorest half of the population is around 27 per cent among the less egalitarian countries and only about 34 or 35 per cent among the more egalitarian ones. How could a difference of not much more than seven per cent be so important? The most plausible answer is that a small change in income shares produces a large change in relative income. Table 1.1 provides an example. Here a seven per cent increase in the share of income going to the bottom 50 per cent means a seven per cent decrease in the share going to the top 50 percent. In this example the result (in the last column of Table 1.1) is that they move from getting only 37 per cent as much as people in the top half of the population, to getting 52 per cent as much. This represents a 40 per cent increase in their relative income. Although the seven per cent increase in the share of total income which we started with may be unimportant in absolute terms, it clearly represents a very substantial change in relative income.

It looks as if the distribution of income is the single most important determinant of levels of health in the developed world. But what is the point of increasing longevity if that just adds a few extra years to people's period of retirement and dependency? The answer is that changes in life expectancy are not a matter of adding a little onto the end of everyone's lives. Instead, life expectancy improves primarily by reducing the number of premature deaths. The socioeconomic differences in health which seem to be affected by income distribution appear to be greatest among people of working age. Indeed, while income distribution widened so dramatically in Britain during the later 1980s it was death rates for men and women aged 15–44 which rose (DOH, 1990). This means that instead of worsening the dependency ratio as the proportion of old people increases, it looks as if a narrower distribution of income would improve it by reducing the loss of younger people.

Relative income and 'psycho-social' influences on health

The importance to health of relative over absolute material standards is shown by the coexistence of three features. They are, first, health's lack of responsiveness to differences in GNP per capita between the developed countries; second, its sensitivity to income differences within countries; and third the close relationship between measures of income distribution and national mortality rates. That the influence of relative income should be so much stronger than absolute income has extremely important implications. It suggests that health is affected less by people's physical circumstances as such, or by their exposure to material hazards in themselves, than by what people feel about their circumstances. The impact of relative standards implies that comparative, cognitive processes, play a central role. It suggests that the psychosocial implications of living in deprived circumstances have a more important impact on health than any direct effect of the material circumstances themselves.

This picture is consistent with a great deal of recent epidemiological research on psycho-social factors in health. Factors such as a lack of social support, depression, low self-esteem, insecurity, stress, high job demand and low control have all been found to be associated with greater ill health or higher mortality rates (House and Landis, 1988; Ross and Huber, 1985; Kamen and Seligman, 1987; Sterling and Eyer, 1981; Johnson and Hall, 1988). Moreover the influence of these psychosocial factors seems broadly based, affecting the immune system as well as the cardiovascular system (Sterling and Eyer, 1981 and Henry, 1982). This would explain why over 90 per cent of the main causes of death are more common in lower than in upper classes.

The view that this relationship works through psycho-social pathways finds support from several other sources. It is, for example, not commonly recognised what a small proportion of the population suffer anything which could be called absolute as opposed to relative poverty. In 1988–9, as well as almost universal ownership of fridges and televisions, each of the following consumer durables were owned by over two-thirds of the *poorest* 20 per cent of households: a freezer, telephone, central heating and washing machine. In addition, between 40 and 50 per cent of these relatively poor households had a video and/or a car (DSS, 1992). A more direct indication of the importance of psycho-social pathways comes from a factory closure study which showed that many of the health effects of unemployment have a psycho-social source. It was found that illness increased when redundancies were first announced—well before people actually became unemployed (Beale and Nethercott, 1988)

Some of the difficulty of accepting that the health effects of relative income depend upon psycho-social processes is no doubt a failure to understand the impact of financial worries, job insecurity, a sense of helplessness and desperation. There is also a failure to appreciate the strength of the evidence linking psycho-social factors with physical health. The evidence comes not only from numerous carefully controlled observational studies such as those referenced above, but also from a number of experimental studies. To give just one recent example, 394 healthy subjects were first assessed for levels of stress and then given nasal drops containing five respiratory virus types. Members of a small randomised control group were given drops of saline solution only. The proportion of those in the experimental group who developed symptoms of respiratory illness was related in a dose-response manner to the initial stress scores—even after controlling for age, sex, education, allergic status, weight, season. Similar results were found for each of the five virus types, and differences in the proportion developing colds varied from 27 to 47 per cent according to stress levels. The differences were not accounted for by 'stress-illness mediators' including smoking, alcohol, exercise, diet, and sleep (Cohen et al., 1991) A failure to appreciate the psycho-social impact of relative deprivation, of financial insecurity and financial stress, coupled with a lack of appreciation of the strength of the evidence demonstrating the power of psycho-social influences on health, leads to an unwillingness to recognise the importance of relative income—and so of income distribution—to health.

The social fabric

If the scale of material inequality has psycho-social repercussions strong enough to have a major impact on life expectancy, then it seems likely that the same psycho-social processes would also affect other areas of life. It would be surprising if major changes in the mental and emotional state of the population did not affect things like the use of alcohol and drugs (whether medically sanctioned or not), the educational performance of school children, crime and family break-up. Even if there are relationships with other social processes to be found, the availability of internationally comparable mortality statistics ensured that it was the health impact of income distribution which first came to light. Any clear evidence of other relationships is likely to remain hidden while differences in definitions and reporting still prevent international comparisons. Some indications can however be gained from looking at trends in other social variables over time within countries. To illustrate that the health relationship may be part of a much broader social process, I shall touch on just two examples: the educational performance of school children and crime.

Although there has been an almost continuous slow increase in relative poverty since the middle of the twentieth century, income differences started to widen very much more quickly in the later 1980s. An analysis of Family Expenditure Survey data by the Centre for Fiscal Studies in Bath showed that top incomes started to grow very much more rapidly than others from around 1985 (Jenkins, 1991 and particularly Atkinson, 1993). With the combined effects of unemployment and the rise in top earnings, differentials widened particularly rapidly among people of working age. The effects on mortality rates are clear. Throughout the second half of the 1980s national death rates rose for both men and women across the age range 15–44 years (DOH, 1991). Such a dramatic widening of income differentials provides a unique opportunity to look for other effects.

That the increase in relative poverty may also have affected the educational performance of school children is shown by an analysis of reading standards among school children aged seven to eight years old in Buckinghamshire (Lake, 1991) The county used the same reading tests on all its school children from 1979 to 1990. An analysis of their records showed that there had been a decline in reading standards each year from 1985. The author says that 1985 was clearly the watershed year. The decline was unrelated to teaching methods but occurred in the schools with the most deprived catchment areas. Nor are these isolated results. In 1990 a group of educational psychologists reported that 'reading standards had declined in eight of the local education authorities in which they had worked in the 1980s, particularly in the period since 1985' (Gorman and Fernandes, 1992) It has always been recognised that educational standards vary inversely with relative deprivation and it is not surprising that both teaching and learning become more difficult as the proportion of children coming from homes in relative poverty rises. Thus, two-thirds of the variation between Local Education Authorities in the proportion of children passing five GCSE subjects with grade C or better in 1991–2 is related to deprivation as measured by the official census-based index (Morris, Blane and White 1994) (The correlation between children's GCSE results and adult male mortality rates is only a little weaker at 0.76.). Between 1979 and 1989 there was a two-and-a-half fold increase in the proportion of children from families living on less than half the national average income—a rise of from one in ten to one in four of the children in the average school class (DSS, 1992) With this came an increase in the number of children expelled from school and an increase in children admitted to mental hospitals (Rickford, 1993).

Crime rates may also be influenced by the same psycho-social effects of income distribution that have such a dramatic affect on health. Again, it is well known that the geographical distribution of crime (and of the victims of crime) follows the pattern of social deprivation. A former Commissioner of the Metropolitan Police claimed that in London their distributions were 'identical'. Research carried out in the Home Office shows an extremely robust statistical connection between crime rates and national economic fluctuations in total personal consumption expenditure. Whenever consumers' expenditure drops below its slowly rising long-term trend line, property crime increases. In other words, crime rates respond to shortfalls in expected income. People may feel their incomes inadequate and experience a sense of relative deprivation as easily in relation to a failure of income to meet their expectations and commitments, as they do in relation to the standards of others in society. Having established that crime responds to one form of relative deprivation, it does not stretch the imagination to think that it might respond to the other. While the Home Office research accounts very accurately for the annual fluctuations in crime, it makes no attempt to explain the all-important long-term upward trend in crime rates. The increase in the recorded crime rate in 1990 was equivalent to the total crime rate in the 1950s (Young, 1992). In the absence of a plausible explanation, there is a tendency to exaggerate the proportion of the ten-fold increase in crime rates during that period which can be explained simply as an increase in reporting of crime. But the trends in recorded crime would look less mysterious if the extent of the rise in relative poverty over this period was better known. As we have already noted, between the early 1950s and 1989 the proportion of the families living in relative poverty increased from about 12 per cent to around 30 per cent (Piachaud, 1988 and DSS, 1992).

If the growth of the modern economy and the increased use of cars and telephones has led to a major increase in the reporting of crime in Britain, one might expect to find similar changes in Japanese crime statistics. However, in contrast to the rise in reported crime in so many developed countries, Japan has seen a long-term decrease. It now has one of the lowest crime rates in the developed world, with fewer muggings in a year than Britain has in a week (Short and McCleod, 1992). Women are able to walk home late at night in Tokyo without fear of attack. Japanese travelling abroad have been so unwary that videos have been produced to warn them not to leave their valuables unattended. That recorded crime has declined in Japan, despite the greater ease of reporting, suggests that changes in reporting do not overwhelm the underlying trends. It also shows how empty is the increasingly popular tendency to assume that economic growth and increasing prosperity lead to more crime by making everyone more materialistic and self-interested. In marked contrast, the Japanese tend to attribute the fall in their crime rate to the decrease in poverty brought about by economic growth (Short and McCleod, 1992). The suggestion that as people become better-off they have less need to steal is plausible enough. But the opposite crime trends in Japan and the West suggest that the key is less a matter of trends in absolute poverty than of the less well known changes in the extent of relative poverty.

There is then circumstantial evidence to suggest that the effects of changes in income distribution may go well beyond health. Indeed, the powerful psycho-social influence of income distribution on health may turn out to be more important for what it tells us about the determinants of the quality of the social fabric of society than for what it tells us about the determinants of health. In this context the extent to which Britain's high sickness absence rates reflect greater ill health, or are a reflection of morale, may be largely an irrelevant distinction. It is enough to say that once again it is Japan which appears to have the lowest rates—variously estimated as not much more than a fifth of British rates (Henke, 1993 and CBI, 1987). No doubt they reflect both the very high standards of health, indicated by Japanese life expectancy, as well as better morale of employees resulting from a more egalitarian ethos in the workplace.

Implications

The significance of the relationship between income distribution and health for society at large is analogous to the significance of sickness absence for a firm's productivity. In both cases the ill health is of course a very substantial economic and social loss. But, in addition to that, a proportion of sickness absence is an indicator of differences in morale and commitment in the workplace. This is likely to mean that where sickness absence is high, people may work less efficiently even when not affected by sickness. In other words, productivity will be lower even after allowing for the extra days lost. The same is probably true on the societal scale. An impact on the educational performance of school children and on the crime rate, even if areas such as drug use and family break-up remained mysteriously insulated, would incur economic and social costs well beyond the costs of the additional ill health.

Although income distribution seems to be the most important known determinant of health in the developed world, it may turn out that what matters most about this relationship is that it suggests how the psycho-social quality of life in modern societies might be improved. Too often the quality of life is equated with the material standard of living measured by the absolute level of income or by GNP per capita. In many ways health can claim to be a better measure of the quality of life. Unlike income or GNP, which measure only the quantitative increase in the consumption of goods and services—warts and all—health is sensitive to both qualitative and quantitative aspects of change, to material, social and psychological life, and in both public and private spheres. If health is more sensitive to income distribution than to economic growth, might that indicate that the real subjective quality of life is now primarily dependent on income distribution? If so, it would accord well with the widespread impression that there is a sharp contrast between the material success and social failure of modern societies. If ways were known of improving the social fabric of society, few people would not give it a high priority.

Given that income differences within a society make such an important difference to health, while differences in economic growth between societies makes so little difference, the possibility arises that everyone's individual desire for additional income cannot be aggregated into a desire for economic growth. It is possible that the individual utility of additional income is in improving ones relative income and position in society. Raising material standards in unison with everyone else may be a case of having to run to stay in the same position. Instead of asking whether redistribution is compatible with economic growth, perhaps we should be asking how much difference each of them makes to the subjective quality of life.

A politically respectable justification for increased economic growth has been the belief that the privations of the poor stem from material standards which are inadequate in absolute terms. But the tendency to assume that the health disadvantage of the less well-off result from the physical rather than the psycho-social effects of material deprivation, reflects a desocialised view of human beings. The emphasis on the psycho-social here comes, as we have seen, from the primacy of relative over absolute income and from the results of a good deal of research on psycho-social factors. But two further points need to be made. One is that the health gradient goes all the way up the social scale so, for instance, administrative civil servants have better health than the executive grades below them. Yet these people are in secure employment and none could be called poor by the standards of our society. The other point is that although the total number of people affected by absolute material deprivation might seem large, as a proportion of the population they are a very small minority—as shown by the figures (above) of the ownership of consumer durables among the poorest 20 per cent of households.

The tendency to over-play the significance of the material in relation to the social position represents a failure to recognise the nature of the unhappiness caused by relative deprivation. There is no doubt that it is less nice to live in a home where some of the decoration is damaged by damp. Similarly a poor diet is less palatable than a good one. But taken out of their social context, these material disadvantages in themselves count for rather little compared to the low self-esteem, insecurity, depression and anxiety which relative deprivation so often engenders. Psycho-social factors can dominate one's consciousness and drain life of its value. What really damages the all-important subjective quality of life is having to live in circumstances which, by comparison with others, appear as a statement of one's personal failure and inferiority.

The implications of the health evidence are therefore three-fold. First, a wider income distribution raises national death rates and leads to greater ill health. The economic costs of premature death are high, though it is perhaps the costs of sickness absence which affect industry most directly. Second, the effect of income distribution on health is almost certainly an indication of the impact of income distribution on human functioning much more widely. This is likely to have a direct effect on productivity through the alienation of employees and on the rest of society through effects on educational performance, the crime rate and the prevalence of a number of other social problems. Third, it is probably wrong to think that the merits of income redistribution should be seen primarily in terms of the contribution they make to economic growth. The health evidence suggests that narrowing the gap in relative standards is now much more important to the quality of life in the developed world than further economic growth. Rather than ignoring the material needs of the less-well off, narrowing the gap means devoting increased production to their needs. By abandoning a pattern of growth which increased the standard of living as fast for the well-off as for the less well-off, we might be expected to improve the quality of life for everyone by simultaneously improving the social fabric and slowing the pace of environmental damage.

2 EDUCATION: OPPORTUNITY, EQUALITY AND EFFICIENCY

Tony Edwards and Geoff Whitty

The dominant assumptions shaping education policy in the 1960s were expansionist and egalitarian. It was in that context that Edward Boyle and Anthony Crosland, ministers in successive Conservative and Labour governments, justified large increases in educational expenditure by combining human capital arguments for investing more widely in the nation's 'pool of talent' with a confidence in the power of educational reform to even out the 'life chances' of children from different social backgrounds (Kogan, 1971). Both lines of argument were rejected by Black Paper opponents as reinforcing a dangerous 'cult of equality'. From the predominantly traditionalist perspective of the first 1969 collections and from the 'libertarian Right' position more clearly visible by 1975, the cult was seen as damaging educational standards, and as unfair to able children because it denied the basic truth that 'You can have equality or equality of opportunity; you cannot have both' (Cox and Boyson, 1975). The outrage which New Right heresies against 'progressive orthodoxy' aroused at the time was dismissed by the heretics themselves as the predictable response of a theocracy whose faith had been challenged. Since then, as often happens, heresy has become 'true' faith. Traditional Conservative belief in 'natural' inequalities has prompted fervent defence of academic standards and individual merit against those 'who promote mediocrity in the name of social justice' by using schools 'as instruments for equalising rather than instructing children' (Hillgate Group, 1987 and O'Hear, 1991). But the strongest influence on recent education policy has been a belief in what Keith Joseph termed 'the blind, uncoordinated wisdom of the market' and in its capacity, once freed from the constraints of 'welfarism', to raise standards and empower consumers (Joseph, 1976).[1] From both conservative and neo-liberal positions, the main charge against public education has been that it has declined in quality as it has become more equal.

It will be argued in this chapter that far from being marred by an egalitarian drift towards institutionalised mediocrity, the main failing of British (and more particularly English) education has been a skewing of provision, towards an academic minority and towards the socially advantaged, which has limited opportunity and wasted ability. Such progress as has been made towards greater equality of opportunity is now threatened by over-confidence in the wisdom of the market, and in the beneficial consequences of a 'free' interplay between educational supply and demand.

Inadequacies of a divided system

Contrary to the frequent assertions of its critics, the weight of evidence indicates that standards in public education have been rising. But this relative success is diminished by international comparisons which show a system doing well by the ablest, badly when the criterion changes to overall standards of attainment, and thus poorly adapted to the labour needs of a modern economy. This was the burden of Sir Claus Moser's warning to the 1990 British Association meeting, a warning which prompted the creation of a privately-funded, independent National Commission of enquiry into education. In his view, the 'major deficiencies' which made this country 'one of the least adequately educated of all the advanced nations', and which threatened 'dire consequences' for its future, were to be found in the scope and quality of what it provided for the majority of its children. Similarly, the CBI's targets for a properly educated workforce relate not to the academic elite whose fortunes have preoccupied the conservative Right, but to bringing at least 80 per cent of school leavers by 1997 to the standard of National Vocational Qualifications level 2 or its 'academic' equivalent of four GCSE passes (CBI, 1991).[2]

The main tendency in British education, however, has been to treat 'real' achievement as necessarily rationed. As Lyn Davies observes, doctors do not normally confront people 'who must be simultaneously motivated to compete to get well' and then assessed against others for their success in doing so, nor are only a fixed proportion of their patients permitted to achieve 'full health' (Davies, 1990). Yet when the 1992 GCSE results showed a fifth successive rise in the proportion of 'good passes' since the replacement of O-level in 1988, the Ministerial response was to suggest that examining standards had slipped. Changing modes of assessment certainly complicate the task

Table 2.1 Performance of pupils in public examinations at 16, England 1980–91 (percentages)

| | *1980-1* | | | *1990-1* | | |
	Boys	Girls	All	Boys	Girls	All
5 or more 'good' (A-C) grades	24.4	25.6	25.0	34.6	41.1	37.8
5 or more A-G grades	70.0	74.1	72.0	78.6	83.4	81.0
No graded result	13.1	9.9	11.5	9.4	7.0	8.2

Source: Department of Education and Science, *Statistical Bulletin* 15/92, July 1992 Table 2

of demonstrating educational improvement or deterioration over time, and the evidence cited here is confined to those public examinations which the government itself treats as providing indicators of LEA and school performance.

In relation to the main school leaving examination in England, Table 2.1 seems to indicate improving standards over a period when schools have been regularly attacked for permitting standards to decline. Indeed, it seems to show a rise in productivity which few parts of British industry have matched during that period. Nor has it been achieved, as might have happened, by concentrating on the more able and so widening the gap between the 'successful' and the 'failed'. For it is also notable that a sharp increase in the proportion with good results, especially marked among girls, has coincided with a fall in pupils leaving with no qualifications at all. Table 2.2 shows a significant rise, again more marked for girls, in the proportions gaining 'good passes' at GCSE in subjects which are usually considered to be the core of a good general education.

The main target of attempts from the Right to explain away such evidence has been the GCSE, accused of having adjusted the testing of performance downwards so as to give an illusion of improvement and so providing by means of 'a universal, low-standard examination' the next best thing to what the Left really wanted—which was to have no examination at all (North, 1987 and Sexton, 1988). Yet Table 2.3 shows a significantly improved success rate in the Advanced-level, regarded by the conservative Right as an oasis of academic rigour which has to be defended against attempts to broaden and thereby dilute it. Indeed, the 1993 results show the highest ever proportion of passes in the three top grades (48 per cent), prompting immediate

Table 2.2 School leavers with good O-level/GCSE grades or equivalent in each of the 3–4 core subjects, England 1981–91 (percentages)

	1981-2			1990-1		
	Boys	Girls	All	Boys	Girls	All
English, Maths, Science	21.5	17.8	19.7	28.2	28.6	28.4
English, Maths, Science and a modern foreign language	9.9	12.3	11.1	16.5	22.0	19.2

Source: Department for Education, *Statistics of Education: School Examination GCSE and GCE 1991*, DFE 1992, Table C4(ii)

Table 2.3 School leavers with A-level passes ((a) as a percentage of A-level entrants; (b) as a percentage of 18-year olds), England, 1980–91

	1980-1		1990-1	
.	(a)	(b)	(a)	(b)
2 passes	22.3	3.9	20.9	4.9
3 or more passes	50.6	8.9	57.6	13.6

Source: Department of Education, *Statistical Bulletin* 15/92, Table 14

predictions of widespread disappointment and anger as larger than ever numbers of well-qualified applicants compete for limited university places. Putting the output of the two stages together, as in Table 2.4, suggests a significant improvement at both the critical points of transition from school to further education or employment.

At least within a national context then, there is evidence of rising standards. But the picture looks very different when the frame is extended. Allowing for inevitable inexactness in establishing equivalence, the proportions of 16–year olds reaching roughly the same standard in mathematics, science and the national language as the 28 per cent who achieved three 'good passes' in England in 1990 were 50 per cent in Japan, 62 per cent in Germany, and 66 per cent in France (Green and Stedman, 1993). Such international comparisons are strikingly consistent in what they show: the top 20 per cent in the

Table 2.4 Highest qualification obtained by school leavers, Britain, 1975–90 (percentages)

	1975-6	*1980-1*	*1985-6*	*1989-90*
2 or more A-levels or equivalent	14	15	15	20
5 or more 'good' grades O level/GCSE/School Certificate	7	8	10	11
No qualification	21	15	13	10

Source: Central Statistical Office, *Social Trends* 23 HMSO (1993), Table 3.11

UK do as well as anywhere, but overall standards of performance are poorer than in most comparable countries and participation in full-time post-compulsory education stage is lower. For example, a cross-national study of achievements in science showed the English system to be relatively efficient at identifying and sponsoring able students, and at maintaining short degree courses with low wastage rates; its output of science graduates was therefore similar to that of countries which offered much wider access to higher education but experienced much higher wastage. At the age of 18, by which stage the English sample was already highly selected, achievements in science were among the highest (Postlethwaite and Wiley, 1991). The costs of that success become apparent when the performance of younger pupils is compared. In a survey of average attainment in science among 14-year olds and 10-year olds, English scores were among the four lowest, ranking just above the United States and alongside two systems—those of Hong Kong and Singapore—which have inherited the English bias towards an academic elite. Significantly for the argument here, Germany and the Netherlands did well in the comparisons of able pupils but also did well when attainment among the bottom third of the ability range was compared (Wallberg, 1991).

The relative fierceness of a sifting process apparently designed to convince a majority that 'real' educational achievement is not for them is most clearly visible in the provision for post-compulsory education and training. In 1990, 29 per cent English eighteen-year olds gained the basic qualifications for entry to higher education compared with 48 per cent in France, 68 per cent in (West) Germany, and 80 per cent in Japan (DES, 1992). The system for which they

Table 2.5   Vocational qualifications in the workforce (percentages)

	Britain (1988)	Germany (1987)	France (1988)	Netherlands (1985)
University degree, Higher vocational diploma	17	18	14	18
Intermediate vocational qualification	20	56	33	44
No vocational qualification	63	26	53	38

Source: S.J. Prais and Elaine Beadle, *Pre-vocational Schooling in Europe Today*, National Institute of Economic and Social Research 1991, p.36

qualify has moved, rather erratically but at an accelerating pace, in the direction of 'mass' higher education. Thus Britain's age participation rate rose from 7 per cent in the élite conditions of the early 1960s to 28 per cent in 1992, when a purportedly market-oriented government tried to apply a brake to expansion in the high-demand areas of arts and social science. Given the persistent view that 'more means worse', it is significant that the proportion of home applicants scoring high grades in their Advanced-level subjects is greater than when university entry was very much a minority activity (Halsey, 1992).

But if Britain's output of graduates is now similar to that in comparable countries, Table 2.5 indicates a serious relative deficiency when attention turns to the provision made 'between' school and higher education for 'intermediate' occupations in the labour market.

Participation in education and training beyond the compulsory stage has certainly risen, and done so steeply in recent years as job opportunities for young people have declined. (Table 2.6) It therefore compares well with the position in the mid-1970s, when half the age group were left to find their way into employment at sixteen with no further training for the skills they might need. International comparisons of its adequacy are complicated by the very different proportions of full-time and part-time provision in different countries (as well as by rather different definitions of what is counted as 'full-time'). In 1990 for example, an overall U.K. rate for the education and training of 16–18 year olds similar to that elsewhere was produced from the highest part-time figure (31 per cent) and the lowest full-time figure (40 per cent) of all the countries compared (DoE, 1993), and it is at least doubtful whether part-time provision of variable quality com-

Table 2.6 Participation of 17 year olds in education, England, 1981–93 (percentages)

	1981-2	1986-7	1991-2	1992-3 estimated
Males				
Full-time	27.0	29.8	45.3	51.5
Part-time	20.8	19.3	17.2	13.7
Females				
Full-time	33.1	35.4	52.8	59.0
Part-time	11.1	12.6	10.0	8.8

Source: Department for Education, *Statistical Bulletin* 16/93, June 1993, Tables 4 and 5

pensates for the relatively low proportion who remain in full-time education in Britain. This is especially so when 'academic' courses for those full-time students have traditionally been so superior in status and in the market value of the credentials to which they lead as to consign 'vocational' alternatives to a poor second-best. Though perhaps somewhat overstated, and being challenged now by the considerable rise in full-time registrations for 'vocational' courses, there is justification for concluding that the tradition of labelling general education beyond compulsory schooling as 'academic' has meant that 'there is effectively no mainstream post-sixteen education for most of the school population' (Smithers and Robinson, 1991).

This is an increasingly serious economic weakness as the proportion of high-skill 'knowledge jobs' rises, and as the high pace of technological change demands of the workforce a developed capacity to learn new skills. While the relationship of educational to economic performance is complex, it is now widely recognised that the quality of labour is decisive in determining the international competitiveness of goods and services. In Britain, the effects both of over-restricted general education and of low quality, low status vocational education have therefore been detected in poorer worker productivity at almost all levels in the labour market, and in particular at those 'intermediate' (technician and equivalent) levels of employment for which other countries expect both a higher level of general education and more extended vocational training (Prais and Wagner, 1987; NIESR, 1989 and Porter, 1990).

To conclude from these deficiencies that education has failed the economy would be too simple. Certainly a pattern of secondary education traditionally preoccupied with identifying and sponsoring

Table 2.7 Average examination scores at 16, by ethnic origin, gender and socio-economic group

Ethnic and socioeconomic group	Average exam score	
	Male	Female
Afro-Caribbean		
Professional/Managerial	27.1	24.9
Intermediate	21.1	18.1
Manual	14.3	15.6
Other*	12.1	16.1
All	(16.4)	(16.8)
Asian		
Professional/Managerial	30.7	27.8
Intermediate	27.2	25.9
Manual	23.3	22.5
Other*	12.9	14.1
All	(21.1)	(20.9)
White		
Professional/Managerial	30.4	32.3
Intermediate	23.7	25.0
Manual	17.6	20.0
Other*	13.0	13.4
All	(20.9)	(23.4)

* This includes those for whom insufficient information was reported

Source: David Drew and John Gray 'The fifth year examination achievements of young people of different social origins' *Education Research* 32(2) 1990, p. 114, Table 5. The data is taken from the Youth Cohort Study, and the scoring of examination results follows the ILEA practice of giving (eg) 7 points for an Ordinary-level grade A, 5 points for an Ordinary-level grade C or a CSE grade 1, down to 1 point for a CSE grade 5

the top 20 per cent has left large numbers unconvinced that prolonging their education would benefit them. This is why the evidence is encouraging that improved levels of attainment in GCSE have raised the aspirations of many 16 year olds, and been more significant than the declining opportunities for immediate employment in increasing the proportion of pupils continuing in full-time education (Gray, Jesson and Tranmer, 1993). There is still an entrenched cultural habit to be overcome however—that of so emphatically denying parity of esteem to different kinds of education that the worth of a course of study and the qualification resulting from it is measured by its distance from a traditional academic model of quality. But that failure is not merely attributable to the conservatism of schools. It reflects the high value of academic credentials in the labour market. Similarly, the low status of vocational education in this country is an effect as much as a cause of the 'low skills problem'. Limited demand by employers for high levels of trained competence reduces the value to individuals of investing in their own preparation for work, while relatively extensive opportunities for young people to enter unskilled jobs which offer no training make decisions to end schooling as soon as possible rational rather than short-sighted for the individuals making them. In what has been called a 'low skills equilibrium', supply and demand are matched but at a level inadequate for a modern economy (Finegold, 1992 and Finegold, Keep et al., 1990)

The argument so far has been that if the education of the ablest is what the English system does best, then the costs of that partial success have been high. They are apparent in a low educational base, with the general education of the majority ending too early and at too low a level and sharply polarised and unequal routes beyond that stage. Within this over-selective system, educational opportunities have continued to be more readily available to the socially advantaged to an extent which is unfair and economically unproductive. Contrary to claims from the Right, educational standards have not fallen. But nor have educational opportunities become progressively more equal.

Reducing inequalities?

By the 1960s, when confidence in egalitarian policies was still high, some progress towards more open access was apparent as a consequence of 'secondary education for all' and of expansion in further and higher education. By the early 1980s, however, it was clear that a substantial narrowing of social class differentials had not been achieved. Using as its measure of an open society an absence of relationship between social origins and social status which in a caste society would entirely coincide, the Oxford Mobility Study showed from evidence of the education and careers of boys born 1913–43 a correlation of 0.36 and therefore a very considerable inheritance of status from one generation to the next. While the chances of getting a university education (for example) increased considerably for working-class pupils over that period, their relative chances in comparison with the sons of professional and managerial fathers widened slightly. The general conclusion reached from the study was that the conventional portrayal of fairly steady progress towards greater equality of educational opportunity between social classes was 'an optimistic myth' (Halsey, 1986, p.134; Halsey, Heath and Ridge, 1980 and Heath and Ridge, 1983).

It could be argued in extenuation that such major structural reforms as 'secondary education for all', the rapid development of comprehensive schools, and expansion in higher education, had not yet had their full effect. It takes time for more open access to be recognised and acted upon by those unaccustomed to seeing educational opportunities for people like themselves. It takes even longer for increased opportunities and achievements in one generation to prompt higher expectations in the next. Yet both effects of educational expansion were among the cautiously optimistic conclusions of the Oxford study. In Scotland, where comprehensive reorganisation occurred earlier than in England and was less diluted by a powerful private sector or by the survival of many grammar schools, educational opportunities improved and general standards of attainment rose in the period between the ending of formal selection and the introduction of 'open' school enrolment (Gray, McPherson and Raffe, 1983 and Willms, 1992). Given the power of statistics to create their own reality where individuals are aware of the likelihood of success for 'people like us', it is reasonable to expect that broadening access to educational institutions or qualification levels will diversify entry to them by prompting 'realistic' aspirations among those who have not considered such access to be a natural continuation of their previous education. Thus the proportion of women in the university student population (though still only 42 per cent) has grown substantially since the 1960s, while there are 'some grounds for optimism' in the 'over-representation' of many ethnic minority groups in both applications and admissions to higher education[3] (Modood, 1993). Given the significance of parents' education, independent of social class, as a predictor of their children's aspirations and attainments, it is also reasonable to expect some levelling out of opportunity as general standards rise (Burnhill, Garner and McPherson, 1988 and 1990). It is at this point that optimism has to be moderated, and the likely consequences of recent educational policy considered.

The evidence displayed in Table 2.7 may dispel any notion of a simple black-white divide in educational attainment, but it also shows the continuing strength of the association of attainment with social class. While male children of white professionals did only 10 per cent better than those of Afro-Caribbean professionals, they did almost twice as well as children of white manual workers. And in the survey from which that evidence was taken, the proportion of professional and managerial households was three times higher in the White sample than among the young people of Afro-Caribbean or Asian origin. Table 2.8 illustrates, on a larger scale, the extent to which educational participation and performance remain closely associated with social origins, unequal educational outcomes in one generation contributing to unequal opportunities for the next. The statistics relate to people who entered the labour force between the mid-1950s and the late 1980s. They show that children of unskilled manual workers were one tenth as likely to gain a university qualification as those of professional parents, and eight times as likely to achieve no qualifications at all. By doing so, they suggest a double inefficiency in the education system which has persisted over time. First, and unless it is assumed that the social distribution of ability in one generation matches closely the occupational positions of the generation before, then an ostensibly meritocratic system has been less than effective even in its own terms in identifying and promoting ability. Secondly and more seriously, the figures indicate a continuing and damaging waste of talent in large parts of the population. For reasons outlined later in this chapter, a situation unlikely to have improved significantly in recent years and is likely now to deteriorate unless current policies change. Thus a recent series of studies of five thousand young people making the transition to adulthood showed that qualifications at sixteen were the best predictor of their occupational prospects, with sharply segregated 'career trajectories' and very different risks of unemployment apparent beyond that stage, and that the nature and level of those qualifications was still closely associated with parents' socio-economic status (Bates and Riseborough, 1993 and Banks et al., 1992).

Given the two-way relationships suggested earlier between opportunity and aspiration, it is interesting that the further improvement in A-level results in 1993 brought immediate predictions, evidently alarming some Conservative Members of Parliament, of middle-class anger as too many well-qualified applicants competed for university places. Yet the worst effects of intensifying competition are likely to be experienced by the less confident, more marginal applicants, by those not being sponsored by 'successful' schools, and by those (of whom a hugely disproportionate number will be girls) whose qualifications do not fit in with the government's promotion of science and technology and its constraints on expansion in arts and social science. The universities' central admissions statistics show that applications from socio-economic classes 3–5 rose by 44 per cent over

Table 2.8 Highest level of qualification of workers aged 25–54 by socio-economic category of father, Britain (1991) (%)

	Degree	Other higher qual.	A level	O level	CSE	None
Professional	32	19	15	19	4	7
Employers/managers	17	15	13	24	9	19
Intermediate lower non-manual	17	18	12	24	7	18
Skilled manual, self-employed non-professional	6	10	8	21	12	40
Semi-skilled manual, service	4	7	6	19	12	50
Unskilled manual	3	5	4	15	10	60

Source: Central Statistical Office, *Social Trends* 23 HMSO (1993), Table 3.26

the period 1977–90 compared with a rise of just under a third from classes 1 and 2, but they also show that the ratio of admissions to applications fell by 10 per cent compared with only 4 per cent for applications from the more advantaged backgrounds. At least on past evidence, increasing pressure of demand on supply is likely to increase such differences in class chances.

By what criteria then, is progress towards reducing educational inequality to be assessed? It has been a traditional conservative position to defend 'natural hierarchies of worth' against 'unnatural' egalitarian efforts to ignore them. Thus Anthony O'Hear insists that 'true education' should be unashamedly 'divisive, elitist and ineglitarian' because it should 'undemocratically' recognise and create real distinctions between people; unequal achievements are entirely acceptable when they are the deserved outcome of talent, enterprise, ambition and hard work (O'Hear, 1991). The logic of that position is that inequalities should not be the undeserved outcome of having had no chances to succeed. There has therefore been a long tradition of constructing ladders of educational opportunity for the 'poor but able', such sponsoring of individual talent being presented as a necessary part of a meritocratic society. The Assisted Places Scheme, introduced in 1981 to enable 'able children from less well-off homes' to attend independent schools on subsidised places, is a recent example of constructing limited escape routes from the supposed inadequacies of public education rather than attempting a more general improvement. It was immediately objected to as part of a profoundly inegalitarian strategy of 'starving the maintained schools of funds, and then rescuing the brightest children from the surrounding wreckage'[4] (Labour Party, 1980).

Such highly selective rescue operations are incompatible with a comprehensive concept of equal opportunity which seeks to reduce structural differences in the education available to children from different social backgrounds. What is sometimes termed the 'weak' version of that approach concentrates on the equalising of access, though the inequalities outlined earlier make that too a formidable challenge to existing provision. The 'strong' version, concerned with securing more equal educational outcomes from the opportunities formally made available, is often travestied from the Right as levelling down to a uniform and therefore undivisive mediocrity.[5] Yet the objective is not uniformity, what the Commission on Social Justice terms 'arithmetic equality', but to reduce the gap between educational 'success' and 'failure' wherever that gap can be shown to be unnecessarily wide. From this perspective, inequalities are unjust and therefore unacceptable when 'opportunities and life chances...are heavily skewed towards an élite', when they are too dependent on the 'accidents' of birth and upbringing, and when they are larger than can be justified by reasonable notions of merit[6] (CSJ, 1993). They are acceptable when they arise from unavoidable differences between individuals in capacities and preferences, and from the exercise of personal choices which in a democratic society cannot reasonably be denied. The inequalities identified in the section which follows are unacceptable because they do not meet those criteria.

Avoidable inequalities

Substantial inequalities in access to educational resources arise from the academic and social selectiveness of what is available beyond the compulsory stage. The 'top 20 per cent' have access to considerably more financial support than the less fortunate majority, a university student for example being far more costly to public funds than even the most fortunate beneficiaries of youth training. As Francis Green's chapter in this volume shows, inequality persists through employment because opportunities for subsequent vocational training are also biased towards professional and managerial occupations. The children of parents in those occupations are themselves much more likely to stay on at school, to follow the prestigious 'academic' routes, and to enter higher education. A notable aspect of that situation is the prominence of privately educated students beyond the compulsory stage, a sector which caters for 7 per cent of children of compulsory school age providing almost half of those who end their schooling with three Advanced-level passes.

At the other end of the educational process, the fact that compulsory schooling begins earlier in the U.K. than in most European countries might constitute an advantage were it not undermined by relatively poor provision for children under five. The proportion of 3–5 year olds attending school or nursery classes rose from 20 per cent in 1971 (when Margaret Thatcher made its extension *a priority*) to 44 per cent in 1981 and to almost 53 per cent in 1991. But it remains among the lowest in European Community, despite incontrovertible evidence of its high correlation with later educational achievement and therefore of its value as social investment. Being discretionary, it has been made particularly vulnerable to central government assessments of (and imposed reductions in) what Local Authorities can spend on their services, and to their consequently reduced scope for defining their own priorities. But it also provides clear example of how much educational access can depend on where a child lives. In January 1991 all thirty-six English Metropolitan Authorities, but only ten of the thirty-nine Shire Counties, provided nursery schools or classes for more than 50 per cent of 3–5 year olds. The size of the variations is illustrated by the figures for Harrow (5 per cent), Stockport (19 per cent), Essex (22 per cent), Greenwich (47 per cent), and South Tyneside (59 per cent).[7] Such differences reflect neither levels of need nor levels of demand in the local populations.

Within the period of compulsory schooling, the most obvious inequalities of the past lay in the process of selection for different types of secondary education offering very different prospects. As A.H. Halsey put it, the typical professional of the 1960s was 'a grammar school boy with education beyond school' while the typical unskilled worker 'went to elementary or secondary modern school and no further'. It was Tony Crosland's view, in urging Local Authorities to end selection, that what was being tested at the age of 11 was so largely a matter of social class background that the existing system carried children from different social origins along segregated educational tracks to segregated occupational destinations (Halsey, 1974 and Crosland, 1974). The confidence that structural reform would transform that situation seems excessive in retrospect, because it was largely unaccompanied by questioning what should be taught in schools which should no longer be sharply differentiated by status and intake. The National Curriculum provides an apparently bold answer to that question, its egalitarian potential highlighted in the notion of common access to a high threshold of skills, knowledge and understanding wherever a child lives and goes to school. This is how the DES partly presented its benefits for the consultation exercise of 1987, yet a common entitlement to 'broadly the same good and relevant curriculum' is not easily reconciled with the 'open', competitive market in education which other parts of the 1988 Reform Act—and more blatantly its 1993 successor—are designed to achieve. It is not surprising then that the National Curriculum has been opposed from the Right as paternalist, over-prescriptive, and incompatible with a proper trust in market forces.

Even within its own terms, the National Curriculum draws attention to the resources needed at LEA and at school level to sustain curriculum breadth and balance and so has reinforced objections to some basic inequalities in funding. Why should it be assumed, for example, that younger pupils can be taught effectively in larger classes than pupils in the later stages of the same curriculum, or that the average per capita funding of children in the last year of Primary school should be £350 less than their Secondary school will receive in the following year? The apparently preferential treatment of city technology colleges, and government inducements (especially in capital expenditure) to schools to opt for grant-maintained status, seem unfair when both categories of school are publicly-funded to teach the same subjects. And although independent schools are encouraged rather than statutorily obliged to meet its requirements, the existence of a supposedly 'national' curriculum highlights the advantages in buildings, facilities and recurrent spending of that part of the private sector which is also highly selective in the pupils for whom it provides.

Along with expectations of rough comparability in the resources demanded by 'broadly the same' curriculum go assumptions about acceptable levels of school performance. It is often asserted that 'the poorest schools' are largely concentrated in inner-city areas 'where they take large numbers of children from disadvantaged backgrounds' (Office of Her Majesty's Chief Inspector, 1992). If that were true, it would still be difficult to establish how far such schools are 'poor' for reasons beyond their control. It is the more difficult because ostensibly technical arguments about how to take socio-economic factors into account in assessing the performance of schools are highly political. It has been the government's preference not to do so at all, on the grounds that it provides schools with excuses for their own failings. Yet the very high correlations between examination performance and prior attainment, and between examination performance and parents' socio-economic status, make it impossible to assess a school's performance fairly without considering what results would be predicted from the character of its intake. The difference that good schools make to their pupils' attainments and aspirations is now a well-documented challenge to environmental determinism, and to that depressing of educational expectations which can arise from finding too much mitigation in the circumstances with which schools have to cope (Mortimore, Sammons et al., 1988; Smith and Tomlinson, 1989; Gray, Jesson and Sime, 1990; Willms, 1993 and Reynolds and Cuttance, 1992). But it is also important not to detach schools from their economic and social environment as though they are entirely responsible for creating their own conditions of work. At LEA level, the controversial 1992 'league tables' of performance showed, predictably, an overwhelming predominance of affluent southern Authorities such as Harrow, West Sussex and Surrey among those with the highest proportions of pupils gaining five or more 'good' GCSE passes and the lowest proportions leaving with no graded passes at all. As predictably, the 'bottom ten' were entirely urban and largely inner-city (for example, Manchester, Knowsley, Lambeth, and Southwark). Yet a decade of research into how best to measure the value added by schooling shows the close association of 'output' with the social characteristics of a school's intake and an LEA's population.[8] The government may partly recognise this in principle, yet the ideological attractions of 'informing' consumers with apparently hard evidence sustain its belief in league tables which take no account of the circumstances in which schools work.

Differences between LEAs in their funding of schools, though partly historical and partly a reflection of local political priorities, also reflect the very different populations for which Authorities have to provide. Those 'high-spending' councils which have figured so prominently in Conservative campaigning against local government also had high scores on the government's own 'index of disadvantage', which recognised (for example) that providing for relatively large numbers of children whose first language was not English or who came from overcrowded, low-income homes justified higher levels of central grant. The recent reduction in the number of variables included in this 'index' on the grounds that they were double-counting the same factors has served to shift resources away from urban areas, and so raises again old arguments about the effectiveness of positive discrimination. An analysis (published in 1984) of differences in LEA expenditure which failed to find any 'direct or predictable' effects of spending levels on educational outcomes, concluded nevertheless that 'by far the best predictors' of pupil achievement at LEA level were 'the proportion of manual workers' children—a proxy for social class— and the indicator of housing conditions' (Lord, 1984). If that conclusion indicated 'limits to what the government can do in terms of equalising educational expenditure by altering grant distribution', it was also a salutary warning against over-estimating the power of educational interventions to compensate for inequalities in home background. In the same year, the highest-spending LEA in the country noted a lack of evidence in London that the extra resources being provided by the Authority were compensating for 'less favourable pupil characteristics and environmental circumstances' by producing improved pupil performance (ILEA, 1984). Yet inadequate educational provision reinforces other disadvantages when, for example, an ethnic minority group already suffering unusually high levels of overcrowding, unemployment and low income was also severely under-provided with school places and when parents' strong interest in their children's education was undermined by feelings of helplessness. In that case, argued the researcher, it was unlikely that a generally well-intentioned LEA would not have acted more vigorously, or that the DES would not have intervened, 'if the authority had been predominantly white and middle class' (Tomlinson, 1991). Yet it is also unreasonable to expect the school system to 'compensate for society' by providing educational remedies where the problems lie elsewhere.

There is evidence throughout this book of widening differences in conditions of life through the 1980s. Consequently higher correlations between socio-economic circumstances and (for example) health are readily translated into statements about length of schooling and levels of attainment. Defined in relative terms (which neo-liberals usually reject) as living on less than half the average wage, 25 per cent children were 'in poverty' in 1988–9 compared with 10 per cent in 1979. Even in absolute terms, the bottom 10 per cent of households suffered a 6 per cent fall in real income during that time and there has been a particularly steep rise (to 73 per cent) in the proportion of children living in households with incomes below the national average (HMSO, 1992). Such basic inequalities structure educational attainment through the effects on children of their parents' sense of failure and of insecurity. While there are possibilities of 'escaping from disadvantage' through educational achievement, and while such escape depends partly on individual qualities and aspirations, the chances are markedly better for those individuals who are relatively less disadvantaged in housing, income and or family circumstance (Pilling, 1990). Prolonged parental unemployment, and awareness of high levels of unemployment among relatives, friends and acquaintances, must be added to that list of disadvantages as a potent source of educational inequality and a potent threat to educational standards. More generally, a major consequence of the competitive, consumer-driven market in schooling which the government wishes to see is that it will heighten the advantages of children whose parents have the knowledge, time and confidence to apply for the 'best' schools and make their applications count. At the same time, it is likely to discriminate against those whose parents have more pressing immediate concerns than being an educational 'consumer' and who are struggling to survive increasing social and economic problems with decreased social support (Brown, 1990).[9]

Conclusion

There was a strong tendency in the 1960s to assume that the obvious handicaps of poverty had diminished sufficiently for egalitarian attention to focus largely on the school system. That view is not tenable. Yet the directions currently being taken by government policy make it necessary to return finally to the education sector itself as a source of avoidable inequalities because the emerging 'framework for schools', promoted as providing the same opportunities...for every pupil everywhere' (to quote the Prime Minister's foreword to the 1992 White Paper *Choice and Diversity*), is more likely to extend inequality and so intensify the inefficiencies which this chapter has described.

What is intended is the transformation of a public service into a competitive market. At the post-compulsory stage, as Francis Green describes, the mechanism of training credits to be 'cashed' by trainees with the supplier of their choice is intended to promote a wider range of supplying agencies, many of which will be operating for profit. At school level, the use of state power to equalise educational opportunities is to be replaced by an 'empowering' of individual parents to choose their children's schooling in an increasingly diversified and competitive market unconstrained by traditional notions of welfare. Subjecting schools to the disciplines of consumer preference, it is argued, will make them more effective; forcing them to be responsive to consumer demand will make them less homogeneous as well as less mediocre; and a system which is diversified by the pressures of consumer choice will also ensure better opportunities for all. The approach embodies a belief that schooling will become more efficient as it becomes freed from the egalitarian prejudices of the 'education establishment' and thus more heterogeneous and more unequal.

The various reforms designed to achieve that aim constitute a highly ambitious experiment with the nation's schooling. In the context of those international comparisons of educational performance cited earlier, it is notable that supposedly open enrolment to schools, league tables of school performance, and the undermining of public accountability have not been considered necessary reforms in the relatively high achieving systems with which British schooling is often compared. Within the British context, the creation of a market (or quasi-market) in education is being driven forward by faith in market forces as the best means of distributing goods or services. From that perspective, the outcomes of such distribution are necessarily unequal or there would be no incentives for the able and ambitious; but they are not unfair because a market is a neutral mechanism for matching supply and demand, the inequalities between individuals which it produces being neither intended nor predictable. In practice however, markets display a strong tendency to redistribute resources from the weak to the strong. And if it is predictable that the operation of a market in education is likely to further disadvantage those already limited in their opportunities, then there is a collective responsibility to avoid that outcome.[10] The particular predictions which follow lead to a general conclusion that the deficiencies of an already over-selective and divided system are likely to be made worse by the government's promotion of a more competitive, selective and hierarchical school system.[11]

The traditional academic model of secondary education, the supply of which is by definition limited, is likely to retain and increase its dominance in a competitive and supposedly more diversified market. It is argued from the Right that schools will respond to the consumer demand released by open enrolment by seeking some distinctive market appeal. It is much more likely, however, that 'successful' schools will be identified largely by their conformity to the dominant academic model.[12] Those schools whose success is 'demonstrated' by their position on the league tables of examination performance to which the government is committed are highly likely to be schools considerably advantaged by their intakes. Since the relationship of results to the composition of the intake is a social fact known to schools and to prospective parents, schools which are over-chosen are much more likely to use their market position to become more selective than to expand. They thereby worsen the position of less successful competitors. In Scotland, where open enrolment was introduced earlier than in England and Wales, there has been considerable evidence of such 'band-wagon effects, and little evidence of the market functioning as a self-correcting mechanism' because the 'trap' of declining parental demand is so difficult to escape (Adler, 1993).[13] Schools enabled to be selective, whether overtly or covertly, by a high level of demand are likely to do so directly by 'academic aptitude' and indirectly by social background. The main outcome of such selection will be a disproportionate representation of already socially advantaged children in the most 'successful' schools, both as cause and as effect, and of already socially disadvantaged children in schools identified as 'failing'.

There is nothing new in that situation. What is new is a government policy of deliberately increasing funding differences between schools on the grounds that they are deserved by relative success or failure. A funding formula driven mainly by pupil numbers ensures that popular schools are rewarded, while the significantly larger unit of resource for older pupils further benefits those with intakes likely to produce large sixth forms. The resulting inequalities, which LEAs progressively constrained in the money they can retain for planning purposes are increasingly unable to alleviate, present a fundamental challenge to that equal access to the same 'broad and balanced' curriculum to which the Government also declares itself committed. They are made worse by the government's encouragement of schools to become more entrepreneurial and more selective by opting out of the network of schools and the ethos of co-operation which LEAs at their best embody. Instead of that overall enhancement of quality which markets are claimed to produce, there is likely to be a hierarchy of schools and types of school increasingly stratified in status and funding which will diminish the prospects of many pupils.

The argument of this chapter is that a system which has been inefficiently unequal would then, become more inefficient by becoming even more unequal.

3 TRAINING: INEQUALITY AND INEFFICIENCY

Francis Green

> Over the last decade, there has been a revolution in Britain's education and training. The Government have introduced far reaching reforms and backed them up with increased resources. As a result, parents and their children now have choices and opportunities that simply did not exist for previous generations.
> (John Major, in Department of Education and Science, 1991)

Education and training in Britain have undergone considerable changes in the last decade. In the schools, the Government has developed a National Curriculum. It has altered the assessment system with the introduction of GCSEs and it is pressing forward with a system of testing in the classroom. It has been wrenching control of schools and colleges away from local government. Meanwhile there has been a substantial change in the way that government support for training is organised and in the level of that support. More than a million people have passed through the Youth Training Scheme (later Youth Training) since its inception in 1983. Schemes such as TVEI and Compacts have been introduced, aiming to bridge the gap between school and work. The Manpower Services Commission, with its vestiges of corporatism, has been abolished and replaced by the system of locally-based and business-dominated TECs and LECs, funded directly by the Government. In an attempt to develop a 'training market' the Government is moving towards a system of providing training credits, improved career guidance and career development loans, while at the same time exhorting companies to improve their training via its 'Investors in People' accolades. Alongside these changes, employers have themselves been providing more training to employees across the age range, and across all socio-economic groups. Young people have begun, in the later part of the 1980s to stay on longer at school. More are attaining A levels, and many more are going on to higher education. One indication that

65

some of these changes represent real advances, at least in terms of the Government's resource commitment to education and training, is given by the squeeze this introduces on Treasury finances in the current era of fiscal austerity.

This range of activity may appear at first sight to indicate, not only that the Government is seriously tackling the often-mentioned skills deficiencies of the British economy (in relation to other countries' economies), but also that a meritocracy is being created with universal chances to participate. A rhetoric of free choice has accompanied many of the policy innovations, and it has been generally harnessed to the prospect of equal opportunity. Such objectives command widespread support. It is, however, open to question as to how far the objectives are being fulfilled.

Consider some immediate worries. The prospect of equal opportunity for all is a hollow one for those with insufficient resources (the majority) to fund a superior private education for their children, or for those who cannot afford to take the risk of giving up work to obtain further qualifications. There are also major barriers on the available routes for personal economic development deriving from the operation of the economic system. Training and the development of advanced work skills cannot be divorced from the workplace itself, which is a centre both of production and of learning. Therefore, in order to have wide opportunities for training and the acquisition of advanced and satisfying work skills, individuals have to be able to find employers who can provide the appropriate setting. Most employers would need to be committed to high-skilled methods of production, and to operate in the relatively advanced sectors of the global division of labour for this to be so. To ensure this is the case, employers cannot be left alone to decide for themselves on the skill content of their workplaces. Much training is for transferable skills, a fact which, with imperfectly competitive labour markets or missing capital markets, implies there are externalities (Stevens, 1993) involving the risk of skill 'poaching'. These externalities call for state intervention and other forms of regulation to support the acquisition of skills. Not least, the macroeconomic support needs to be provided to enable continuity of full employment, so as to give employers the confidence to invest in workforce training for the long term, to allow workers to choose their employers and to prevent the atrophy of individuals' skills characteristic of prolonged periods of unemployment. In this light, Britain's experience of mass long-term unemployment and its employers' tradition of using relatively low skill methods of production across large swathes of the economy, pose some severe limitations on the opportunities for many individuals. Coupled with the abolition of Industrial Training Boards, which alongside the Manpower Services Commission had been the prime regulatory means of circumventing the externality problem, there must remain some cause for concern that the free market for training is leading to inefficiently low rates of skill acquisition.

It is necessary, therefore, to examine the reality lying behind the official rhetoric of the 'education and training revolution'. This chapter focuses on the issue of training, broadly considered. It examines the extent of inequality in access to training in Britain, and the relationship of this inequality to what is widely regarded as 'Britain's skills problem'. In the next section Britain's 'low-skills equilibrium' is briefly outlined. In Section 3, the available facts are documented: the dimensions of inequality over access to training are reviewed, and the evidence on the effects of training is examined to see if this suggests that the training that takes place is likely to be reducing economic inequality and/or raising productive efficiency. Section 4 concludes by briefly examining the link between inequality in access to training and the government's training philosophy.

Britain's skills problem

The relationship between training in Britain and the so-called skills problem confronting the British economy needs to be placed in a global and historical context. First, we must note that the world economy has still not stabilised after the major shocks it received from the late 1960s onwards. This date marked the end of the so-called 'golden age of capitalism', a period in which the advanced countries experienced unprecedented economic growth, when economic crises were comparatively infrequent, living standards were steadily increasing and mass unemployment was seemingly a thing of the past. The period since then has been one of structural change in the wake of much more numerous economic problems and crises, of which the celebrated oil shocks of 1973 and 1979 are only two examples. Most, but not all countries, have seen a return to the boom and bust cycle, and increasing unemployment. Few countries have avoided double digit inflation.

Underlying these events, two fundamental related changes were going on. First, there was an increasing internationalisation of the economy. Not only was trade growing faster than each country's GNP, we see also the growing internationalisation of finance, and in particular the growing strength of multinational corporations. And for the first time, many of these multinational corporations started to locate their manufacturing facilities in parts of the third world, especially Latin America and the Asian NICs. The second major change has been termed the end of 'Fordism', that is, the end of the era when the mass production assembly line was the technological paradigm for efficient production. In the new and modern economy, with the aid of the increasingly pervasive information technology, 'flexibility' in production became the watchword for dynamic efficiency. This meant that low-skilled manufacturing work would be the kind that was parcelled out to the low-wage areas of the economy, while the more highly skilled work, necessary at the research, design and management end would be concentrated in the newly modernised countries in Europe, Japan and the US.

This outline characterisation of the present period is deficient in one serious respect. On the one hand, a small number of notionally third world countries have already raised their skill levels above many regions of the so-called advanced world, and are able to take on even the more technologically advanced lines of production—Singapore is a good example, but similar trends are found in Taiwan, South Korea and Hong Kong. On the other hand, considerable volumes of low-skilled work persist in the advanced nations, despite the fact that wages remain much higher than in the third world. Hence, it is more accurate to think of two tracks for the countries of the advanced world, one based on the production of goods and services at the frontiers of innovation and quality, the other focused on price competition and low wage production. These two responses correspond to a two-fold characterisation of the developed economies, now much in vogue, as either in a 'high-skills equilibrium' or in a 'low-skills equilibrium' (Finegold and Soskice, 1988).

Although this dual characterisation is something of a simplification, it has served as a useful device for examining the location of national economies within the world market. The implications for efficiency are straightforward, from the point of view of a nation's citizens. For those in a low-skilled economy, inefficiency derives from their low productivity and pay compared to what they could with existing technology have been producing and earning in a high-skilled economy.[1] From the point of view of businesses, however, the efficiency ranking is ambiguous: a low-skilled/low-pay system could as easily provide higher as lower profits. For this chapter I adopt the former concept of efficiency because the issue at hand is the relationship between the inequality among, and productive efficiency of, those living in a particular economy.

The following findings tend to support the hypothesis that Britain has conformed most to the model of a low-skills developed economy:

- Compared to competitor nations education participation rates are especially low in Britain. (see chapter 2)
- British school children perform relative poorly in internationally comparable tests. With regard to science, English 10-year olds and 14-year olds on average lag behind children of the same age in most of 17 other countries (International Association for the Evaluation of Educational Achievement, 1988)
- The British workforce has a relatively low level of certified qualifications. To cite some recent evidence, by way of example, the British workforce compares unfavourably in this respect with Canada (Ashton, Green and Lowe, 1993), with Germany (Mahoney, 1992; Mason, Ark and Wagner, 1992), with the Netherlands (van Ark, 1990a; Mason, van Ark and Wagner, 1993), with France (van Ark, 1990b; Mason, Ark and Wagner, 1993) and with Japan (Prais, 1987). Moreover, a number of these studies have been able to trace a substantial connection between qualification levels and labour productivity. Earlier studies from the National Institute of Economic Research showed that a particular deficiency in Britain was in intermediate-level skills. Ryan (1991) argues that the shortage of key technicians and craft-level skills has been a major source of inefficiency.
- There is also a good deal of case study evidence that there are substantial sectors of industry, particularly in the sectors of low paid employment, where training is regarded as unnecessary for workers and a waste of time. (Keep and Mayhew, 1993).

Set against this negative portrayal, there are some positive signs. In 1984, less than 10 per cent of employees had received job-related training in the previous four weeks; by the early 1990s, the figure was around 15 per cent (Felstead and Green, 1993). Although the average length of training has been decreasing (Greenhalgh and Mavrotas, 1993), the 1980s saw a widening of exposure to training, especially among older workers. This expansion has been halted by the recession, but there has been no collapse of training. Certain forms of regulation and intervention, such as the Food Safety Act 1990 and other industry and occupation specific regulations have provided a floor to training levels. Moreover, the intensification of competition combined with the spread of the BS 5750 quality control standard has compelled many firms to step up their provision of short training courses (Felstead and Green, 1993). The question therefore arises: is training in British workplaces transforming the British economy, moving it more towards a high-skills plane? Is the training being made available across all sectors of society, so as to start to address low skill levels? Is the training for the less advantaged strata of society of sufficient quality to benefit both them and the economy generally in terms of increased wages and increased productivity?

Inequality in access to training

An economy with a generally low level of skills is clearly inefficient, in that the effectiveness of the labour force is low. But there is nothing necessarily inegalitarian about it. It is possible that a workforce, from the most highly qualified surgeon or engineer to the least qualified manual worker, could be equally poorly educated and trained. Their work might all be of similarly low productivity and their pay correspondingly depressed. But the low skills equilibrium characterising the UK has a strongly inegalitarian thrust involving a high proportion of relatively badly paid and unproductive jobs. In training, the problem is not simply a low average level but also unequal access which helps to reproduce and intensify the inequalities generated in the education system.

Access

The distribution of training experience depends both on the individual wanting training and on the opportunity being available. There is evidence of considerable excess demand for training among the British population: in a 1987 Government survey some 43 per cent were estimated to have had unsatisfied training demands (Rigg, 1989). The proportion was greater amongst older males, and amongst those with only a few, or no qualifications. Financial constraints and domestic constraints were the most often quoted reasons for not getting the training people wanted, with domestic constraints being the most crucial for women. But for those in employment the key factor is likely to be whether the employer provides the training. Hence much of the distribution of access to training—especially amongst the employed, but also amongst the rest of the population—reflects the distribution of opportunities for and constraints on training.[2]

We can examine the extent of inequality in access to training in Britain along a number of dimensions, the most salient being income, occupational status and gender. According to the same above-mentioned survey (Rigg, 1989; Ryan, 1993) there was a clear correlation between receipt of recent vocational education or training and income: only 18 per cent of those earning under £4,000 per year had received such training, while the proportion rose to 32 per cent for incomes up to £10,000, and to 46 per cent for incomes above that. Since 'recent' in this study refers to the period three years prior to interview it could conceivably be argued that some of the higher income is the result of the training, which could have raised both productivity and wages. No such argument can be made in respect of the evidence from the General Household Survey, also in 1987 (see Figure 3). Here, the period concerned is the previous four weeks and the same correlation is found. Those earning between £8 and £10 per hour, were more than twice as likely to be receiving training as those in the lower income brackets of less than £4 per hour.

A large proportion of income inequality is of course a reflection of variations in occupational status. Training incidence is nowadays regularly tracked by the Labour Force Survey, which also records respondents' occupations. Table 3.1 shows that, even after all the innovations in Government training schemes, and after the growth of training throughout the 1980s, training remains very unequally distributed amongst people of different occupations. Training is far more prevalent among professional and managerial groups than among the lower-ranked non-manual and the manual groups. The least likely to be receiving training are the unskilled, followed by agricultural workers, and semi-skilled workers. The only qualification to this finding is that the unskilled workers who are receiving training tend to attend for longer hours.

If an employer is not currently providing training, it is possible that workers may nonetheless have already been offered some training in the past. Table 3.1 shows that this offer is also skewed in broadly the same way: those in the higher occupational groups, in particular those in managerial or professional positions, are far more likely to have

Table 3.1 Access to training for people of working age* by
socio-economic group, Britain 1992

	% receiving training in last 4 weeks	% of those not in training, who have ever been offered training by current employer	Hours of training in last week, for those in training
Employers and managers			
Large establishments	21	74	13.3
Small establishments	11	50	11.5
Other professional workers	25	74	15.1
Non-manual workers			
Intermediate	23	70	13.5
Junior	14	45	15.1
Personal service workers	13	30	19.4
Manual workers			
Foremen and supervisors	1	54	13.0
Skilled workers	11	37	13.1
Semi-skilled workers	8	33	14.1
Unskilled workers	6	19	18.0
Agricultural workers	7	29	18.4

* All those in employment within previous 8 years, excluding those currently
self-employed, farm employers and HM Forces.

Source: *Quarterly Labour Force Survey*, Spring 1992

had some training in the past than those lower down the pecking
order.[3]

Another important dimension along which training is unequal is
that of gender. Here, however, the inequality does not lie primarily in
the overall frequency with which men and women receive training. As
Table 3.2 shows, only slightly more males than females were receiving
some training in Spring 1992, and, while men appear to receive on
average longer training sessions than women, the differences are not
enormous. There was also a difference in the proportions of those who
were not training but who had been offered training in the past by
their current employer. However, while females fared worse than
males on this score, the difference may be partially an artefact of the
question asked, since females on average will have worked less years
for their current employer.

Table 3.2 Access to training for people of working age by sex, Britain 1992

	% receiving training in last 4 weeks	% of those not in training who have ever been offered training by current employer	Hours of training in last week, for those in training
Males	13.3	52	21.3
Females	12.5	45	19.0

Source: *Quarterly Labour Force Survey*, Spring 1992

Discrimination between men and women in the frequency of access to training shows up in studies which compare the training access that women would expect to have if they were treated in the same way as men with the amount of access they actually get (Booth, 1991; Green, 1991, 1993). The analyses show that the relationship of income to training propensity is largely a reflection of a number of other salient factors—chiefly occupational status, educational qualifications, age, length of job tenure and size of the work establishment. Nevertheless, after accounting for the impact of these and other measurable factors on the probability that an employee will receive training, there exists a significant difference between the access of men and women to training. On the basis of 1987 data, it is estimated that if the average full-time female employee had been treated in the same way as the average male employee, her probability of getting training would have been some 15 per cent higher. If part-timers are included the figure goes to 45 per cent.[4]

A yet more far-reaching problem with the gender distribution of training opportunities is that they tend to reproduce the segregation of the majority of women into relatively few occupations. Contrary to the rhetoric of equality of opportunity which surrounded the Youth Training Scheme (and its successor YT), young women YTS trainees have been highly segregated—with one in three being trained for clerical and administrative occupations. Very few young women (less than 5 per cent) have been represented among the trainees for more typically male occupations such as construction, engineering or vehicle repair (Clarke, 1991: 13; Cockburn, 1987). Such segregation is at the heart of the differences in men's and women's pay. It has its origins not only in forms of employer discrimination but also in gender differences in subjects chosen in school, and more fundamentally in Britain's patriarchal culture. There has been no appropriate attempt from government to counter this restriction on the training opportunities for women.[5]

The impact of training

The evidence of inequality in access to training undermines the concept of the 'education and training revolution'. It is also hard to be at all optimistic that the substantial increase in training incidence through the 1980s has had much impact on the low-skills nature of the British economy and raised its efficiency. To begin with, as regards the terms of international competition it is discomforting to note that training has been far less prevalent in those industries that actually compete on world markets than in the non-tradeable sectors (Greenhalgh and Mavrotas, 1993).

Unfortunately, there is not a great deal of solid evidence regarding the connection between training and the acquisition of skills. The meaning of training is known to vary widely between individuals, and the level of skills obtained can range from the 'ability' to turn up neat and tidy for work, through craft or technician skills, to high-level management coordination skills. Training might in one circumstance lead to a productive general skill, while in another it might involve the development of company culture and company loyalty. Among all the training episodes reported in the Spring 1992 Labour Force Survey, only 45 per cent were leading to any kind of qualification, and some 40 per cent of the episodes were due to last at most one week. The Government has now taken some responsibility for the achievement of NVQ level 2, or the academic equivalent of 4 GCSEs, among 80 per cent of young people by 1997 and has set the National Advisory Council for Education and Training targets to monitor progress. This is a modest objective, as the council's chairman notes, but its achievement is said to be unlikely on present performance (*Financial Times*, 1 April 1993).

The evidence (Booth 1991) is that training does have a positive effect on earnings. The effect appears somewhat greater for women than men (Booth, 1991; Greenhalgh and Stewart, 1987), confirming the inefficiency of the poorer access to training of women described above. There is no comparable data for the effect of training on earnings within different categories of workers to set against the very unequal access shown in table 3.1.

The evidence from national surveys suggests that the costs of training are likely to be higher for the less well-off. Column 1 of Table 3.3, based on the Labour Force Survey, examines the proportions of those receiving training (whether employed or not) who had to pay their own fees. More women (1 in 5) had to do this than men (less than 1 in 6). The difference among occupational groups is also noticeable: managers in large establishments and professional employees were particularly unlikely to have to pay for their own training, while unskilled manual workers, junior non-manual workers and personal service workers were most likely to have to pay. Amongst employees, unskilled manual workers, agricultural workers and personal service workers were also most likely to have to forgo their basic wages during training (column 2), while managers and professionals were very unlikely to be so penalised.[6] The loss of wages hits women hardest. This finding is confirmed by the General Household Survey: in 1987 about 15 per cent of male, but 22 per cent of female employees gave up some or all of their wages while training. Consistently, the average hourly pay for all those employees who lost wages during training was £5.42 compared to £5.80 for those who continued to receive full wages.[7]

If training within firms appears to be concentrated on, and more attractive for, those who are more qualified already and in better paid jobs, have government training schemes done anything to correct such inequalities? The YTS scheme, being explicitly aimed at those at the bottom of the educational ladder seemed to have just that objective. According to the Government it was aimed at providing 'the opportunity for all young people who enter the labour market to gain the skills and qualifications which will enhance their job prospects and meet the demands of the labour market' (*Hansard*, 29 March 1988).

The unofficial studies of YTS schemes in progress bear out the charge that, in the rush to guarantee large numbers of places, with insufficient resources for monitoring and for subsidising the more costly training courses for many intermediate skills, a majority were providing training of low quality (Marsden and Ryan, 1991). This pessimistic evaluation has been matched by formal evidence on the outcomes of YTS. From the start it was a stated intention that YTS

Table 3.3 Elements of training cost for those receiving off-the-job training, Britain 1992

	% of those receiving training who paid their own fees*	% in training whose employer paid no basic wages during training
Males	15	7
Females	20	13
Employers and managers		
Large establishments	7	3
Small establishments	17	5
Other professional workers	8	3
Non-manual workers		
Intermediate	15	7
Junior	18	15
Personal service workers	17	37
Manual workers		
Foremen and supervisors	10	7
Skilled workers	11	5
Semi-skilled workers	14	16
Unskilled workers	22	39
Agricultural workers	15	27

* payment by self, family or relative

Source: Quarterly Labour Force Survey, Spring 1992

should be more than just a make-work scheme, and that it should provide genuine training to help the individuals concerned and the countrys long-term skill needs. In the context of this objective, empirical studies have been devoted to seeing whether YTS has succeeded in raising participants' chances of getting a job. In fact the studies show only relatively small effects of YTS on the chances of getting a job (Main and Shelly, 1991), whilst one study (Dolton, Makepeace and Treble, 1992b) found that being on the two-year YTS actually reduced the likelihood of employment.

An obvious objective of YTS was to raise participants' productivity and their wage if they did find work. An alternative objective was in Nigel Lawson's words 'to make young people's pay expectations more realistic', that is to lower youth wages relative to adult levels and thus increase their attractiveness to employers. Here the evidence seems unambiguous. YTS lowered the wages of participants—the most detailed study (Dolton, Makepeace and Treble, 1992a) puts the effect at some 15 per cent. Whilst this might be counted as success in making the labour market more flexible, it certainly does not suggest that YTS did much to enhance productivity. Within YTS there is plenty of evidence that schemes were divided into good and bad (or 'sink') schemes. Furlong (1992) shows that YT as a whole constitutes a 'disadvantaged' route from school to work, reinforcing existing inequalities by placing young people in insecure service jobs.

It seems, therefore, from the formal evidence, that this major plank of the Governments contribution to training in the 1980s has provided neither the wide opportunities for personal betterment that have been claimed for it, nor the prospect of a significantly better-skilled workforce. The official stance on training is confirmed perhaps more vividly still in the Government's treatment of adult training, in particular its decision to wind down and eventually abolish the Training Opportunities Programme (TOPS). An evaluation study (Payne, 1991) showed that this had been a very effective scheme in a number of ways. It enhanced the skills of the workforce, in some cases to intermediate or higher levels, in a way which reduced existing inequalities.

In the late 1970s around 90,000 adults were completing training under this scheme every year. Schemes lasted between a month and a year, and involved off-the-job training courses which were more expensive than job-based schemes with less training involved. TOPS was replaced by Employment Training (ET), available only to the long-term registered unemployed. Consequently it gave access to only a small proportion of women, whereas women had constituted some 43 per cent of TOPS graduates. For a 'typical' married woman of 35, TOPS raised employment probability in the sample period from 80 per cent to 90 per cent; for a 'typical' man employment probability was raised from 69 per cent to 86 per cent. For both men and women, expressed job satisfaction for those in work was significantly increased through TOPS. For both men and women without A levels, TOPS raised pay in jobs for which they had been trained.

TOPS was in effect an equalising scheme raising pay for the less well-off young and poorly-qualified workers. It was a successful programme in improving individuals' prospects. It also can be said to have been helping to meet the widely-recognised need for a more highly-skilled workforce in the country as a whole. Only 4 per cent of trainees were being trained at operative level; some 76 per cent were being trained at skilled-level (manual or non-manual), and 20 per cent at technician level or above. There was a fairly reasonable spread of occupations, including the relatively higher-level computing and engineering occupations. This contrasts with ET which concentrated its training among generally lower-level occupations, and from which there is almost a complete absence of training in areas of high technology. By the end of the 1980s, there were many more people on ET, some quarter of a million people, so in that sense training was more widespread. This was, however, just an unemployment-driven phenomenon. In contrast to TOPS which had been closed down, ET was making a negligible contribution to enlarging the stock of high-skilled workers, which the Government has set as its stated aim.

Conclusion

That training should be found to be unequal is not unique to Britain. Although it is very hard with present data to make adequate comparisons of the average level of training in other countries, and impossible to compare the degree of inequality in training access, similar factors are found to have an impact on training in other OECD countries (OECD, 1991). Nevertheless, contrary to the ideology that an education and training revolution has opened up wide avenues of opportunity for the acquisition of skills in Britain, this paper has shown that access to training remains very unequally distributed, with the less well-off experiencing less training than those further up the income scale. The less well-off appear, moreover, on average to pay more for their training. The many young people who have resorted to the Youth Training Scheme have been rewarded if anything with lower wages. The only substantial government scheme which was unequivocally both egalitarian and efficient in raising skills, the Training Opportunities Programme, has been abolished.

The Government's training philosophy has been driven by two principles. On the one hand it has wanted employers to take the lead. This idea underpinned the abolition of the Manpower Services Commission and the subsequent development of the Training and Enterprise Councils. On the other hand, it has advocated the fostering of the market for training. This meant that the Industrial Training Boards were reduced in number and eventually abolished, together with their powers to subsidise training in industry. Recently, this philosophy has informed the development of the idea of training credits and of career development loans, such that individuals should be supported in their search for employers who are prepared to provide training.

In allowing people to choose the extent and direction of their training, as a training market implies, there is the basic fact of the capital market to contend with, namely that those with low incomes cannot afford to finance their own training and cannot provide the collateral with which to borrow funds as easily as those with higher incomes to draw upon. This factor undoubtedly underlies some of the inequality in training documented in this paper. It is recognised by the Government to some extent in that it accepts the obligation to finance at least some of the training for young people, and still sees the need for loans to students in higher education, even if it is gradually phasing out the grant system.

The consequences of the relatively low level access to training for many of those on the lower rungs of the economic ladder in Britain, as documented in this paper, are both a reinforcement of their under-privileged status, and for the economy a loss of their potential productive output. There being no available measures of the social rate of return to training it is impossible to estimate how large is this loss of economic efficiency. But in any case the strong link between the training system and other institutions of the economic system means that a complete evaluation of the effectiveness of the training policies could not be carried out without at the same time examining the effectiveness of a range of economic institutions and policies. Training policies need to be accompanied by a sustained attempt to address the fundamental weaknesses in the British economy, such as the low levels of investment. If all one did was to enlarge greatly the supply of skills, for example by an expansion of education and training in colleges and universities, with no policies at the same time to influence the demand for highly-skilled workers, one would obtain a highly but overly trained workforce—an 'over-accumulation' of human capital. Hence policies to widen access to training of good quality also require policies to ensure there is a demand in Britain for the skills created.

4 CRIME, INEQUALITY AND EFFICIENCY

John Hagan

Contemporary theory and research on crime provides an important perspective from which to consider links between inequality, individualism and efficiency. The common view critically examined throughout this book holds that social inequality enhances individual initiative and is therefore necessary to achieve economic efficiency, or in other words, economic productivity and success. Conversely, social equality is assumed to dampen individual initiative and to produce inefficient, unsuccessful economic outcomes. This suspicion of social equality plays a central role in justifying what we call in this chapter capital disinvestment policies—policies that divert investment from declining communities and from disadvantaged families and individuals.

The contrasting position increasingly given voice in contemporary criminological theory and research is that investment in expanded social and economic opportunities can provide a foundation for broadened participation of citizens in the production of economic wealth and the reduction of mounting social costs. The latter costs notably include crime and its control through detection and punishment. These costs impede economic growth and social well-being more generally.

Social inequality declined during much of the post World War II boom that lasted into the early 1970s in the advanced capitalist economies, but generally increased during the economic slowdown of the last two decades. During the period of the economic slowdown of the last two decades, problems of street crime have become pronounced in countries with high inequality, such as the United States, and in the parts of these countries where inequality is most concentrated, in minority low-income communities. The dimensions of the social costs imposed by crime and its punishment can be devastating. Consider the dimensions of the American crime problem: rates of violent crime and imprisonment far exceed those of other Western industrial nations, more than quadrupling those of neighbouring Canada (Hagan, 1991a). While the time spent in prison per violent crime nearly tripled in the United States between 1975 and 1989, violent crime did not decline (Reiss and Roth, 1992). The effects have been devastating for residents of minority low-income communities. The imprisonment rate for blacks is four times that for whites (Irwin, 1991), and three quarters of black male school drop-outs in the United States are under supervision of the criminal justice system by the time they reach their early 30s (Freeman, 1991). The escalation of criminal sanctions has not reduced the black homicide rate. Homicide is the leading cause of death among young black males (Fingerhut and Kleinman, 1990), and this death rate soared more than 50 per cent during the 'War on Drugs' of the mid to late 1980s (Jencks, 1992:183).

In the remainder of this chapter we present a theoretical perspective and review recent research which links inequality to crime in the United States, especially in its minority low-income communities. We begin with an overview of our theoretical perspective and then move to a more detailed discussion and the review of recent studies. Although this presentation focuses on the United States, it is important to emphasise that its implications are broader. Other advanced capitalist countries, for example Great Britain, have experienced substantial increases in crime in recent decades, and these increases are linked to changes in the British economy (Field, 1990). Toward the end of our review of research, several studies are introduced from Canada and Great Britain. These studies are suggestive of the broader implications of the analysis.

Overview

The theoretical perspective that organises this discussion begins with the premise that structural changes beyond the control of affected individuals have brought increasing inequality into the American economy and its most distressed communities, with rising levels of crime as one of the associated costs. Three theoretically distinct but empirically interconnected processes of macro-level capital disinvestment have intensified the crime problems of these communities: residential segregation, racial inequality and the concentration of poverty. These processes of capital disinvestment are intensified by business and government practices that are premised on the belief, questioned throughout this volume, that efforts to increase social equality diminish economic efficiency. Meanwhile, these disinvestment policies impair the formation of human, social and cultural capital, especially the ability to structure socially organised activity toward the achievement of approved goals in distressed communities and families. In this way, capital disinvestment encourages subcultural adaptations by the affected individuals, who often organise their efforts through groups and gangs. These individual and group based adaptations are often forms of recapitalisation; that is, they represent efforts to reorganise available (albeit usually illicit) resources to reach attainable goals.

Often these efforts at recapitalisation occur through the development of 'ethnic vice industries' and the formation of 'deviance service centres' in distressed community settings. When these industries and centres evolve with little interference from external authorities, they can sometimes develop as virtual free enterprise zones of crime. One of the most enduring of these illicit industries involves illegal drugs. This illicit enterprise has sometimes provided an external source of financial capital that can serve a redistributive function in distressed ethnic communities and that can recapitalise the economic and social lives of individuals involved. Involvement in this illicit enterprise can provide short-term capital gains, in social and economic terms, bolstering self-image and feelings of social competency at the same time that it generates income. However, the more recent American experience with drugs, especially with crack, is more violent, exploitative and disruptive than experiences with alcohol during prohibition and other kinds of narcotic drugs during the more recent past. Furthermore, as consumption of such drugs has become more concentrated within minority communities, drug sales have redistributed declining amounts of money from outside the affected communities, and have encountered mounting interference from external authorities. The results are increasingly disruptive and dangerous to the communities and individuals involved, as when individuals become so embedded in crime networks that they have few opportunities to leave. The combination of little schooling, poor job experience, and arrest records provide little or no social capital for affected youths to pursue legitimate career paths.

Capital disinvestment processes

The three disinvestment processes that discourage societal and community-level formations of conventional social capital—residential segregation, race-linked inequality, and concentrations of poverty—overlap one another in America, but each is distinct enough to require its own introduction.

Residential segregation

Despite declines in social inequality and the passage of the Fair Housing Act and other civil rights legislation during the golden age of American economic expansion described in the introduction to this volume, the United States has remained a highly racially segregated society. Massey (1990) calls this pattern 'American Apartheid' and links it to housing market discrimination against African and Puerto Rican Americans who share a black racial identity.

Massey demonstrates with simulation models that racial segregation concentrates social and economic disadvantage. A consequence is that shifts in black poverty such as those observed during the 1970s have the power to transform poor black neighbourhoods very rapidly and dramatically, changing a low-income black community from a place where welfare-dependent, female-headed families are a minority to one where they are the norm, and producing high rates of crime and related problems. In Massey's terms, 'segregation creates the structural niche within which a self-perpetuating cycle of minority poverty and deprivation can survive and flourish' (350).

The effects of segregation began to hit black American communities especially hard during the 1970s, when the economic slowdown of the last two decades began. Results of this slowdown initially were felt most intensely in the 'rustbelt' of Northeastern and Midwestern American cities, such as New York City, Chicago, Philadelphia and Baltimore (Kasarda, 1989). Massey reasons that the results were most devastating in these settings because they were not only primary sites of manufacturing, where large numbers of core sector jobs were lost, but also because these were the most segregated cities in America. The loss of core sector manufacturing jobs drove poverty and crime rates up most sharply in these cities where blacks were most segregated residentially. Practices of racial segregation are processes of capital disinvestment that make affected communities extremely vulnerable

83

to economic downturns and social and cultural adaptations involving crime in response to the concentrated poverty that follows.

Racial inequality

During the golden age of the third quarter of this century in the United States, African Americans made substantial gains in the labour market relative to whites. The demand for black workers increased and the racial gap in earnings among younger adults with similar schooling may even have nearly disappeared. However, during the last quarter of this century when core sector manufacturing jobs were lost, African American economic conditions worsened and wage inequality and unemployment grew. Black college graduates and blacks with high school or less education had the biggest losses in relative earnings, while dropouts had the largest drop in relative employment (Bound and Freeman, 1992).

The earlier declines in racial economic inequality were associated with social policies designed to increase investment in the social and human capital of minority Americans, in large part through the Civil Rights Movement and the War on Poverty. These policies included implementation of employment discrimination provisions of the 1964 Civil Rights Act, affirmative action programs, and court enforcement of anti-discrimination laws. The later increases in racial economic inequality were associated with an array of actions that included opposition through the courts to affirmative action laws and regulations, as well as a decline in the real minimum wage (Bound and Freeman, 1992). These are policies of capital disinvestment and they impacted most heavily on young African Americans with low levels of education.

Blau and Blau (1982) argue that when economic inequalities are associated with an ascriptive characteristic such as race they produce 'a situation characterised by much social disorganisation and prevalent latent animosities' (119) that lead in turn to 'diffuse aggression.' The problem is that in a situation made more salient by the visible marker of race, 'pronounced ethnic inequality in resources implies that there are great riches within view but not within reach of many people destined to live in poverty' (119). The results are socially structured and objectively based subjective feelings of resentment, frustration, hopelessness, and alienation. Blau and Blau suggest that these feelings in turn lead to widespread social disorganisation and violent crime. Race-linked economic inequalities are an expression of capital disinvestment in particular groups that in this case most prominently include black Americans, with consequences that often are unplanned, criminal and violent.

Concentration of poverty

A third process of capital disinvestment involves the concentration of poverty that began in the cities of the Northeastern and Midwestern United States in the 1970s and has continued through the last quarter of this century. William Julius Wilson (1987; 1991) in writing about *The Truly Disadvantaged* observes that pockets of central city poverty have grown during this period in the United States, with substantial increases in the severity of economic hardship among the minority poor in these areas, and concentrations of poverty that affect racial minorities more than whites. The nature of this process of capital disinvestment is summarised as follows:

> the social structure of today's inner city has been radically altered by the mass exodus of jobs and working families and by the rapid deterioration of housing, schools, businesses, recreational facilities, and other community organisations, further exacerbated by government policies of industrial and urban laissez-faire that have channelled a disproportionate share of federal, state, and municipal resources to the more affluent (Wacquant and Wilson, 1989:10).

A key concept in Wilson's discussion of the concentration of poverty is 'labour force attachment.' The historical, demographic and economic trends already noted have weakened labour force attachment among the ghetto poor, and Wilson (1991) observes that 'a social context that includes poor schools, inadequate job information networks, and a lack of legitimate employment opportunities not only gives rise to weak labour force attachment, but increases the probability that individuals will be constrained to seek income derived from illegal or deviant activities. This weakens their attachment to the legitimate labour market even further'(10).

The central point is that the concentration of poverty plays a key role in intensifying the linkage between weak labour force attachment and crime. Wilson explains this in the following way:

> I believe that there is a difference, on the one hand, between a jobless family whose mobility is impeded by the...economy and

the larger society but nonetheless lives in an area with a relatively low rate of poverty, and on the other hand, a jobless family that lives in an inner-city ghetto neighbourhood that is not only influenced by these same constraints but also by the behaviour of other jobless families in the neighbourhood.

The latter family confronts the effects of not only its own difficult situation but also the compounding effects of the situation that surrounds them.

In terms we have used to organise this discussion, the concentration of poverty produces divergent and oppositional adaptations to pervasive deprivations. That is, the concentration of poverty is a capital disinvestment process that produces adaptations, including deviant formations of social and cultural capital that diverge from and oppose convention. These adaptations are ways of obtaining what disinvestment in ghetto neighbourhoods and its restriction of access to legitimate opportunities will not otherwise permit. In this sense, deviant formations of social and cultural capital represent adaptive efforts to recapitalise the lives of individuals and the communities in which they live.

The new ethnographies of poverty and crime

A number of recent studies document the significance of the processes of capital disinvestment and adaptation we have described (see, for example, Sullivan, 1989; Sanchez-Jankowski, 1992; Moore, 1991; Hagedorn, 1988; Padilla, 1992). These studies characteristically operate on two levels, as studies of communities, and as studies of the life course experiences of individuals. These studies also focus on the role of illegal markets, especially for drugs, and on what we earlier referred to as the development of ethnic vice industries and deviance service centres. This is important because while the processes of capital disinvestment we have described above stress the consequences of the diversion and withdrawal of economic and social resources from disadvantaged communities, there often in these same communities is a process of recapitalisation that involves the development of deviance service industries.

The process of recapitalisation involved in the development of deviance service industries is partly indigenous to communities and partly a product of the actions of external authorities. The key to deviance service industries is that illegal markets emerge whenever desired substances and services—such as narcotic drugs, prostitution, and gambling—are made illegal. Authorities with responsibility for the enforcement of such laws, whether they wish to or not, have the power to regulate the development and operation of these markets, and members of communities that are denied access and involvement to legal markets often pursue these illegal opportunities. A succession of ethnic groups (e.g., Irish, Jewish and Italian Americans) have participated in such markets as a mobility mechanism during this century in the United States (Ianni, 1972). However, as illustrated in the ethnography discussed next, these kinds of activities are more dangerous and less rewarding for the individuals who pursue them today.

Three New York City neighbourhoods

In an study provocatively titled 'Getting Paid', Mercer Sullivan (1989) and his collaborators interviewed members of cliques about their life histories in three New York City neighbourhoods: an African American public housing project, an Hispanic neighbourhood adjacent to a declining industrial area, and a white working-class community. The latter predominantly white neighbourhood serves as an essential reference point because it has not experienced the loss of core sector jobs and more general capital disinvestment that has occurred in the comparison minority communities. Various forms of social capital remain intact. The community retains viable legitimate labour market networks that offer opportunities for obtaining jobs through personal contacts. There are still unionised core sector jobs in which adults have some security. Two-parent households are also more viable, and family and community controls are more stable. This has implications for the life course experiences and chances of the youth of this neighbourhood. For example, when youth in this neighbourhood get into trouble with the law, they are more likely to be reintegrated into their families and community, and they are less likely to be permanently marginalised from labour market opportunities.

Conditions were much different in the Hispanic and African American communities studied. Here the consequences of capital disinvestment became strikingly apparent. Sullivan links this process to changes in the world economy we have discussed, including the transition over the past two decades to a post-industrial economy in which lower wage and insecure jobs in the information and service sectors only partly and inadequately have replaced the loss of higher wage and more secure jobs in the manufacturing and industrial sectors. He notes that our cities in effect have exported jobs and imported unemployment in a set of intra- and international realignments that we are only beginning to understand (see also Revenga, 1992).

A result is that the Hispanic and African American neighbourhoods Sullivan studied are physically isolated from core sector employment. Many of the parents in these neighbourhoods have no jobs, while those parents who are employed tend to work in government jobs that recruit by bureaucratic means rather than through personal contacts. Sullivan finds that, 'without family connections even to low-paying jobs, these youths had to rely on more impersonal methods' (80). In contrast, for white youths, 'social ties between residents and local employers reinforced physical proximity to produce a much greater supply of...jobs' (104).

These patterns are reflective of a process of capital disinvestment that has corroded the social and cultural capital of these communities and that is associated with a recapitalisation of community life around underground economic activities that include drugs and crime. We come, then, to the provocative title of Sullivan's book, which plays on the ghetto jargon of 'getting paid' or 'getting over' to describe the illegal economic strategies that include the muggings, robberies and other forms of theft and drug-related crime common to American city life. Sullivan's point is that these are not intergenerationally transmitted expressions of cultural preferences, but rather cultural adaptations to restricted opportunities for the redistribution of wealth. Put another way, these youth have substituted investments in subcultures of youth crime and delinquency for involvements in a dominant culture that provides little structural or cultural investment in their futures. Their subcultural adaptations represent investments for short term economic gains. Drawing on the classic analysis of Paul Willis (1977), Sullivan argues that this participation in youth crime temporarily achieves a 'penetration of their condition.' However, he then turns his eye to the life course consequences of these involvements and notes that,

Over time, this penetration becomes a limitation, binding them back into [the social] structure as they age out of youth crime and accept...low wage, unstable jobs.... Alternatively, some will die; others will spend much of their lives in prisons or mental hospitals (250).

For these youth, problems connected to youth crime are prolonged into adulthood. It is important to emphasise the role of the police, courts and prisons in the development of these youthful criminal careers. Sullivan found in the more stable white neighbourhood that parents 'sought to manipulate the system—and were often successful in doing so—by means of money and personal connections' (196). In contrast, in both of the minority neighbourhoods youths began to move further away from home to commit violent economic crimes and encountered more serious sanctions when they did so. These crimes produced short-term gains, but they also further separated the minority youth from the legal labour market and stigmatised them in terms of job prospects. Sullivan writes of the minority youths he studied that, 'their participation in regular acts of income-producing crime and the resulting involvement with the criminal justice system in turn kept them out of school and forced them to abandon their earlier occupational goals' (64). Court appearances and resulting confinements removed these youths from whatever job referral networks school might provide and placed them within prison and community-based crime networks that further isolated these youths from legitimate employment.

The new quantitative studies of crime, class and community

The new ethnographies of poverty and crime provide a picture of distressed communities in which capital disinvestment processes have made economic prospects bleak, and in which crime has become a short-term adaptive form of recapitalisation for youth whose longer term life chances are further jeopardised by these involvements. A new tradition of quantitative research provides further support for this view of crime in urban America.

Community studies

Community-level studies persuasively link street crime in America to the capital disinvestment processes of residential segregation, racial inequality and the concentration of poverty emphasised in our earlier discussion and in the new ethnographies of poverty and crime. For example, recent studies in large US cities reveal high levels of homicide victimisation for African Americans in areas with high concentrations of poor families. However, the same studies show low levels of homicide victimisation for both blacks and whites in higher socioeconomic areas (Lowry et al., 1988; Centerwall, 1984; Munford et al., 1976). Since poor black communities are much more distressed economically than poor white communities, and since it is only in higher socioeconomic communities that it is possible to establish real similarity of black and white life conditions, these studies imply that racial differences in homicide rates have their origins in differing socioeconomic experiences.

However, it is sometimes difficult in community-level studies to more fully disentangle the effects of racial segregation, racial inequality and racially concentrated poverty. Although there is recent evidence of a direct effect of the degree of poverty in a neighbourhood on violent crime (e.g., Curry and Spergel, 1988; Taylor and Covington, 1988), and although evidence from a review of many studies suggests the existence of a 'positive frequently significant' relationship between unemployment and property crime (Chiricos, 1987:203), such relationships are not universally found (Bursik and Grasmick, 1993b). And in a systematic review of macro-level studies, Land et al. (1990) located a cluster of factors (including median income, per cent families below the poverty line, an index of income inequality, per cent black population, and per cent single parent families) that had a clear and persuasive causal influence on homicide rates; however, these factors could not be fully decomposed into more specific causal effects. These factors are probably too closely intertwined to be specifically distinguished. The implication is that capital disinvestment processes operate in a more general and interconnected way.

Still, it is important to know more about how capital disinvestment processes might exercise their community as well as individual-level effects, and important advances are being made along these lines at both theoretical and empirical levels. Much of this work is tied together by an underlying concern with the effects of changing labour markets on youth attempting to make the transition to adulthood in racially segregated and impoverished communities.

Greenberg (1977) points out that youth in our money and media driven society are under unique pressures to consume. Young males are under further pressures to express age linked notions of masculinity, as well as to accomplish the transition to adulthood, in the absence of adequate access to labour markets. Inadequate availability of employment is a major obstacle to successfully traversing the gap between a troubled adolescence and the entry into a more stable adulthood. This gap is especially problematic for the one third or more of residentially segregated and concentrated inner city minority youth who are unable to find stable work in the United States.

Blau and Blau (1982; see also Messner and Rosenfeld, 1993 and Messner, 1989) describe this highly visible spectre of racial inequality as resulting in 'prevalent disorganisation' and as sparking 'diffuse aggression,' while Sampson and Wilson (1994; see also Bursik and Grasmick, 1993a) conceptualise this concentrated poverty as producing a 'dislocation' and 'disorganisation' of social control.

Diffuseness of aggression and dislocation or disorganisation of social control are much evident in related research. In a study of over 150 US cities in 1980, Sampson (1987) found that the scarcity of employed black males relative to black women was directly related to the prevalence of families headed by females in black communities, and that black family disruption was in turn substantially related to rates of black murder and robbery, especially by juveniles (see also Messner and Sampson, 1991). Simpson (1991) further notes that the major increase in poverty in recent decades has occurred among those living in households headed by a single-parent mother, that in America one third of these women are black, and that this economic marginalisation is an important factor in the violence of young black women as well as men. By 1990, 51 per cent of black children compared to 16 per cent of white children lived in single-parent families headed by women (O'Hare et al., 1991:19), and there is compelling evidence that class, race and family disruption have interconnected influences on delinquency (Matsueda and Heimer, 1987).

The structure of community social organisation also involves informal social networks and formal institutions that influence and monitor leisuretime youth activities (Bursik and Grasmick, 1993a). For example, the prevalence of unsupervised teenage peer-groups in a community has large effects on rates of robbery and violence by strangers (Sampson and Groves, 1989).

Allan and Steffensmeier (1989:110) connect several strands of research on economic conditions and social control by noting that a 'lack of suitable employment may contribute to a climate of moral cynicism and alienation that attenuates the effectiveness of social controls.' They find that availability of employment produces strong effects on juvenile arrest rates, that low quality of employment (e.g., low pay and bad hours) is associated with high arrest rates for young adults, and that generally such effects are stronger in relation to minority (Hispanic and African American) underemployment than in relation to white underemployment (Allan, 1985).

All of this work can in a more general way be understood in terms of the concepts of social and cultural capital. In conventional circumstances, the presence in a community of intact families and informal social networks and formal institutions are all sources of social capital that can be converted into cultural capital to improve the life chances of youth as they become adults. However, in distressed communities this process is jeopardised. Youth have less hope of finding the stable core sector jobs that will allow them to successfully traverse the gap from adolescence to adulthood, both because the economy is not providing them, and in turn because their communities and families are not well positioned to help them prepare themselves for such jobs or to find them when they are available.

Individual-level studies

There is reason to believe that juvenile offenders in low-income, high unemployment communities may be more prone to adult criminal involvements and a cluster of other difficulties in adulthood that include unemployment and diminished socioeconomic attainments. This possibility is suggested in the ethnographic studies noted above, and it is apparent as well in the combined findings from several long-term quantitative studies that follow individuals from childhood and adolescence into adulthood.

For example Robins (1966) followed two groups into adulthood: a clinic-based sample of predominately low-status 'severely antisocial children' and a 'control group' who were without adolescent behaviour problems and were matched with the clinic sample on race, sex, age, intelligence and socio-economic status. As adults the clinic sample experienced more behavioral problems than the control group, as well as unemployment, depressed earnings, more credit problems and greater reliance on public assistance.

The Gluecks (1950) applied a similar matched group design to study white males from predominately lower income Boston neighbourhoods who, because of their persistent delinquency, were committed to one of two correctional schools in Massachusetts.

Sampson and Laub (1990; 1993) reanalysed these data and reported a tendency for the delinquent group to be more criminal as adults, as well as to experience economic, educational, employment, and family problems (1990:616).

However, research focused on milder forms of drinking, drug use and delinquency in more predominantly middle class settings reveals fewer problems in adulthood. For example, Jessor et al. (1993) tracked a broadly representative sample of Colorado high school students into early adulthood. Although the authors found some continuity in problem behaviours in adulthood, these behaviours did not affect work and status attainment (see also Ghodsian and Power, 1987; Newcomb and Bentler, 1988). They suggest several plausible reasons for this:

> First, our research involved normal rather than clinical samples, and the extent of their adolescent/youth involvement in problem behaviour—even at its greatest—has to be seen as moderate for the most part. Second, our samples were largely middle class in socioeconomic status, and the openness of the opportunity structure for them and their access to 'second chances' have to be seen as far greater than might be the case for disadvantaged youth who had been involved in problem behaviour (Chapter 9).

Jessor et al. optimistically conclude that the course of psychosocial development is not inexorable, that past actions do not necessarily foreclose future options, and that there can be resilience in growth and change: 'at least in social contexts that are not malignant' (Chapter 9).

This reference to social context is crucial because it directs attention to differences in family and community settings of the kinds we have emphasised in this chapter. Recall our argument is that when communities and families can invest social capital in their youth, it is more likely that these youth will develop cultural capital through education and other institutionalised mechanisms that improve their life chances. However, in communities that suffer from capital disinvestment and in families that have little social capital to invest in their children, youth are more likely to drift into cultural adaptations that bring short-term status and material benefits, but whose longer term consequences include diminished life chances. These ideas have recently been tested in a study of nearly 500 youth of varied class backgrounds followed from adolescence to adulthood in Toronto, Canada (Hagan, 1991).

This research focuses on a range of cultural preferences associated with adolescence, from going to rock concerts to involvements in delinquency. Two subcultures are identified: a 'party subculture' focused around partying, rock concerts and drinking, and a 'subculture of delinquency' that involves theft, vandalism, fighting and running from the police. Both of these subcultures derive salience from their separateness from conventional sources of social and cultural capital, including schools and parents. Identification of youth with these subcultures is linked to weaknesses in the school and family ties that might otherwise direct youth into more reputable cultural domains. In the Toronto study, the consequences of involvement in the subculture of delinquency consist of reduced occupational attainments among the sons of working class fathers, but not among daughters or sons with more advantaged class backgrounds. This pattern is consistent both with the findings of Jessor et al. (1993) that adolescent deviance has few negative effects among predominately middle class Colorado youth, and the findings of Robins and Sampson and Laub of significant longer term negative socioeconomic consequences of juvenile misconduct in the more distressed socioeconomic settings of St. Louis and Boston.

Of course, an important way in which youth from disadvantaged community settings become locked into downward trajectories is through contacts with the police and courts. There is evidence of this in the Toronto study and elsewhere. Being caught by the police and caught up in the criminal justice system are especially hazardous for youth from disadvantaged backgrounds because of the risks that becoming embedded in crime can produce not only for future criminality, but also in terms of later chances of finding employment.

These risks are reflected in a recent analysis of youth tracked from childhood through adulthood in a London working class neighbourhood (Hagan, 1993). This study reveals that intergenerational patterns of criminal conviction make youth especially prone to subsequent delinquency and adult unemployment (see also Hagan and Palloni, 1990; Ward and Tittle, 1993). Other studies similarly show that working class males with conviction records are uniquely disadvantaged in finding employment (Schwartz and Skolnick, 1964), and that a criminal arrest record can have negative effects on employment as much as eight years later (Freeman, 1991; Grogger, 1991). Sampson and Laub's (1993:168) long term study of predominately lower socioeconomic status Boston delinquents also indicates that 'incarceration appears to cut off opportunities and prospects for stable employment in later life.'

Much of what we have learned in this chapter about capital disinvestment processes and their impact on life course experiences can be synthesised in a final discussion of community and individual-level involvement in the illegal economy of drugs.

Capital disinvestment and the criminal economy of drugs

During the same approximate period of capital disinvestment when access to legitimate job networks linked to core sector jobs declined in many distressed US minority communities, networks of contacts into the world of drugs and drug related crime proliferated, paving the way for many youth to become embedded in the criminal economy. Fagan (1992) finds in field studies with over a thousand participants in the Washington Heights and Central Harlem neighbourhoods of New York City that this criminal economy employs large numbers of individuals in support roles as well as drug sales and in a greatly expanded sex trade. This activity can assume an important role in the neighbourhood economy, with white as well as blue collar customers bringing cash into the community, and at least some of the funds being redistributed within the neighbourhood. This criminal economy is a contemporary institutionalised link to the deviance service centres and ethnic vice industries of America's past.

However, today's illegal drug industry is also much more competitive, violent and unstable than in the past. Where drug distribution was once centralised through relatively small networks of heroin and later cocaine users who retailed drugs on the street, the more recent experience with crack has involved a less regulated market with violent competition for territory and market share (Williams, 1989). As well, while entry level roles and the market for drugs more generally have increased, the redistribution of profits has declined. This contrasts with an earlier period when marijuana sales predominated. Drug income now is less often invested in local businesses, and profits more often are concentrated among individuals elsewhere in the city and outside the country (see also Ianni, 1974).

Yet low level participation in the drug economy, despite its poor career prospects and declining returns to the community, is still a cultural adaptation with compelling short term capital attractions: in the absence of better sources of employment, drug selling is a primary route to gaining both the material symbols of wealth and success in the neighbourhood. The drug industry also offers the hope, however illusory, of self-determination and economic independence, as contrasted with the petty humiliations and daily harassment faced in secondary service sector jobs (Fagan, 1992).

This is why one in six African American males born in 1967 in Washington DC are estimated to have been arrested for drug selling between 1985 and 1987, with rates of actual participation in drug selling presumably being much higher (Reuter et al., 1990:46). Street level sellers are estimated to have incomes ranging from $15,000 to $100,000 annually (Williams, 1989). A Boston study concludes that disadvantaged youth would have had to take sharp reductions in income to move from drug selling to legal jobs (Freeman, 1990). Drug selling is simply more profitable per hour invested than legitimate employment (Reuter et al., 1990). So the illegal drug industry is an important source of social and economic capital for individuals. Unfortunately, this capital is quickly depleted, with excess earnings dispersed through family and social networks, consumption of drugs and conspicuous spending. And we have seen that imprisonment and unemployment further deplete this capital.

Capital disinvestment processes and changes in the illegal drug industry also have influenced the lives of many minority women. The increasing number of female-headed households and families placed new demands on minority women to generate income. The disappearance through deaths and imprisonment of numbers of young adult males may also have relaxed barriers to female participation in street-level drug selling. And the emergence of crack escalated the demand for drugs. These factors have increased the participation of minority women in drug use and sales and also in prostitution.

The ethnic vice industries and deviance service centres that surround drugs and drug-related crime pose great policy dilemmas in the New York City neighbourhoods that Fagan studied. As exploitative and corrosive of the community and individuals as these activities may be in the long term, their short term benefits are difficult to resist:

First, since neighbourhood residents benefit from the redistributive aspects of drug selling, this undercuts their efforts at formal and informal social control. Residents may be less willing to disrupt drug selling since some directly benefit, and especially when economic alternatives do not compete well or the risks are not acute or immediate. As suppliers of a commodity to others in the city, funds flow into the neighbourhood and are recirculated to some extent before accumulating to individuals. What will happen if this circulation is interrupted? Unless risks increase from drug selling or living in its milieu, it is unreasonable to ask people to act against their economic well-being (Fagan, 1992).

In the end, these are the kinds of dilemmas that social inequality and capital disinvestment can provoke.

Criminal inequalities

Theory and research on crime increasingly focus attention on the criminal costs of social inequality. They do so against the backdrop of a dominant political creed which asserts that social equality is economically inefficient. This belief is inconsistent with the last half century of economic development in the advanced capitalist nations, when, if anything, declining social inequality accompanied economic expansion, and increases in social inequality were joined with reduced economic growth. Meanwhile, increased social inequality and reduced economic growth are both associated with increases in crime, as illustrated in America's low-income minority communities. It is difficult to avoid the conclusion that high levels of crime among black American youth are causally associated with the concentration of poverty in distressed urban neighbourhoods. The major policy response to this crime problem has involved the increased use of imprisonment.

The economic slowdown and increased inequality of the last part of this century in the United States has been accompanied not only by increased crime but also by a shift in systems of criminal justice from an emphasis on rehabilitation and treatment to an emphasis on just deserts, incapacitation, and deterrence. In criminology this transition has involved a resurrection of theories of crime which emphasise the consequences of punishment, with an associated view toward the protection of society. The reemergence of deterrence theory and strategies of selective incapacitation are a part of this shift of attention. Associated with this shift is increased use of institutionalisation and incarceration, especially with minority offenders.

The aggregate numbers in US state prisons, which hold 92 per cent of this nation's inmates, are in themselves dramatic. In little more than a decade, commitments to prison increased nationally nearly two and one-half times, from less than a hundred thousand in 1974 (96,073), to over two hundred thousand in 1986 (232,969). Langan (1991:1568) reports that as of 31 December 1989 state prisons nationwide held a record 610,000 inmates, 63,000 more inmates than a year earlier.

There also has been growth in the use of institutional placements for juvenile offenders, although this growth has been less pronounced than is the case for adults. In 1975, juveniles were confined in juvenile facilities at a rate 241 per 100,000 juveniles between 10 and the age of majority. By 1987, the figure was 353 per 100,000 such juveniles. Over the 1975–89 period, children in custody in public facilities increased by 19 per cent from nearly 47,000 in 1975 to over 56,100 in 1989.

There are many reasons why the use of imprisonment could have grown over this period, including increasing levels of reported crime and arrests, more specific increases in drug crime and arrests, and changes in the proportion of young people in the population. However, Langan's (1991) analysis indicates that changes in overall reported crime and arrest account for only nine per cent of the increase in imprisonment from 1974 to 1986, while changes in drug arrest and imprisonment explain eight percent. Changes in the proportion of young people in the population are responsible for 20 per cent of this growth. However, the largest factor by far, accounting for more than half of the change, is simply a renewed preference for imprisonment.

Because crime is concentrated so heavily among youth and minorities in American society, the increased use of imprisonment falls heavily on young minority males. For example, during the 1974–86 period, the national rate of incarceration for African Americans was more than six times as high as the rate for white Americans (Chilton and Galvin, 1985). Between 1978–82 alone, the percentage of adult black males in the US population sent to prison increased by 23 per cent (Bureau of Justice Statistics, 1985:5).

A recent report of the US National Academy of Sciences concludes that, 'the US justice system is overburdened, and...its emphasis on punishment is expensive, unproductive of the desired gains in reducing levels of crime, and probably productive of increased hostility toward itself in ghetto communities' (1993:167). Growing fear of crime and concern about the demoralisation of our cities is an added cost of street crime (Skogan, 1990; Skogan and Maxfield, 1981). One reflection of this fear and demoralisation is that the number of guns in

America has more than doubled over the past two decades, from less than one hundred million prior to 1970, to about two hundred million in 1990. The American experience with crime is an especially striking illustration of the social and economic costs of inequality. It is difficult to reconcile these costs with concerns about efficiency in social and economic planning.

5 HIGH PAY, LOW PAY AND LABOUR MARKET EFFICIENCY

Paul Gregg, Stephen Machin and Alan Manning

Two thirds of gross household income in the UK is made up of earnings from employment, and much of the remainder is derived from wage-related pensions. This makes wage inequality a crucial component in household income inequality. Any substantial change in the distribution of household income is therefore dependent on change in the distribution of earnings. However, orthodox economic teaching insists that the distribution of earnings is the outcome of the efficient working of the market with workers remunerated according to their capabilities. It follows in this model that any attempt to make the distribution of earnings more equal will cause inefficiency. For example, a minimum wage will disrupt the efficient outcome by pricing low-ability workers out of a job; attempts to compress skill differentials will decrease the incentives to acquire skills.

Most economists appear to recognise that the labour market does not work perfectly all the time, but the imperfections are usually seen as short-term deviations from the efficient market model. In this chapter, by contrast, we argue that such an assumption may be unwarranted: a great deal of wage inequality is a symptom of the endemic inefficiency and market failure in the labour market. Therefore, measures to reduce inequality may, under some circumstances, go hand in hand with improved efficiency.

This kind of discussion is important if one considers what has been happening to the distribution of earnings in Britain in the 1980s. In Figure 5.1 we plot the difference between the 90th and 10th percentiles of the log (real hourly wage) distribution for male and female workers between 1972 and 1991. Both show a dramatic widening out of the distribution with the best-paid workers doing much better amongst both men and women after the late 1970s (the widening is somewhat greater for men).

In Table 5.1 we also show what kinds of workers are more likely to be low paid (ie beneath the Low Pay Unit's low pay threshold) and

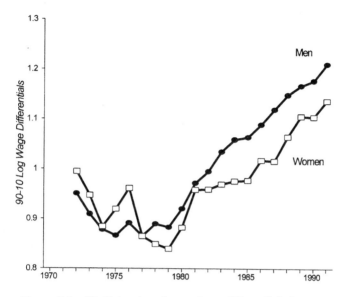

Figure 5.1   90–10 log hourly earnings differentials for men and women in the UK, 1972–91.

Source: New Earnings Survey

how this has changed between 1984 and 1991. Even in this simple descriptive exercise it is clear that some workers are much more likely to be low paid than others (women, those with no educational qualifications, those in the North, non-whites) and that the situation has worsened in the 1980s. The scale of these changes should be borne in mind in the discussion that follows.

In the next section we describe the conventional view of the labour market and discuss the implications to be drawn from it for the effects of policies to reduce inequality. We then discuss evidence against the view that wage inequality is the outcome of an efficient market and attempt to identify whether certain policies to reduce inequality could increase efficiency.

It is important to note that drawing a link between inequality and inefficiency is not straightforward. We focus on areas of pay determination at the top and bottom ends of the labour market where one can be more confident about such links. Our analysis shows that patterns of pay in these two extremes of the pay distribution do not conform to the conventional labour market model; therefore, the inequality of these markets may be inefficient too.

Table 5.1   The incidence of low pay in the UK, 1984 and 1991

percentage of workers below the low pay unit's definition of low pay

	1984		1991		Change	
	Men	*Women*	*Men*	*Women*	*Men*	*Women*
TOTAL	16.8	44.8	26.2	44.9	7.4	0.1
Work sector						
manuals	23.4	73.0	38.4	80.7	15.0	7.7
non-manuals	8.3	36.1	13.7	36.6	5.4	0.5
Education						
degree	5.8	13.6	5.6	10.9	-0.2	-2.6
no qualifications	29.0	83.4	42.3	84.4	13.3	1.0
Region						
North	18.4	50.7	30.1	52.8	11.7	2.1
South	15.8	40.8	22.9	40.2	7.1	-0.6
Race						
white	24.3	—	29.1	—	4.8	—
non-white	27.6	—	35.7	—	8.1	—

Source: *New Earnings Survey, General Household Survey*

Note: Low pay means two-thirds of male median earnings. We would like to thank Steve Woodland for preparing this table.

The competitive labour market

In a competitive labour market the basic principle that determines the distribution of earnings is that every worker should receive a wage equal to the value of what they produce (in economists' language, their marginal product of labour). Competition for workers among employers will mean that a worker paid less than their marginal product will be offered a slightly higher wage by another employer and in this way their wage will be bid up. An additional implication of this view of the labour market is that all workers of the same ability will receive the same wage. Pay variations then reflect the distribution of abilities, both innate and those learnt through education, training and experience. To account for differences in the non-monetary attractiveness of various jobs one needs to modify this account. For example, unpleasant jobs need to pay higher wages to attract workers of a given quality and, for workers in pleasant jobs, employers can get away with paying less. But the principle of equal pay for workers of equal ability re-emerges as the principle of equal satisfaction in all jobs for workers of a given ability (this is known as the theory of compensating differentials). Another implication of the orthodox theory that each worker receives a wage commensurate with their contribution to production is that workers have the appropriate incentive to increase their productivity by training or education or any other means. Such investment in human capital will be desirable if the returns to it in the form of extra output equal the cost; if the worker's increase in wages is equal to the extra output then they have the appropriate incentives to acquire skills (see Becker, 1957).

In this framework, any attempt to alter the distribution of earnings is likely to lead to inefficiencies. Consider, for example, the introduction of a minimum wage. If all workers are initially receiving a wage equal to the value of what they produce then the effect of a minimum wage will be to make the employment of those workers initially paid below the minimum wage unprofitable and hence they are likely to lose their job. The minimum wage may reduce wage inequality but at the cost of inefficient unemployment. Critics of minimum wage policies who use this type of argument would also say that while the inequality among those who remain in work may be reduced, inequality as a whole may be increased because those who lose their job are worse off than before. If the minimum wage covers only some sectors, those workers displaced from the covered sector will look for work in the uncovered sector and push down wages there. A similar type of analysis can be applied to policies designed to compress income differentials, like progressive tax policies. If implemented, such policies would mean that workers who increase their productivity by acquiring new skills do not achieve the full returns to their investments and hence the incentive to invest will be reduced and this is obviously inefficient.

There are relatively few economists who believe that the above description of the labour market applies in all places at all times. But, the majority view among labour economists is that deviations from perfect competition are only temporary or apply only in special cases. The evidence which follows suggests very strongly that this is not the case and, therefore, that wage inequality resulting from labour market inefficiency—mainly resulting from imbalance of power—is more important and pervasive than commonly thought.

Empirical evidence

Building on work initially developed in the late 1950s (Mincer, 1958) much attention has been devoted to looking at the relationship between individual characteristics and wages; what have come to be known as earnings functions. In a competitive labour market the wage that an individual receives should be determined by their personal characteristics relevant to their productive ability. Those individual characteristics not relevant to ability should not be related to wages, nor should the characteristics of the employers for whom they work be relevant. The archetypical earnings function considered by Mincer related earnings to levels of education and labour market experience which were taken to measure (at least some dimensions of) labour quality. On one level these equations were very successful in explaining who gets paid more or less: earnings did seem to be significantly related to these quality related explanatory variables. Large numbers of empirical estimates of such earnings functions reported significant positive effects of both schooling and work experience.

The limited success of the so-called human capital earnings function approach soon became apparent. First, the explanatory power of the individual characteristics used to explain wages was rather limited. This was often explained away by the difficulties in observing ability, but the residual unexplained component of wages was too large to be entirely explained by omitted ability variables. In addition, individual characteristics which one would reasonably think are unrelated to ability were found to be important in explaining the variation in earnings. The most dramatic example concerns labour market discrimination. Sex and ethnicity are always found to be important determinants of wages even after controlling for differences in observable characteristics. Typical findings are that women and non-whites receive significantly lower pay for a given set of characteristics. Even within gender and ethnic groups, characteristics unrelated to ability are found to be important in explaining wages (for example, marital status and number of dependent children).

It is not only personal characteristics unrelated to ability that appear to be important determinants of earnings, but also that characteristics of the employer seem to matter. In the context of earnings functions, this conclusion was forcefully stated by Krueger and Summers (1988) who found that wages for workers with identical observable characteristic differed significantly by industry. In many ways these econometric studies simply reproduce the findings and conclusions drawn by American labour economists in the 1950s (e.g. Slichter, 1950) and later in Britain (e.g. Mackay and Reid, 1970) that, even in very tightly defined labour markets and within very tightly defined jobs, significant wage differentials exist. The general conclusion from these studies is that large, more profitable and productive firms pay higher wages.[1]

Those who believe in the competitiveness of labour markets typically dismiss these empirical findings as 'disequilibrium' phenomena. For example, a popular approach to explaining the existence of discrimination is that people are prejudiced (Becker, 1957). If employers are prejudiced against the employment of black workers then the relative demand for black workers will be less and their wages will be lower than that of whites. But employers who are not prejudiced will be able to take advantage of the cheaper black labour to lower costs, make higher profits and ultimately drive the prejudiced employers out of business. Hence, discrimination should disappear. But there is precious little evidence for such an optimistic view. In the absence of policies designed to reduce or eliminate discrimination, it seems to have very consistent effects on earnings. For example, in the UK, prior to the Equal Pay Act, the relative earnings of women had been about 60 per cent of those of men for as long as records last (about 100 years).

It seems that much of the inequality that we observe does not reflect rewards to ability as suggested by the conventional approach. In addition, this inequality seems to have been remarkably resilient over time (and has even begun to rise dramatically since the late 1970s: Gregg and Machin, 1993). This suggests that there is potential for policies that reduce inequality without adversely affecting labour market efficiency (and which could possibly increase it). But, to make such a case more convincing we need to try to explain why the labour market does not work perfectly.

Low wage labour markets

In the perfectly competitive labour market all workers get paid their marginal product because competition among employers for workers is very intense. In reality, the process of labour mobility to maintain wages is far from instantaneous. An employer who cuts wages may find that their workers are more likely to leave than before and may have increased difficulty in recruiting workers, but these processes are very slow and take time. This means that an employer is not constrained to pay a going market wage for a particular quality of labour and has some discretion in setting pay levels. In the language of economics, employers have some market power in setting wages, a situation that is known as monopsony. A monopsonistic employer does not pay a wage equal to the marginal product of labour; they pay a wage that lies beneath and the gap is greater the more that employers find it necessary to bid up wages to attract workers. That is, this gap depends on how strong are the forces for labour mobility. It should be obvious that these forces are stronger for some groups of workers than others so that workers who may have the same productivity end up with different wages.

This sort of model of the labour market tends to fit the description of the distribution of earnings given above very well. For example, women in households with small children typically end up with the responsibilities for childcare which means that they are only available for part-time work. The time and money costs of going to work become more important the fewer the hours available so that choice of employers is restricted and women with dependent children would be expected to earn less than equivalent men or women of the same ability. In a labour market where labour mobility is limited, employers who are more profitable will want to have larger workforces so will be forced to pay higher wages, which explains the correlations found between wages, profitability and employer size.

If the labour market is monopsonistic then there are inefficiencies associated with it. These are basically two-fold. First, as workers receive a wage below their marginal product there will be some workers who would want to work if they received the full value of what they produce but who do not find it worthwhile to work at the going wage. Employment is therefore inefficiently low. Secondly, the incentive for workers to increase their productivity is too low because they do not get the full return. The result is an inefficiently low level of skills in the economy.

A good measure of the extent of monopsony in the economy is the gap between the wage and the value of what workers produce. Machin, Manning and Woodland (1993) present a way of computing the average gap between the wage and productivity. Briefly, they assume (unlike the perfectly competitive model) that, because workers have some kind of attachment to certain employers, a firm which cuts (raises) wages will not instantaneously lose its workers (be flooded with new recruits). This may happen over a longer time period, but these kinds of frictions will endow the employer with some degree of monopsony power.

Machin, Manning and Woodland (1993) collected their own data on a specific low wage labour market, private sector residential nursing homes. The average employer size is relatively small (approximately 10 employees) in this sector. Pay is extremely low: in April 1992 the median rate of pay was around £3 per hour and 95 per cent of workers received hourly pay of under £4.00. One quarter of workers received pay rates of less than £2.65 per hour. When one considers that the Labour Party was intending to introduce a national minimum wage at £3.40 per hour in 1992 one can see that the majority of workers (82 per cent) in this sector would fall below this minimum. Alternatively, the Low Pay Unit's definition of low pay is less than 2/3 of male median earnings: this corresponded to £4.65 in 1992 (96 per cent of workers were paid below this level).

Machin, Manning and Woodland (1993) estimated that, on average, workers in this sector are paid 15 per cent less than the value of what they produce: one quarter of workers are paid at least 21 per cent less than their marginal product. It is extremely important to place this average estimate of 15 per cent into perspective. For example, it is worth noting that the Conservative Government has spent 14 years strongly attacking a union wage premium that is estimated at eight per cent on average. There are also reasons for believing that the 15 per cent figure is an under-estimate. First, as discussed above, low wages reduce the incentive to acquire skills. Higher wages themselves encourage higher productivity. Secondly, the availability of workers at low wages encourages the entry of low productivity firms into the market who could not survive if the labour market worked perfectly. In an imperfect labour market, the productivity of workers depends not just on who they are but also on who they work for so that this effect also tends to depress productivity.

It is evident that if wages lie beneath marginal products as these estimates suggest, this is evidence for the notion that low pay is symptomatic of inefficiency in the manner described above. Given this, it is possible to examine the feasibility of policies that may alleviate inequality and inefficiency at the same time. It is the potential of one particular policy, minimum wages, to which we now turn.

Minimum wages

If the labour market is monopsonistic then a minimum wage policy may have the desirable effect of reducing inefficiencies. Introducing a minimum wage raises the incentives to work and the incentives for workers to acquire skills. As the wage is initially below the value of what the workers produce they remain profitable to employ. However, for many years, the consensus among economists was that minimum wages reduced employment as predicted by the competitive model (see Brown et al., 1982). Conservative politicians used this argument extensively in the 1992 general election. This conclusion has recently been re-examined. For the United States, in studies based on the big rises in minimum wages there in the late 1980s, a number of papers have concluded that minimum wages have no effect on or even raise employment (Card, 1992a, 1992b; Katz and Krueger, 1992; Card and Krueger, 1993; Card, Katz and Krueger, 1993). In the UK the system of minimum wage legislation (until the recent Trade Union and Employment Rights Bill of 1993 which abolished the system) was the industry based Wages Council system which set minimum rates of pay for a large number of workers (about 2.5 million in 1990) in a number of low wage sectors (catering, clothing, retail and hairdressing being the largest). Two recent papers (Machin and Manning, 1992; Dickens, Machin and Manning, 1993) have directly confronted the jobs/wage trade-off, and examined the effects of minimum wages in these sectors. They use data on Wages Council covered workers from the late 1970s to 1990 to establish empirically that:

(i)   throughout the 1980s the ratio of minimum to average wages for Wages Council workers fell dramatically;

(ii) these falls went hand-in-hand with rises in pay dispersion;

(iii) contrary to competitive models (but in line with monopsony models) the decline in the minimum relative to the average wage was associated with declines in employment (alternatively, there was a positive correlation between the 'toughness' of the minima and employment).

In this context, abolition of the UK Wages Councils would seem to be synonymous with rises in inequality and inefficiency. Dickens et al. (1993) estimate that Wages Council workers are likely to see their pay fall after abolition and that this will mainly affect the household income of those households in the bottom two deciles of the income distribution. Hence, abolition is likely to lead to increased poverty, widening inequities in pay and income, with no offsetting efficiency gains in the form of higher employment.

The Equal Pay Act

Another good example of a policy which reduced inequality, but may well have increased efficiency, is the Equal Pay Act which was passed in 1970, but which came into force at the end of 1975. This had the effect of causing a substantial rise (about 10 per cent) in the ratio of female to male hourly earnings over a period of about five years. This rise was historically unprecedented and resulted in a large fall in earnings inequality.

The competitive model makes a strong and unambiguous claim about the introduction of such a policy: as the female wage rises relative to the male wage, female employment should fall relative to male employment, since female labour has become relatively more expensive. However, when one looks at what actually happened, it proves very difficult to find evidence for this predicted fall in relative employment. Rather, in the 1970s female employment continued to rise and appeared to be unaffected by the big relative rise in the female wage. Manning (1993) has investigated this in some detail and concludes that one can easily rationalise these trends in terms of the female labour market being better thought of as monopsonistic rather than competitive. That is, because prior to the Act women workers were paid substantially beneath the value of what they produced, it proved possible to raise their wages without having a detrimental effect on employment. Indeed, as women were getting a better return to their skills after the Act, it is likely that labour market efficiency was enhanced by the Equal Pay Act.

High wage labour markets

Even the most ardent free marketeers rarely claim that salaries received by high paid executives are what they would receive in a perfectly competitive model with full information. Rather, high levels of managerial pay are often justified in terms of what, in economics, is referred to as principal-agent theory. In this framework, shareholders or company owners (who collectively are the principal) delegate decision-making authority to managers (agents). An informational problem then occurs because the interests of managers can potentially diverge from those of owners. This informational asymmetry then generates a source of market failure because it is not possible directly to monitor managers' actions. To the extent that managerial effort is important to the owners' returns, but extra effort has a cost, there will be a conflict of interests between the principal and its agent(s). In situations where managerial actions and effort and their impact on firm performance are not perfectly observed, and where there is a monitoring cost facing owners, the resulting market failure provides an incentive for owners to link managerial pay to company performance. An optimal incentive contract can be designed to minimise the conflict between the parties' interests (see Jensen and Murphy, 1990). One consequence of this is that managers will receive a level of pay which lies above that which is needed to recruit and retain them.

One should note that any employee with delegated authority or autonomy is likely to be in this moral hazard situation. It is also evident that, as one moves higher up the corporate hierarchy, one would expect this such autonomy to become more important and, according to this theoretical approach, the need for stronger pay-performance links to be generated. One might alternatively argue that the high pay received by top managers comes about as a consequence of the exercise of monopoly power. It is evident that, by the nature of their job functions, top managers are likely to possess knowledge or skills that are scarce or difficult to replace. As such, these managers have 'insider power' on the basis of them being costly to replace, and they are able to use such power to push their wages above competitive levels. Hence, there may be a link between pay and corporate performance, not as a result of optimal incentives, but because of a greater ability to secure a share of the firms' economic rents. Such an outcome would be exacerbated if shareholder control over such issues is limited.

A second source of monopoly power comes about because of replacement costs exceeding mobility costs. In the low wage sectors discussed above we emphasised that employers set wages and, because workers face difficulties in moving from one employer to another, employers can pay workers wages which are less than the value of what they produce. For managerial workers, it seems more plausible to think of them setting wages themselves. Since the costs of replacing workers becomes more important than costs of moving employer, then managerial workers can force wages above competitive levels: it is evident that managerial pay is often set by other managers (see below) and this kind of system may be thought of as generating high wage outcomes.

Finally, monopoly power may be generated in situations where incumbents are able to control the supply of new entrants. This is a mechanism that operates in many of the professions (doctors, solicitors, accountants, etc.) where a body of representatives sets limits on the number of new entrants to the profession. The mechanism works either through direct appointment with a limited quota of jobs (e.g. QCs in the legal system) or by setting examination (or similar) requirements to restrict supply. Of course, this monopoly power enables wages to be set above competitive levels.[2]

High pay at the top end of the labour market has become a national political issue. In Gregg, Machin and Symanski's (1993) study of 288 UK quoted companies between 1983 and 1991 the median salary plus bonus for the highest paid director was £106,000. To illustrate this in relative terms, the ratio of the highest paid directors' remuneration to that of the median male employee in the New Earnings Survey of 1982 was 7.8; by 1992 this had dramatically risen to a massive 16 times higher. There have been a number of investigations of the importance of optimal incentives in executive pay determination in both the US and the UK (see Main, 1992, or Gregg, Machin and Szymanski, 1993, for the UK; Jensen and Murphy, 1990, or Gibbons and Murphy, 1992, for the US). Evidence in favour of the important pay-performance links suggested by optimal incentive models is scarce: typically, the extent to which directors' remuneration is linked to company shareholder returns is very minimal and quantitatively very small. Over the period 1983 to 1991 the Gregg, Machin and Szymanski (1993) study finds no evidence of a statistically significant link between directors' pay and their companies' previous stock market performance. Rather, it appears that corporate growth and size are much more important determinants of the compensation rewards of top directors (i.e. greater rewards are received by the top directors of bigger, faster growing corporations). An extremely revealing insight of the Gregg, Machin and Szymanski study is that the situation (in terms of pay-performance links) appears to have worsened through the 1980s when the relative fortunes of those at the top dramatically improved. Gregg, Machin and Szymanski uncovered a positive (albeit extremely small[3]) statistically significant relationship between the growth in directors' compensation and stock market performance; after 1988 the relationship disappeared entirely. Given the relative improvements in the pay of those at the top this poses some extremely serious questions for the applicability of the principal-agent approach.

The second consideration of the theoretical analysis concerned the possession of monopoly power by top managers. Several pieces of evidence lend some credence to this view. First, Conyon and Gregg (1993) have reported evidence of the impact of various company-specific shocks on the pay of top directors. Like other studies they isolate a strongly positive sales growth impact. However, they also decompose sales growth into that related to mergers and acquisitions and that related to organic growth by the firm. The results point to a one-off rise of about 12 per cent in pay over and above that linked to organic growth. They also report results that increased debt issue is an important determinant of bigger directorial pay increases. Hence, directors seem to have achieved larger rewards as a consequence of rapid expansion; other evidence on the 1990–3 recession (Geroski and Gregg, 1993) suggests that this kind of rapid expansion which took place in the 1980s had drastic effects on companies during the recessionary period. A second piece of evidence pointing to the substantial pay setting power possessed by top directors emerges from Conyon's (1993) survey of pay setting institutions in 279 of the top 1000 UK companies. He found that by 1993, in line with the Cadbury Report's recommendations, 94 per cent of quoted companies and 75 per cent of all companies had remuneration committees for setting top pay. He also found that in 41 per cent of companies with remuneration committees the Chief Executive Office was a member. Furthermore, in 75 per cent of cases the company chairman and/or other executive directors were present when the committee met. Clearly these studies point to a degree of monopoly power in pay setting held by those at the top of the corporate hierarchy. This monopoly power interpretation of the executive labour market clearly suggests an ability of top managers to achieve supra-competitive wages.

Conclusions

We have explored the efficiency implications of high and low pay and attempted to assess the importance of labour market failures in the link between equality and efficiency. We find it hard to rationalise, both from a theoretical and empirical perspective, the notion that pay setting in these areas is the outcome of an efficient market, and argue that much of the observed variation in wages is rather a symptom of inefficient workings of the labour market. These claims are substantiated by theoretical models and empirical data on pay determination at the lower and upper ends of the pay distribution. In the former there appear to be inefficiencies linked to wages being paid beneath marginal products, whilst in the latter there appear to be inefficiencies linked to monopoly power held by those at the top. It appears possible to alleviate such inequalities by the design of appropriate policy responses which may also, contrary to conventional viewpoints, also contribute positively to the efficiency of the labour market.

6 UNEMPLOYMENT, INEQUALITY AND INEFFICIENCY

6.1 The Rise in Economic Inactivity

John Schmitt and Jonathan Wadsworth[1]

One in five men, some 3.7 million people, aged between 16 and 64 are now without a job in Britain. They can be classified as either actively seeking work—the unemployed—or as having withdrawn from job search—the economically inactive. Since 1986, the number of economically inactive, working age British men has consistently exceeded the number classified as unemployed. Between 1977 and 1992, the economic activity rate amongst the non-student male population of working age fell from 96 to 88.5 per cent. This represents a reduction in labour supply of some 1.3 million individuals,[2] so that by 1992, 2 million men of working age were no longer actively seeking employment in addition to the 1.7 million officially recognised unemployed. Consequently, the official unemployment rate now seriously understates the extent of joblessness and labour market slack in Britain. Further, as we show below, the fall in participation, whilst apparent across all age groups, has been confined almost exclusively to those who lack any formal qualifications.

The rise in male unemployment during the 1980s has been extensively documented and analysed. Much less attention, however, has been focused on the doubling of the numbers of economically inactive. During the same period, the activity rate for women rose from 65.4 to 71.7 per cent, most of whom entered work. The activity rate amongst unqualified women, however, remained unchanged. Neither has the fall in male labour supply resulted in a redistribution of working time within the household, since the majority of the rise in female participation has come from within households already containing employed men. Rather, this trend has enhanced the

114

unequal distribution of employment across households.

Why then has inactivity amongst men risen so steeply and so inequitably? This chapter documents the retreat of working-age men from the labour force and investigates the principal determinants of the fall in participation. We use pooled Labour Force Survey and General Household Survey data (LFS and GHS) from 1977 to 1992 to outline recent developments in the British labour market in an attempt to provide an explanation for these events. The evidence indicates that a shift in demand away from low skilled work, rather than any voluntary reduction in labour supply, was responsible for the rise in inactivity. The result is a stagnation of relative real wages and opportunities for low skilled men. Faced with increased competition for existing jobs from new labour force entrants and increased preferences amongst employers to hire a casual or part-time workforce, this may then have elicited a discouraged worker effect—which has contributed to the rising numbers claiming state benefits other than those traditionally associated with unemployment. Section 1 outlines the main features of the fall in participation, whilst section 2 tests the rival explanations of the events underlying section 1. Section 3 concludes the chapter.

The rise in inactivity

Figure 6.1.1 charts movements in non-employment rates, the sum of unemployment and inactivity, of the non-student working age population over time. The growth in non-employment amongst men and in particular the secular rise in inactivity is striking. The majority of the inactivity increase occurs before 1986, though this was renewed in 1992. The short-run, cyclical variation in non-employment seems to be captured by movements in the unemployment rate. Hence declines in unemployment follow downturns in employment. The inactivity rate is much less responsive to the economic cycle. For women, non-employment and in particular the inactivity rate have fallen steadily over the same period. Table 6.1.1 provides some numbers.[3]

Table 6.1.1 highlights the contrast between changes in the male and female labour markets. Male employment fell by 11.9 percentage points between 1977 and 1992. The inactivity rate rose by 7.4 points and the unemployment rate by 4.6 points. Hence, sixty per cent of the decline is accounted for by a rise in non-participation, the rest being attributable to an increase in recognised unemployment. By 1992, 21

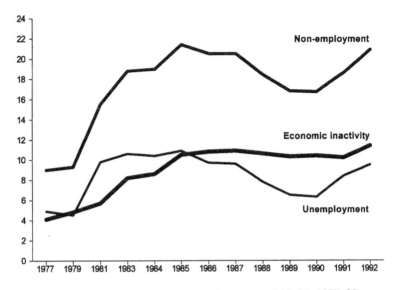

Figure 6.1.1 Non-employment of men aged 16–64, 1977–92
(percentages)

per cent of the adult male workforce were without a job and eleven per cent of the workforce were no longer actively seeking work. As male employment rose in the late eighties only those still actively seeking work were absorbed into the workforce. The inactivity rate remained static.

Conversely, the employment rate for women rose by 6 percentage points over the same period. This was almost entirely accounted for by increased labour force entry, so that the vast majority of women who entered the labour market found employment, primarily part-time work. The increase in female employment has not been large enough, however, to offset the decline in employment of men.

Tables 6.1.2 and 6.1.3 repeat the exercise, disaggregating the population by age and by educational attainment respectively. Employment amongst men has fallen most and participation rates risen fastest amongst the peripheral age groups. Declining activity rates account for over 85 per cent of the fall in employment for men aged 55, over 46 per cent of the fall for prime-age men and 31 per cent for young men. Amongst women, only prime-age workers have experienced any employment growth and increases in participation. Table 6.1.3 highlights the importance of educational attainment in

Table 6.1.1 Employment, participation and unemployment rates, 1977-92 (percentages of population)

	Employment	Labour Force	Unemployment
Men (16-64yrs)			
1977	91.0	95.9	4.9
1986	79.5	89.2	9.7
1990	83.4	89.7	6.3
1992	79.1	88.6	9.5
Change 1977-92	-11.9	-7.3	4.6
Women (16-59yrs)			
1977	60.8	65.4	4.6
1986	61.8	68.7	6.9
1990	68.3	73.3	4.9
1992	66.9	71.7	4.8
Change 1977-92	6.1	6.3	0.2

Note: Table excludes students. Participants on active labour market programmes are classified as employed.

reducing the likelihood of job loss and labour force withdrawal. The largest employment fall was amongst workers lacking any formal qualifications; 33 per cent of the unqualified workforce are without a job. This means that one quarter of the stock of unqualified workers lost their jobs over the period. In addition, over two thirds of this decline has been accounted for by a rise in non-participation rather than unemployment, so that by 1992 the unqualified inactivity rate was 20.3 per cent. The unqualified unemployment-population ratio grew by some seven points to reach nearly 14 per cent by 1992. In contrast, the rise in non-employment amongst graduates and those with intermediate qualifications,[4] whilst less severe, has been distributed equally between unemployment and inactivity. Most of the employment fall amongst the unqualified occurred prior to 1986. In contrast, joblessness amongst the intermediate group has been particularly strong during the current recession.

Even amongst prime-age men (22–54 years), traditionally thought to be less exposed to employment fluctuations, over 15 per cent were without a job in 1992 and 6 per cent were economically inactive. Amongst unskilled prime-age workers, 26 per cent were without work, with the inactivity rate at 13 per cent. This pattern is remarkably similar to the findings of Juhn, Murphy and Topel (1991)

117

Table 6.1.2 Employment, participation and unemployment rates by age, 1977–92 (percentages)

	Share of population	Employment/ population	Lab. force/ population	Unemploy./ Lab. force
Men				
Age 16-21				
1977	10.4	89.1	98.6	9.5
1986	11.0	75.8	94.0	18.3
1992	8.2	71.9	91.9	19.3
Change 1977-92		-17.2	-7.4	9.8
Age 22-54				
1977	71.3	93.6	98.0	4.4
1986	71.3	84.8	94.1	9.2
1992	74.8	84.5	93.7	9.2
Change 1977-92		-9.1	-4.3	4.8
Age 55-64				
1977	18.3	81.5	85.9	4.4
1986	17.6	60.3	66.4	6.1
1992	17.0	58.7	65.0	6.3
Change 1977-92		-22.8	-20.9	1.9
Women				
Age 16-21				
1977	10.9	77.6	86.0	8.4
1986	12.8	69.0	83.7	14.7
1992	8.4	69.2	79.9	10.7
Change 1977-92		-8.4	-6.1	2.3
Age 22-54				
1977	78.0	59.4	63.8	4.4
1986	77.5	62.5	68.7	6.2
1992	82.5	68.3	72.8	4.5
Change 1977-92		9.0	9.0	0.1
Age 55-59				
1977	11.1	53.8	56.2	2.4
1986	9.7	48.0	51.0	3.0
1992	9.1	51.6	53.7	2.1
Change 1977-92		-2.2	-2.5	-0.3

Table 6.1.3 Employment, participation and unemployment rates by educational level, 1977–92 (percentages)

	Population share	Employment/ population	Lab. force/ population	Unemploy./ Lab. force
Men				
Degree				
1977	9.0	95.7	97.6	1.9
1986	13.5	92.1	95.6	3.5
1992	18.2	89.5	93.9	4.4
Change 1977-92		-6.2	-3.7	2.5
Intermediate				
1977	39.6	94.1	97.7	3.6
1986	45.3	86.8	95.6	8.8
1992	56.9	81.7	92.0	9.3
Change 1977-92		-12.4	-5.7	5.7
None				
1977	51.4	88.2	94.7	6.5
1986	41.3	68.2	80.7	12.5
1992	25.0	66.0	79.7	13.7
Change 1977-92		-22.2	-15.0	7.2
Women				
Degree				
1977	9.9	71.3	75.2	3.9
1986	8.3	77.6	82.3	4.7
1992	11.6	82.5	85.7	3.2
Change 1977-92		11.2	10.5	-0.7
Intermediate				
1977	23.4	67.7	72.3	4.6
1986	47.1	68.4	75.9	7.5
1992	55.7	71.3	76.2	4.9
Change 1977-92		3.6	3.9	0.3
None				
1977	66.7	57.0	61.7	4.7
1986	44.6	52.1	58.7	6.6
1992	32.7	54.0	59.0	5.0
Change 1977-92		-3.0	-2.7	0.3

Note: Intermediate denotes any qualifications below degree level

Table 6.1.4   Reasons for non-participation in the labour market, 1979–91 (percentages)

	Long-term sick	Retired	Looking after home	Believes no jobs	Other
Men					
1979	57.7	28.3	1.3	3.8	8.8
1986	41.4	21.3	4.4	17.0	15.5
1991	52.8	24.9	5.3	6.0	11.1
Change 1979-91	2.6	1.1	0.4	0.4	0.7
Women					
1979	4.8	1.9	76.5	0.5	16.1
1986	9.2	2.4	68.2	2.6	17.6
1991	13.2	3.8	66.9	1.0	15.1
Change 1979-91	3.4	0.9	-8.7	0.2	-1.6

in the United States, where the non-employment rate for the prime age male workforce in 1989 was 10.9 per cent, of which 6.5 points was accounted for by inactivity. As in Britain, non-participation has risen strongly over the past fifteen years and is concentrated amongst low skilled groups. Other countries have experienced similar problems, but not of a similar magnitude. The OECD (1992) shows that the 14.9 per cent average prime age, male non-employment rate for Britain during the 1980s was the highest in the seven largest industrialised countries. For women, only unqualified workers have experienced falls in demand for their labour. Participation rates for unqualified women have fallen, whilst those of the other skill groups have risen to such an extent that they account for the entire change in employment.

Table 6.1.4 outlines the reasons given for inactivity. For men, the majority appear to be long-term sick, though this proportion dipped during the eighties. The official discouraged worker rate, those who believe no work is available, peaked in 1986 at 17 per cent. Thereafter these workers appear to have been absorbed into the numbers of long-term sick. Rows 4 and 8 give the increase in the inactivity rate attributable to these responses.[5] The majority of the rise in male inactivity, 2.6 points of the 5.2 point increase, can be attributed to an increase in the numbers self-classified as long-term sick. Likewise the majority of the rise in participation amongst women has come from

Table 6.1.5   Benefit recipients amongst inactive men aged 20–59,
1977–91 (000s)

	Sickness/ invalidity benefit	Other income support	Unemploy- ment benefit	Estimated inactive men
1977	419	78	n/a	420
1981	330	87	90	530
1986	338	119	440	1140
1991	473	381	109	1050

Source: Columns 1, 2 and 3 from *Social Security Statistics* (DSS), Column
2 excludes those also receiving contributory based payment and
was Supplementary Benefit prior to 1988. Column 3 is based on
percentages claimants classified as inactive by *Labour Force
Survey*. Column 4 is based on estimated grossed LFS inactivity
rates

those previously looking after the home. In addition, over 30 per cent
of the male inactive population profess a desire for work. This is not
confined to the official category of discouraged workers but incorporates other classifications.

What sources of income do the inactive draw on? Table 6.1.5
shows a steady increase in the number of men in receipt of various
forms of state support other than those normally associated with
unemployment. Sickness and invalidity benefit are contributory based
payments. Those with insufficient national insurance contributions
can claim a disabled premium on top of basic income support (IS).
This premium is only payable to those incapacitated for at least 7
months.[6] Many of these could presumably be short term sick. The
GHS for 1991 confirms that 72 per cent of those receiving invalidity
and sickness benefit and 73 per cent of those receiving the Disabled
Premium had no qualifications.

At the same time as the number of long-term sickness benefit
claimants was rising, there has been a dramatic fall in the proportion
of inactive men in receipt of unemployment related benefits. Over 30
per cent of inactive men were unemployed claimants in 1986, but the
claimant proportion had declined to around 10 per cent by 1991.[7] The
Government's Restart counselling and advice initiative for the long-
term unemployed also began in 1986. It seems plausible, therefore,
that one of the results of the Restart initiative may have been to move

some of the long-term claimant unemployed who are classified as inactive according to the LFS, onto sickness related benefits.[8] Certainly the numbers in Table 6.1.5 give broad support to this hypothesis. The 330,000 decline in inactive claimants, is more than matched by the increase in numbers in receipt of other forms of state support over the same period. This is also consistent with the finding of White and Lakey (1992) that 67 per cent of unemployed men in a 1989 survey who left the register for reasons other than employment began receiving other forms of state benefit. The authors go onto show that Restart was particularly helpful in boosting this flow for unemployed men with durations of between 6 and 12 months. In addition Schmitt and Wadsworth (1993) show that the increasing administrative tightness of the benefit entitlement legislation in the 1980s has reduced the numbers qualifying for unemployment benefit by around 200,000. A direct consequence of this has been to lower the search activity of those unemployed excluded from the system, principally by denying them access to the training and support schemes of the Employment Services. The consequence of this could have contributed to the rise in inactivity. Once outside the claimant system, these individuals will no longer be eligible for the Government sponsored support schemes, e.g., Job Clubs, Restart courses and commitment to search, aimed at helping the unemployed back into work.

The number of inactive people at any point in time depends on the number of individuals flowing into inactivity and on the number leaving it. Changes in the inactive stock therefore reflect changes in both the chance of becoming inactive, the inflow rate, and the probability of leaving, the outflow rate. Table 6.1.6 documents these inflow and outflow rates over time, disaggregated by education, in order to assess the contribution of each toward changes in the numbers of inactive.

Table 6.1.6 shows a simultaneous rise in inflow rates and a fall in outflow rates over the period. However, most of the explanation behind the rise in inactivity seems to be because more people are at risk, higher inflow rates, and not because individuals are staying inactive much longer than in the early 1980s. Again the protective impact of education is apparent. Graduates are less at risk from inactivity since they are both less likely to experience it, (lower inflow rates), and find it easier to get out, (higher outflow rates). Throughout the late 1970s and early 1980s, the probability of entering inactivity rose whilst that of leaving fell. By 1986 the inflow into

122

Table 6.1.6 Inflow and outflow rates associated with inactivity and unemployment (men 22-54 years)

| | | Inactivity | | Unemployment | |
		Inflow %	Outflow %	Inflow %	Outflow %
1977	Degree	0.2	92.5	1.2	63.7
	Intermediate	0.3	58.7	2.4	65.9
	None	0.8	26.8	3.6	47.7
1986	Degree	0.4	85.8	2.3	48.7
	Intermediate	1.2	46.8	4.0	41.2
	None	3.6	1.5	5.0	36.4
1990	Degree	0.4	83.1	1.2	72.4
	Intermediate	0.6	33.7	2.8	58.1
	None	1.0	16.1	5.3	42.3
1992	Degree	1.3	70.8	3.3	67.7
	Intermediate	2.1	28.0	5.5	45.8
	None	4.8	14.6	7.4	38.6

inactivity for the unqualified and intermediate categories was 4 times larger than in 1977. The outflow rate by 1990 was 40 per cent lower than in 1977. Around two-thirds of the total rise in the inactive stock of low skilled workers between 1977 and 1992 is due to the increased risk of entering. By 1992 more than half of the unqualified unemployed were moving out of unemployment only to become inactive. Once inactive, an unqualified male can expect to remain so around 40 per cent longer than in 1977.

The determinants of inactivity

We now attempt to determine the likely causes of rising joblessness amongst the low skilled. Essentially there are two competing explanations for increases in inactivity amongst men. The first is that this is a labour supply response by the individuals concerned. As society becomes wealthier, people may be in a position to choose to work less, retire early or adjust patterns of labour supply within the household. If so, then declining activity rates may be consistent with efficient, optimising behaviour on behalf of the individual. The second explanation is that these movements were demand induced. Falling demand for low skilled labour generates rising unemployment. If these conditions persist, displaced workers can no longer obtain employment and they effectively withdraw from the labour market.

One method of addressing the labour supply argument is to

Table 6.1.7 Household composition by male labour market status and education, 1983–91 (percentages)

	1983	1986	1991
Labour market status			
Employed			
Married	73.3	70.4	67.3
Working spouse	50.7	52.8	59.1
Unemployed			
Married	52.6	49.1	44.5
Working spouse	29.1	23.2	30.8
Inactive			
Married	69.8	65.5	64.6
Working spouse	22.1	20.9	24.0
Education			
Degree			
Married	80.6	75.4	72.8
Working spouse	47.0	48.1	55.5
Intermediate			
Married	63.9	62.3	63.3
Working spouse	48.4	50.3	56.8
Unskilled			
Married	73.5	70.9	64.4
Working spouse	43.5	42.2	44.7

recognise that these observations could theoretically arise from a change in the population distribution in favour of groups with higher propensities to withdraw from the labour force, primarily the old and the unskilled. Yet Tables 6.1.2 and 6.1.3 show clearly that the share of unqualified workers in the population has fallen sharply over the period. Increased educational attainment reduced the number of workers without formal qualifications by 56 per cent. Similarly, the share of older male workers has risen by just over one percentage point. In other words, inactivity has risen primarily within skill/age groups and not because there are more individuals in the population who are prone to inactivity.

Neither is there evidence of a labour supply induced fall in male participation caused by a redistribution of economic activity within households. As Table 6.1.7 shows, inactive and unemployed men are more likely to be single. Even if married or cohabiting, their spouse is less likely to work. Further, whilst participation of women has risen across all groups over the period, it has grown most within households headed by employed men. A similar result holds if we disaggregate the male population by education. Women are more likely to work in skilled and presumably wealthier, households. Thus not only has the distribution of employment across skill groups become progressively unequal, this rising inequality has been reinforced by the concentration of employment in two earner households.

Is a demand-led explanation therefore consistent with these observations? Table 6.1.8 demonstrates how the pattern of employment has moved away from industries that were dominated by male labour without formal qualifications but often endowed considerable experience of the job, notably in manufacturing, mining and construction, and towards the service industries. There is a clear dichotomy of entry patterns between the retail industries for the unqualified and the financial services for more educated groups. The contraction of industries that were traditional employers of low qualified workers has resulted in a 12 per cent decline in employment for the unqualified group relative to graduates, and a 6.2 per cent fall with respect to the intermediate groups between 1981 and 1991.[9] These numbers underestimate the true extent of the shift in relative demand. In addition to the shift in employment across industries, there was an even greater movement away from low skilled work within industries. Not only did the metal good manufacturing firms contract, they reduced employment of unqualified male labour by more than the average. Consequently, employment of graduates rose by 4 per cent over the period, whilst that of the unqualified fell by 26 per cent.

The employment share change across occupations also supports this pattern. The most significant change is the 28 per cent decline in unqualified men recognised as employed in skilled manual occupations. This has been only partially offset by an increase in the proportion of self-employed manual workers. The majority of unqualified skilled workers have simply disappeared from the employment stock.[10]

One implication of a fall in demand for unqualified workers is that their wages should fall compared to other workers in greater demand by employers. Figure 6.1.2 uses data from the General Household Survey (men aged 20–69), to show that the relative wage position of the unqualified who remained in work did indeed deteriorate over the period (see also Schmitt 1992, Gregg and Machin 1993). Between 1977 and 1991, the average wage, adjusted for inflation, of male graduates relative to those with no qualifications rose by 32 percent-

Table 6.1.8 Industrial and occupational distribution of employment by educational level, men aged 20–64, 1981–91 (percentages)

	Degree		Intermediate		None	
	1981	1991	1981	1991	1981	1991
Industry						
Agriculture	1.0	1.0	2.4	2.4	4.8	5.3
Energy and water supply	4.5	4.5	4.2	3.8	5.8	3.3
Other mineral and ore extraction	4.4	4.5	4.7	4.2	6.4	6.1
Metal goods, Engineering	14.8	14.9	16.9	14.4	16.9	13.4
Other manufacturing	5.3	5.0	10.3	10.2	13.4	13.2
Construction	5.2	6.9	9.6	13.2	13.9	14.2
Distribution, Retail	6.2	8.0	14.3	15.9	15.3	19.1
Transport and communications	4.1	4.2	9.4	10.4	10.2	10.7
Banking, Finance	15.8	23.0	9.3	10.0	3.1	4.2
Other services	38.7	28.1	19.1	15.5	10.3	10.5
Occupation						
Professional, Managerial	57.2	67.0	24.2	26.4	9.2	16.9
Intermediate non-manual	29.3	19.1	10.3	10.1	2.1	3.8
Junior non-manual/ personal services	6.7	4.7	17.1	9.3	7.1	6.4
Skilled manual	3.1	5.4	30.4	29.7	43.1	31.2
Other manual	1.7	1.4	11.7	12.1	29.9	28.8
Self-employed manual	1.9	2.2	6.2	11.4	8.7	13.1

age points. The intermediate to unskilled differential rose by some 4 points.[11] The average graduate wage is now twice that of the average unqualified male wage. Real wage levels have risen for all workers. However, figure 6.1.2 suggests that since 1988 even the real wage level for those without qualifications may have begun to fall.[12]

These patterns are consistent with a fall in demand for the type of jobs filled by prime age unqualified men. Had the rise in inactivity been initiated by a reduction in unskilled labour supply, then their relative wage position would have been expected to improve as employers raise wages to attract the scarce resource. Clearly the reverse is happening. The fact that unskilled wages appear to have remained broadly flat, rather than falling, over the period may be attributable to the continued union presence in male dominated industries.

Should real wages be allowed to fall in order to induce employers to employ more low skilled labour? This argument seems to have little credibility. The growing real wage gap between graduates and the

Table 6.1.9 Earnings increases by industry and education for full-time male employees, aged 20–64, 1981–91 (percentages)

	Degree	*Intermediate*	*None*
Agriculture	*	-15.8	19.0
Energy and water supply	27.0	17.5	26.3
Other mineral and ore extraction	11.0	33.3	23.0
Metal goods, Engineering	30.6	22.2	11.9
Other manufacturing	34.5	7.9	9.9
Construction	24.7	19.8	15.7
Distribution, Retail	6.5	24.2	9.5
Transport and communications	*	9.9	8.3
Banking, Finance	55.2	13.8	1.0
Other services	22.4	13.3	16.7
Total	27.3	16.5	11.3

Note: * denotes sample cell size less than 20, estimates not shown

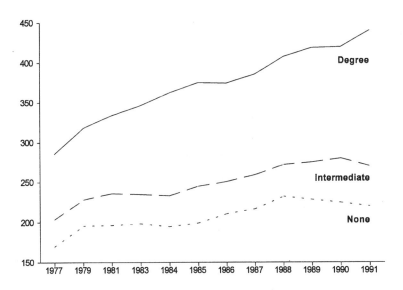

Figure 6.1.2 Real weekly earnings by educational qualification for men aged 20–59, 1977–91 (£s, 1991 prices)

unqualified, means that the unqualified are now cheaper to hire than at any time in the past twenty years, yet their employment has not risen. In the United States, where union presence is negligible, real wages of low skilled workers have fallen by some 30 per cent over a similar period. This has not prevented the non-employment rate for these workers rising to 33 per cent (Juhn, Murphy and Topel 1991). Inactivity seems to have grown because of a dearth of employment opportunities for low skilled workers. Unqualified workers displaced from traditional high-wage industries may be reluctant or unable to take jobs in the low-wage secondary sector. Hence a form of queue unemployment develops, as workers try for jobs comparable to those they previously held, which subsequently manifests itself in a decline in participation if the unemployed are unable to locate work. The GHS indicates that a redundant miner in 1991 would have to take a real wage cut of one third in order to pursue a career in the retail industry. The differential in 1981 was less than 18 per cent.

Yet even this understates the extent of the problem, since full-time jobs are increasingly hard to find. Faced with the choice of low wages, part-time service sector job and competition for these places from married women and younger workers, or the chance of a higher paying job and an even lower employment probability, then the willingness of the unqualified to withdraw from the labour force may have increased. Indeed, one result of the increased casualisation of the labour market is that individuals are less likely to qualify for contribution-based unemployment benefits[13] which further weakens the link with the labour market. In addition, increased competition for jobs from those covered by the Restart scheme now makes it harder for those who withdraw to re-enter employment.

Conclusion

The unemployment rate now seriously understates the extent of joblessness in Britain. A shrinking working population is supporting a growing non-working population. Further, this decline in economic activity has been borne disproportionately by the sector of the population who lack formal qualifications. Neither is this pattern attributable to individuals opting to enjoy more leisure, by retiring early or sharing work within households for example. Inactivity is a problem that affects all ages. Inactivity has gone on rising despite falls in the numbers of individuals with traditionally higher inactivity rates. In other words inactivity has risen because more members of the high risk groups have withdrawn from the labour force not because the at-risk population has grown. Further, it is most prevalent amongst those members of society who earn least. Indeed the rise in labour force participation of women over the period has compounded this problem, since working women are concentrated in households where the spouse is already in employment. Hence employment opportunities, household income and the distribution of working time across households have grown progressively unequal over the last fifteen years, working against those with low educational attainment.

Rather, the explanation seems to lie in a decline in demand for low skilled workers employed in production. Traditionally employers of unqualified male labour at relatively high wage rates, such jobs in these industries have declined dramatically. The alternative source of employment in Britain is now the service industry which prefers to employ a more flexible workforce, often not unionised, part-time and female with whom displaced manufacturing workers must compete. A prime-age male manufacturing worker without formal qualifications faces real wage reductions of around one third if they obtain an increasingly rare, full-time job in the service industries. Fifteen years ago labour withdrawal was often a temporary move, now with a dearth of employment opportunities it is more of a permanent phenomenon. The result is a discouraged worker effect, in which men unable to find work withdraw from the labour force.

In order to improve future employment prospects, then, maintaining a worker's attachment to the labour force must be a priority. Educational attainment undoubtedly helps since it is the single most important factor likely to influence the chances of obtaining employment. Average educational attainment has improved over the period, but it has been insufficiently strong to prevent inactivity from rising as demand for labour fell faster. In the short run, attempts need to be made to integrate the inactive back into labour force. For example, the role of the Employment Service in improving the skills of the workforce could be widened to incorporate all those without a job and not just unemployment benefit claimants, whose proportions have declined in recent years due to increasingly stringent eligibility criteria. Britain has too many low skilled workers. If active policies were pursued to rectify this then labour market efficiency would increase and the associated inequality which currently results in 3.7 million jobless men, primarily low skilled, could be avoided.

6.2 The Incidence and Cost of Unemployment

John Philpott

The incidence of unemployment

The stock of unemployment at any time will include people from all walks of life and all social and ethnic backgrounds. All age groups and skill levels will be represented. However, some people are more likely to be unemployed than others. Younger people and older people of working age are more prone to unemployment than prime-aged people. Manual workers and the less skilled have higher unemployment rates than non-manual workers and the highly skilled. In Britain, men are more likely to be unemployed than women, while men and women from ethnic minority backgrounds are more likely to be unemployed than their white counterparts. Unemployment rates also differ regionally and locally throughout Britain, although in recent years the 'North-South' divide in unemployment rates has narrowed.

Unemployment and age

Table 6.2.1 shows that unemployment rates are highest for younger people, decline into prime-age and then rise again for people aged 50 years and over (although one should note that 25–50 year olds typically account for half of all the unemployed at any time). The table—like all those in this section—is derived from the Labour Force Survey (LFS) which counts as unemployed people who want to work, are available for work and have sought work at some point in the month prior to the survey. The survey count is preferable to the count of people unemployed and claiming unemployment related benefits which omits those who are unemployed but not entitled to benefit (for example 16–17 year olds without a Youth Training placement) or do not have to 'sign on' in order to receive benefit (such as some older long-term unemployed people). Even the LFS figures, however, may not fully reflect the true labour market position of younger and older people. Many of the government employment and training programmes, for example, have been targeted (explicitly or implicitly) at the 18–25 year olds. Moreover, older people may decide to take early retirement rather than remain in the labour market.

Young people tend to suffer disproportionately during economic

Table 6.2.1   Percentage unemployment rates by age group

	16-29	*20-24*	*25-34*	*35-49*	*50-64*	*65+*	*All ages*
1984	22.0	17.7	12.3	8.1	8.6	7.4	11.7
1986	20.4	16.4	12.2	7.7	8.1	6.7	11.1
1990	11.5	9.1	7.1	4.7	6.2	4.3	6.7
1992	16.4	14.0	10.1	7.1	8.4	3.8	9.6

Source: Labour Force Survey

Table 6.2.2   Percentages of manual and non-manual unemployment

	1984	*1990*	*1992*
Non-manual	20.3	20.5	26.6
Manual	40.4	41.0	47.4
Unstated	39.3	34.0	26.6

Source: Labour Force Survey

downturns. If entering the labour market they will find few job openings; if already employed they will be those most prone to informal 'last in, first out' rules. But the fact that young workers exhibit relatively high unemployment rates even during buoyant economic periods suggests the phenomenon is partly structural— possibly indicating that youth pay is too high relative to the value of the productivity of many younger workers. Older workers, by contrast, might be expected to benefit from their experience when faced with fluctuations in the economic cycle. However, the response of many firms in hard times is to restructure their workforces and in such circumstances the experience of older workers may not compensate for the fact that any skills they have will be of an older 'vintage'. Moreover, firms may find it easier to shed older workers since such workers are often more amenable to voluntary redundancy and early retirement packages (Trinder, 1991).

Table 6.2.3 Percentage unemployment rates by former industry

	1984	*1989*	*1992*
Agricultural	5.6	4.5	6.1
Manufacturing	9.1	4.8	10.4
Construction	11.9	6.8	17.6
Distribution, hotels and catering	9.4	5.4	9.0
Transport and communications	5.6	3.5	8.1
Banking and finance	4.0	2.7	5.1
Other services	5.0	3.9	5.0

Source: Labour Force Survey (excludes people unemployed for more than three years)

Unemployment, occupation and skill

As table 6.2.2 shows people from manual occupational backgrounds account for nearly half of Britain's unemployed. Looking at change over time, it is difficult to discern a precise trend because such a large proportion of unemployed respondents to the LFS do not state a previous occupation. Nonetheless, it would appear that non-manual workers now account for a greater proportion of all unemployed people than was the case in the early 1980s. What is also clear, however, is that manual workers have suffered most during the 1990s. This runs counter to the widely held impression that the 1990s recession has been a 'white collar recession'.

The more vulnerable position of manual workers is also conveyed indirectly by table 6.2.3 which shows unemployment rates by the previous industry of the unemployed. Former manufacturing and construction workers tend to have the highest unemployment rates, and these sectors have borne the brunt of job losses in the early 1990s (table 6.2.4)

Turning to skill, Table 6.2.5 shows that unemployment rates rise as one descends the occupational skill hierarchy. In a modern economy subject to rapid technological advance, a fall in demand for unskilled workers might be expected to raise the unemployment rate of the unskilled over time, especially if training programmes fail to equip the unskilled unemployed for new jobs. Earnings data suggest a weaken-

Table 6.2.4 Employment changes by sector, Britain 1984–92

	Primary	Manuf.	Constr.	Services	All
in thousands					
1984	1272	5717	1757	14310	23056
1990	1122	5731	2026	16841	25720
1992	1077	5209	1687	16575	24478
% change					
1984-90	-11.7	0.2	15.3	17.7	11.5
1990-92	-10.2	-9.1	-16.7	-1.5	-4.8

Source: Labour Force Survey

ing in the labour market position of unskilled workers in Britain since the 1970s, their earnings having fallen in relative and (latterly) absolute terms. It is somewhat surprising, therefore, to discover that the unskilled unemployment rate has changed little since the early 1980s while the position of *skilled* manual workers appears to have deteriorated considerably (although as we saw in the previous section change in the relative labour market position of the skilled and the unskilled may be gauged more accurately by examining 'non-employment' rates rather than unemployment rates given the growing tendency of unskilled men without jobs to withdraw from the labour market). The changing fortunes of skilled manual workers undoubtedly reflects the shift away from manufacturing employment and the 'de-industrialisation' of Britain's workforce. Skill in itself, therefore, clearly offers no guarantee of immunity from unemployment.

Female and ethnic minority unemployment

As table 6.2.6 shows, men have higher unemployment rates than women. These LFS data avoid the well known deficiencies of the claimant count based measure of unemployment which understate the extent of unemployment amongst women who, for a variety of reasons, are often not entitled to unemployment-related benefit. However, even the LFS may fail to capture the full extent of women's unemployment. For example, some women who would like to work may not be available for work because they will often first have to make arrangements for child care. Moreover, there is some evidence that women's self-assessment of whether they are unemployed does

Table 6.2.5 Percentage unemployment rates by occupation and
skill level

	1984	*1989*	*1992*
Professional	2.2	1.4	3.1
Intermediate	3.8	2.5	4.3
Skilled non-manual	6.4	3.8	6.4
Skilled manual	8.7	5.1	11.4
Semi-skilled	11.2	7.3	13.5
Unskilled	13.6	9.7	14.6

Source: *Labour Force Survey* (excludes people unemployed for more than
three years)

Table 6.2.6 Male-female percentage unemployment rates

	1984	*1990*	*1992*
Male	11.8	6.8	11.3
Female	11.4	6.5	7.2
All	11.7	6.6	9.5

Source: *Labour Force Survey*

not appear to conform well with standard definitions of unemployment; many married women will undertake more housework when without jobs and seek work only when labour market conditions are more buoyant (Dex, 1989).

In most countries female unemployment exceeds male unemployment, so the British experience is unusual. There is no satisfactory explanation for this but it has been suggested that lower female unemployment rates in Britain reflect the nature of employment and social security legislation (Wells, 1992). What is clear from table 6.2.6, however, is the degree to which female unemployment has fallen relative to that of males since the early 1980s and especially during the 1990s recession. Female employment has held up to a far greater extent than male employment in recent years largely because of

Table 6.2.7 Employment change by gender and working patterns, Britain, 1984–92

	Full-time			Part-time		
	Female	Male	Total	Female	Male	Total
In thousands						
1984	5340	13038	18378	4286	549	4836
1990	6366	13878	20244	4843	769	5612
1992	6099	12858	18956	4876	826	5702
% change						
1984-90	19.1	6.4	10.1	13.0	40.0	16.1
1990-92	-4.2	-7.3	-6.4	0.7	7.4	1.6
	Total male			Total female		
% change						
1984-90	7.8			16.0		
1990-92	-6.6			-2.0		

Source: Labour Force Survey

the relative buoyancy of part-time employment given that over 80 per cent of part-time employees are women (table 6.2.7).

Whether male or female, people from the ethnic minorities are more prone to unemployment. Throughout most of the 1980s the unemployment rate for ethnic minorities was nearly double that for whites. From 1981 the rate for whites (male and female) rose from just below 10 per cent to a peak of nearly 12 per cent in the mid 1980s, before falling sharply to below seven per cent prior to the onset of the 1990s recession. For ethnic minorities both the rise and fall were sharper, unemployment peaking at over 21 per cent before eventually dropping to below 10 per cent. This is a common pattern: as soon as jobs start to be lost, ethnic minority unemployment rises much faster and to a higher peak than white unemployment, while recovery in the job market sees minority unemployment falling faster (Brown, 1990). The pattern has been repeated in the most recent economic cycle: having narrowed substantially during the boom of the late 1980s the differential between ethnic minority and white unemployment has widened again. By the autumn of 1992 the ethnic minority unemployment rate had risen to 19 per cent compared to 10 per cent for whites. Amongst the minorities, people from Pakistani and Bangladeshi backgrounds had the highest unemployment rate, at 32 per cent. The unemployment rate for those from Afro-Caribbean backgrounds was 24 per cent and for Indians 12 per cent. High

Table 6.2.8 Percentage unemployment rates by ethnic origin, age and sex, 1989–91

| | Males | | Females | |
	White	Ethnic	White	Ethnic
Age 16-24				
with qualifications	9	18	7	17
no qualifications	22	34	20	n/a
Age 25-44				
with qualifications	4	8	6	10
no qualifications	14	17	9	n/a
Age 45-64				
with qualifications	5	n/a	4	n/a
no qualifications	10	17	6	n/a

Source: *Labour Force Survey*, taken from 'ethnic origins and the labour market', *Employment Gazette* February 1993

unemployment amongst ethnic minorities can to some extent be explained by the younger age profile of ethnic minorities and the fact that many are concentrated in lower skilled manual occupations. Discrimination is almost certainly a factor, however, as suggested by the much higher unemployment rates for people from ethnic minorities whatever their level of qualifications (table 6.2.8).

Regional unemployment

There has been a narrowing in regional unemployment rate differentials in recent years with the result that the 'North-South Divide' in unemployment that was prevalent throughout the 1980s has all but disappeared. Part of the narrowing can be attributed to the relatively severe impact of the 1990s recession on the South—by the spring of 1992 South East unemployment, for example, was almost equal to the national average—but there is some indication of a narrowing of unemployment rate differentials prior to the recession during the boom years of the latter 1980s.

Unemployment flows and the duration of unemployment

So far we have been looked at the incidence of unemployment in relation to the various components of the stock of unemployment. But the stock is subject to frequent turnover with flows of people continually entering or leaving unemployment (Daniel, 1990). Those entering each week, month or quarter will consist of people losing or quitting jobs and entrants to the labour market unable to find work. Those leaving, by contrast, consist of those who find jobs and those who retire or leave the workforce because of illness. These respective flows can be very large, often several times larger than the stock in the course of a year. In 1992, for example, 4.5 million people flowed into unemployment and 4.1 million flowed out, in comparison to the average stock during the year of 2.75 million.

Flows into and out of employment and economic inactivity as well as unemployment are examined later in the chapter in the context of the growth in non-employment. All that need be pointed out here is that inequality shows up in the pattern of unemployment flows, while the precise nature of these flows determines the duration composition of the stock of unemployment (i.e., the relative proportions of short-term and long-term unemployment). A degree of inequality can be seen in the inflow to unemployment since some people are more likely to lose their jobs than others. For the majority of people in work, the chances of entering unemployment are relatively slight—only 5 per cent of people in employment a year ago are now unemployed. But unskilled and semi-skilled people are four times more likely than average to lose their jobs and flow into unemployment. Similarly, inequality shows up in the outflow from unemployment; while most people who flow into unemployment flow out again quite quickly, some experience long periods of unemployment. Claimant data show that of those people entering unemployment at any particular time around 25 per cent leave within a month, 50 per cent within a quarter and two-thirds within six months. However, although only 15–20 per cent of the inflow will remain unemployed for more than a year this is a high proportion by historical standards. Outflow rates from unemployment are today considerably lower than in the 1970s so far more people leave unemployment within a year. This is significant because long-term unemployment acts like a kind of 'trap'. Once a person has been unemployed for more than a year he or she is four times less likely to leave unemployment within the next three months than somebody entering unemployment for the first time.

The combined effect of fewer people leaving unemployment within a year and the lower propensity of those unemployed for more than a year to leave unemployment means that nowadays a far higher proportion of the unemployed remain without jobs for relatively long periods. At present, over one-third of all unemployed people have been unemployed for more than a year compared with one-fifth a generation ago. So even though only a relatively small proportion of the inflow to unemployment end up long-term unemployed, there has been a substantial build-up of long-term unemployment. Moreover, as well as people who remain continuously unemployed there are those who fail to gain a firm foothold in employment and experience frequent spells of unemployment. Such people will only show up as short-term unemployed in labour market statistics but their weakness and sense of insecurity in the labour market may be as great as that of the continuously unemployed. Unfortunately, relatively little is known about people who experience frequent repeat spells of unemployment although a sample survey of people making appointments to make new claims for unemployment related benefits in June 1991 shows that 20 per cent had had one spell of registered unemployment in the preceding two years while 13 per cent had had two or more spells (Erens and Ghate, 1992).

The observed difficulty of leaving long-term unemployment—the 'trap effect'—might simply reflect the fact that those most likely to filter through into long-term unemployment are the least productive amongst the unemployed and thus the least able to leave. It is certainly true that individuals with long durations of unemployment appear to be less skilled and less well qualified than all economically active adults. Just as less skilled people are more likely to flow into unemployment they are more likely to remain unemployed (and as we shall see later, even if they leave unemployment their destination is more likely to be economic inactivity than employment). But as table 6.2.9 indicates although the long-term unemployed are somewhat less skilled and well qualified than the short-term unemployed the difference is not that great. It seems likely therefore that there may also be something about the very experience of long-term unemployment that renders escape more difficult—an effect known as duration dependence'.

Long-term unemployment and 'duration dependence'

How does one explain duration dependence? One possibility is that individuals suffer some sort of depreciation of skills as a result of being without work. Similarly, long periods without work might reduce peoples' motivation and cause them to forgo active job search or make them less attractive to employers. There is unfortunately no proper evidence available with which to assess the extent of possible

Table 6.2.9 Percentages of short and long-term unemployed with skills and qualifications in Britain, Spring 1992

	Unemployed	
	Short-term	Long-term
Skill level		
Professional/Managerial	2	1
Intermediate	13	10
Skilled non-manual	18	10
Skilled manual	26	26
Semi-skilled	21	22
Armed forces	1	-
No answer or unclassified	11	21
Qualification		
Degree	5	4
Professional	7	4
City & Guilds/Apprenticeship	20	19
A level or equivalent	5	3
O level or CSE	26	17
Other	7	7
No qualification	30	46

Source: Labour Force Survey

skills depreciation but there is firmer evidence which suggests lack of effective job search on the part of the long-term unemployed. For example, a wide ranging Employment Department study of the London labour market conducted in the late 1980s found that around a quarter of people unemployed for over six months had not sought work during the previous week, and while over 80 per cent of those who were searching had consulted newspaper advertisements once a week only 55 per cent made at least one weekly visit to their local Jobcentre (Meadows et al., 1988). It may of course be that Jobcentres are—perhaps with some justification—considered by many unemployed people to be an ineffective avenue of job search since many employers recruit by informal channels. But it would appear from these studies that the majority of the long-term unemployed do not attempt to compensate for this by engaging in what is described as 'employer contact' job search. Moreover, half of those who were searching did not visit a jobcentre weekly and 40 per cent of the long term unemployed never approached possible employers. There may of course be a link between poor job search and the conditions under which benefits are made available to the unemployed, but since in

139

recent years the stipulations placed upon people in receipt of unemployment related benefit have been tightened considerably the problem is far more likely to be one of inefficient job search rather than reluctance on the part of the unemployed to seek work. Those long term unemployed who do search effectively may nonetheless be discriminated against by employers.

It has long been known that most employers 'screen' potential recruits for required qualifications, experience and work histories etc. but it would also appear that many employers also explicitly or implicitly use unemployment duration as a selection criterion. A study performed in the mid-1980s by the Institute of Manpower Studies (IMS) of recruitment practices of some 500 employers in a variety of local labour markets discovered a marked wariness of the long-term unemployed (Meager and Metcalf, 1987). In general employers explained this by reference to a lack of certain aptitudes for jobs in question. In some cases this was related to skill requirements but more often than not simply to a 'lack of motivation'. Some, for example, considered the long-term unemployed unlikely to be able to conform to normal working practices, to be less punctual and perhaps more prone to absenteeism (around a quarter of the employers surveyed attributed this to the experience of long-term unemployment, while another quarter considered it a trait of individuals which made them less able or willing to work).

In addition, some employers expressed the view that long-term unemployment signalled some underlying problem with applicants. But significantly, such suspicion was often felt irrespective of whether the employers concerned had any actual experience of, or direct contact with, long-term unemployed people. The IMS study therefore clearly suggests that the long-term unemployed may be 'discriminated' against and rejected for no other reason than that they are *assumed* to be in some sense inadequate and hence a risky prospect. Their chances of being called even for a job interview may thus be extremely slim, applicants appearing to be at risk of being rejected solely by virtue of being long-term unemployed.

The expectation was that the London study would find evidence of a serious 'mismatch' between the skills and qualifications of the long-term unemployed. This expectation proved to be unfounded as did the assertion that the long-term unemployed had unrealistic pay expectations. Instead, there was a clear indication that employers were discriminating against the long-term unemployed. In general, although the distribution of job vacancies was found to be more skewed towards skilled occupations than the distribution of previous jobs held by long-term unemployed people, a substantial proportion of vacancies were nevertheless available in occupations with minimal skill requirements or well within the scope of the long-term unemployed. Despite this, the long-term unemployed were less successful when applying for jobs irrespective of the skill requirements. Whilst one in five applicants for non-management posts filled just prior to the study period were thought to be long-term unemployed, only one in 50 long-term unemployed applicants were known to be recruited. This was in large part a consequence of employers' unfavourable perceptions of the long-term unemployed, even though such perceptions were unlikely to be based upon actual experience of long-term unemployed people.

The cost of unemployment

The cost of unemployment can be considered in a number of ways. The most obvious cost is the output lost when people are unemployed rather than helping to produce goods and services. The burden of this output loss is borne in part by the unemployed in the form of lost income, in part by businesses in the form of reduced profits, and in part by the Exchequer in the form of benefits payments to unemployed people and lost tax revenues. In addition to these economic costs there are essentially non-monetary costs incurred by the unemployed (psychological distress, ill health, marital breakdown etc.) and society at large (for example, increased levels of crime). For example, the statistical association between unemployment, suicide and parasuicide (i.e., deliberate self-harm) is well documented. Platt and Krieitman (1984), for example, found that the risk of parasuicide amongst the unemployed relative to the risk amongst the employed was related strongly to the duration of unemployment: it was nine to one among those unemployed for fewer than four weeks; five to one among those unemployed for five weeks to six months; ten to one among those unemployed for six to twelve months and nineteen to one among those unemployed for more than a year. But these issues are not the main focus of this chapter.

The output cost of unemployment can be estimated by means of a number of procedures. The simplest is to assume that every person who is unemployed would if employed produce as much as the average person in employment. In 1991 the value of GDP per person employed was £22,000—at current levels of unemployment this would suggest a loss of £66 billion of potential output (11.5 per cent of GDP). Matters are complicated, however, by the fact that it is far from certain how much output would be produced by unemployed people if they were to be placed in jobs. It is not obvious what jobs the unemployed would perform and it is unlikely that they would all be as productive as the average person in work.

Not only (as we have seen) is there a higher incidence of unemployment among the less skilled but also the experience of unemployment (especially long-term unemployment) may itself deplete the productive potential of unemployed people. Rather than base estimates of the output cost of unemployment on a measure of what people in work produce it is therefore preferable to consider what the unemployed might produce. This of course requires an element of subjective judgement but a guideline is provided by official survey data which detail the incomes of people in and out of work. These data suggest that if employed the average unemployed person could expect to earn two-thirds of the average full-time wage (Erens and Hedges, 1990). Taking the relative earnings of the unemployed as a proxy measure of their relative productivity, and adjusting GDP per person employed accordingly, it seems reasonable to conclude that the output lost as a result of unemployment in 1992–3 amounted to at least eight per cent of GDP. Of this roughly half is borne by the public purse in the form of benefit outlays and lost taxes.

Despite the fact that the availability of benefit payments means part of the cost of unemployment is shifted from unemployed people onto the taxpayer, those who become unemployed nonetheless incur a substantial financial loss. The cost to unemployed people can be estimated by calculating a replacement ratio indicating the proportionate loss of income incurred by a person when unemployed. The calculation of replacement ratios is far from straightforward; much depends upon the individual circumstances of unemployed people. The replacement ratios shown in table 6.2.10 (which relate to 1991–2) should thus be considered as illustrative since they are calculated according on the basis of certain broad characteristics of unemployed people (Layard and Philpott, 1991).

As the table indicates, transfers from the taxpayer cushion the financial blow of unemployment most for people with dependent children. It is important to note, however, that married heads of household with dependent children account for only a minority of the unemployed. It is clear therefore that for the typical unemployed person the financial loss of being without a job is considerable.

Table 6.2.10 Comparisons of weekly incomes in and out of work, 1991–92

	Benefit income £	Net earnings in work £	Replacement ratio %	Unemployed man in family %
Single	67.35	139.28	48	53
Married				
0 children	89.55	185.47	48	18
1 child	120.95	163.72	74	10
2 children	142.70	173.79	82	11
3 children	162.45	192.87	84	5
4 children	180.80	215.14	84	3

Note: Benefit figure included housing benefit minus 20 per cent community charge; earnings figures are net earnings minus community charge.

Source: Layard and Philpott (1991)

Moreover, it should not be forgotten that higher unemployment represents the single most important factor contributing to the growth of poverty in Britain since the late 1970s (Piachaud, 1991). Between 1979 and 1988–9 the proportion of unemployed in the bottom decile of the income distribution (after accounting for housing costs) almost doubled—rising from 16 per cent to 30 per cent (Giles and Webb, 1993). The proportion will almost certainly have risen further as a result of the sharp rise in unemployment in the early 1990s. Not surprisingly in the light of our earlier discussion of the structure of unemployment, the poverty caused by unemployment is concentrated amongst groups such as younger and older people, the less skilled and ethnic minorities. But perhaps the greatest hardship is experienced by the long-term unemployed. Not only do they suffer prolonged financial hardship and risk being trapped into dependency on welfare benefits but—as we discuss later in the chapter—they also experience various forms of social exclusion.

As already mentioned, benefit payments comprise only part of the cost of unemployment to the Exchequer, the remainder being the tax revenues and National Insurance payments that are foregone when a person is unemployed. As with replacement ratios, precise calculation of the Exchequer cost of unemployment requires information about the characteristics of the unemployed and estimates of what they can expect to earn when employed. Estimates which relate to the 'average' unemployed person suggest that the annual cost to the Exchequer per person unemployed in 1991–2 was just over £8,000 (Layard and Philpott, 1991). The estimate is similar to others using slightly different methodologies (Unemployment Unit, 1992).

Long-term unemployment and wage pressure

In addition to the cost of unemployment as outlined above, it is increasingly argued that long-term unemployment represents a particular form of economic inefficiency. Although unemployment represents a waste of resources some amount of unemployment can in a sense be considered 'efficient' in a market economy. If there were no unemployed, employers would be engaged in a desperate scramble for labour and wages would be bid up in an ever rising inflationary spiral; even in the post-war era of 'full employment' in Britain policy makers tolerated some unemployment. Unfortunately, since the mid-1970s the goal of full employment has been abandoned and ever higher levels of unemployment have been used to contain inflation. Mass unemployment, however, represents a grossly inefficient and profoundly inegalitarian form of anti-inflation policy. Moreover, it would appear that whatever the overall unemployment rate, long-term unemployment makes no difference to the degree of inflationary pressure in the labour market.

A number of factors may explain this but it is normally posited that duration dependence effects result in the long-term unemployed having barely any influence upon the behaviour of wage bargainers (Layard et al., 1991). Employers will not lower wage offers simply because there is available a large number of long-term unemployed people whom they perceive as 'unemployable', and similarly incumbent workers will not moderate wage demands since they do not consider the long-term unemployed effective competitors for their jobs. Behaviour of this kind has been established by econometric studies which suggest that although there is a relationship between unemployment, wage inflation and price inflation it is only short-term unemployment (i.e., less than one year) that really matters. Long-term unemployment, by contrast, appears to make virtually no difference whatsoever. Therefore, while all unemployment is wasteful, long-term unemployment appears to be a total waste since it fails even to offer a pay-off in terms of controlling inflation.

6.3 Employment, Unemployment and Social Security

Eithne McLaughlin

It is difficult to overstate the political and associated policy influence of the idea that the provision of out-of-work income (through social security systems) constitutes an inherent disincentive to find, take or keep employment (McLaughlin, Millar and Cooke 1989). It is possible to trace these ideas as far back as the late 1300s (Stone, 1985). Both the 'old' and the New Poor Laws and the Beveridge-inspired modern system of social security have been rooted in the idea that unless able-bodied men are forced to work through economic necessity they will not otherwise do so. Thus the distinction between the deserving and the undeserving poor in social security policy involves a separation of those who cannot reasonably be expected to work from those who could, and should (Ditch, 1987). The significance of this dual, essentially moral, categorisation of the poor has been phenomenal because it has directly shaped the nature and level of social security provision for unemployed people, while indirectly it has also constrained the development of adequate forms of income support for sick people, disabled people, lone mothers and elderly people (see, for example, Alcock, 1987; Bradshaw and Deacon, 1983; Ditch, 1987; Novak, 1988 and Thane, 1978 for more extended accounts).

In the 1980s, the importance of preserving work incentives has influenced social security policy in three main areas: in the rules governing access to benefits, in the level of benefits available, and in the introduction of benefits intended to supplement low wages (see also Brown, 1990). This part of the chapter will summarise empirical evidence of decision-making, attitudes and behaviour to show that within each of these areas, the emphasis on work incentives in the construction of public policy has unintended effects on individuals and families which are not efficient in terms of the working of the labour market, and which result in attitudes and actions bearing little resemblance to those on which the policies are based.

The problem of incentives in social security provision

The strength of the view that social security provision is inherently problematic for reasons of disincentives may be rooted in class conflict

(Alcock, 1987 and Novak, 1988), but it finds its rational appeal in, and seeks legitimacy from, neo-classical economic theory. We have argued elsewhere (McLaughlin, Millar and Cooke, 1989) that this theory is fundamentally flawed on a number of grounds. Neo-classical economic theories of labour supply all rest on the assumption that individuals 'choose' between two options—work, which is necessary for material survival, and leisure, which is 'naturally' pleasurable— within the constraint that the number of hours for allocation is fixed. Individuals then seek to find the combination of the two which gives them the greatest overall satisfaction (or utility), and (once basic survival has been achieved) yield leisure to work if, and only if, an increase in income results. These assumptions lead inevitably to the conclusion that a labour supply problem will arise if basic survival can be achieved outside the labour market:

> In an economy with social security provisions, if the level of
> social security for which an individual is eligible while not
> working is greater than the wage offered by a job a rational
> individual man would be expected not to work. (Dex, 1985:66)

Most economic work into the disincentive effects of benefits has not sought to demonstrate the existence of this effect (which is already assumed and intrinsic to subsequent modelling) but rather to estimate the size of the effect of social security provision on unemployment levels and durations. A substantial body of research, using a wide range of different types of data, has built up on these topics (see Atkinson, 1981; Micklewright, 1986; Atkinson and Mickelwright, 1989 and Dilnot, 1992 for reviews) but has yielded inconsistent or inconclusive results. Overall, it would appear that out-of-work benefits in Britain 'does have some impact on the duration of individuals' unemployment spells, but the effect is a rather small one' (Dilnot, 1992:130). Given that this effect is small, and that no conclusion can be reached as to whether out-of-work benefits have an effect on entry to unemployment, some economists have questioned the validity of the assumptions underlying this kind of modelling— that is, questioning the existence, rather than the size, of a benefit-induced disincentive (see Atkinson et al., 1984; Narendranathan et al., 1985; Micklewright, 1986; Beenstock et al., 1987; Atkinson and Micklewright, 1989 and Dilnot, 1992). To date only a handful of research studies (see, for example, McLaughlin, Millar and Cooke, 1989, Smith with McLaughlin, 1989, Jordan et al., 1993 and Dawes, 1993) have explicitly set out to establish, empirically, the existence of disincentive effects, and thereby to offer a critique of the theoretical assumptions underpinning neo-classical economic theories of labour supply.

The next section will briefly summarise some of the results of this empirical work, especially those aspects which most closely touch on issues of social security policy, though there is not scope in this chapter to document the details and nuances of each of these studies. The theoretical implications of these studies may be summarised as follows:

- the assumption that individuals choose between work and leisure is not true for at least half the population—women—who make three-way choices between paid work, unpaid work and leisure;
- the assumption that individuals will yield leisure to work if, and only if, an increase in income results is incorrect—paid work itself offers both non-financial rewards and indirect financial rewards (for example, access to credit facilities), the latter of which are not necessarily reflected in measures of regular weekly income;
- the assumption that the primary determinant of reservation wage levels (that is, the levels of wages which unemployed people say they need in order to take employment) is the level of out-of-work income otherwise available is not sustained empirically; perceptions of basic needs[1] are however critical;
- the assumption that individuals consider only the level of income available in or out of work is incorrect; individuals give weight to the sources of income as well and the 'real' value of a certain sum (that is, the value attached to it in decision-making) is composed of both its numerical value and its certainty (in terms of outcome probabilities and in terms of the degree of control which recipients may exercise over the sum involved—for example, the perceived probability that the sum may be taken away for reasons unconnected with the recipients' actions); this means that sums from different income sources cannot simply be added up to give total incomes;
- the low levels of out-of-work benefit incomes, together with little access to credit, result in little room for manoeuvre or abilities to build pathways into various forms of employment among long-term unemployed people;

147

- assumptions of perfect knowledge and decision-making under conditions of certainty are of very little value in the study of labour supply.

The empirical studies listed above have found that both the level and structure of contemporary social security provision have effects on labour supply. However, these effects do not take the form predicted by neo-classical theories of labour supply—that is, empirical studies have not found that the level of out-of-work benefits available directly sets the minimum wage levels at which unemployed people will consider a return to work. This section briefly summarises the more complex and, from the point of view of policy, largely unintended, effects that both the level and structure of contemporary social security have.

The level of out-of-work benefits

The history of social security provision in Britain has been dominated by what are seen as two conflicting objectives: on the one hand to provide people with a sufficient income when they are out of work and on the other to ensure that no-one is better off out of work than in work. The resolution of this supposed conflict has been levels of benefits intended to provide the minimum necessary for existence, or 'subsistence' as it has most often been called. The origins of modern social security benefit levels lie in the dispiriting search for the minimum calorific levels needed by different kinds of people, the minimum that is needed for household maintenance, and the minimum margin of error that should be left for 'inefficient spending' (that is, people spending unwisely). The pseudo-scientific nature of this activity can all too easily lead us to overlook why so much anxiety and soul-searching was devoted to it—that is, the idea that it is imperative to hold benefit levels down so that incentives to take paid work are maintained. Apart from the fact that alternative approaches geared to the same objective (such as minimum wage legislation) were noticeable by their absence in British policy, it is important to note that the subsistence needs of children and young people, compared with those of adults, were underestimated in the benefit scale rates proposed by Beveridge in 1942 and even more so in the rates actually implemented in 1948 in Britain (Baldwin and Cooke, 1982). This failure has never been redressed.

The current level of social security benefits available to unemployed people, especially those with children, means that once people have been receiving them for, say six months to a year, day-to-day living becomes marked by: inadequate diet (in terms of nutrition and occasionally in terms of quantity; two important studies in the early 1990s, NCH (1991) and Leather (1992), have documented this particularly well); reliance on second-hand clothing; insufficient furniture; inefficient heating systems (partly because no capital is available to install efficient systems and good insulation); inability to participate in active forms of social life (e.g. days out to the zoo, museums, cinemas, adventure playgrounds, visiting family where an out-of-town journey is involved) and corresponding reliance on passive forms of social contact such as television; social isolation and monotony; and fragile money management, where even relatively minor 'crises' cannot be accommodated, carrying with it high levels of stress and anxiety. Three months into unemployment, two-thirds of young unemployed families can expect to be in debt (Heady and Smith, 1989)—a situation which will worsen as the length of unemployment goes on. Here it is important to note that long-term unemployment rose substantially in the 1980s and by 1993 amounted to about one-third of the registered unemployed alone. It is the long-term unemployed with children for whom current levels of social security spell very serious deprivation.

The effects of these low standards of living on labour-supply have been largely overlooked. Rather it has been assumed that the low standard of living of unemployed people and families must be positive in terms of labour supply since it is evidence of an income gap between those in low-paid work and those in unemployment. This position clearly ignores the long-term health and educational impacts of these standards of living on unemployed individuals and their children— effects will be discussed further below. Here, we should consider one of the more immediate effects on individuals' and couples' labour-supply decision-making—the fragile and precarious nature of unem-ployed people's budgeting. This is a commonplace finding in social research. It has, however, important implications for the ways in which people are constrained or empowered towards employment (or indeed self-employment), implications which are rarely discussed. McLaughlin et al. (1989), Millar et al. (1989) and Jordan et al. (1992) all show how the low level of out-of-work income available constrains the ability of unemployed people, especially parents, to manipulate potential economic opportunities where those opportu-nities do not carry with them an immediate, weekly wage large enough to meet most of the individual's or household's basic needs. With no 'margin of error' in their incomes, and hence tight budgeting practices, the practicalities of moving out of unemployment into low-paid full-time, part-time, temporary (or otherwise uncertain) jobs, or economic opportunities which require some initial outlay (for example, some 'own-account' forms of sub-contracting), or of drawing on in-work benefit sources of income (family credit and housing benefit), all become considerably more difficult, if not impossible, than policy-makers and other commentators appear to understand.

The current 'solution' to incentives/disincentives issues is therefore fundamentally flawed. On the one hand, means-tested in-work benefits are necessarily complex, and individuals' knowledge about them tends to be non-existent or mistaken. It is common, for example, even among those who have heard of these benefits, for knowledge of them to be inexact (in terms of the amount they would receive) and pessimistic (in terms of claiming procedures and the time taken for claims to be processed). A quotation from an interviewee in McLaughlin, Millar and Cooke's study demonstrates both the vagueness of knowledge about these benefits and the typical pessimism about lengths of claim times (usually based on experience of claiming other benefits):

> The jobs I've applied for at the moment they are about £80. I'd be even lower than now with taking a job on that but with the family income supplement, I don't know what it would be. But I'd lose all my other benefits, I'd still be worse off but at the same time I'd have a chance to be among people and be working. I don't like to be idle....But FIS wouldn't cover your losses by taking the lower wage, but I'd take a job tomorrow if I could, any time, cleaning sewers or whatever the case may be. The lowest wage I could take would be £80 plus FIS. If I was to get FIS I'd also get a rent rebate....But there again you have to struggle for six weeks before you get that FIS. You must have six weeks pay packets. Which mean its actually seven weeks because your first week is a lying-in week. So its seven weeks before you can even start to think about claiming it. And then you claim for it and there's no certainty that you get it. And then you can't claim for a rent rebate until you get FIS and in all it works out it could be 12 weeks before you get your full benefit you'd be entitled to at that particular time (quoted in McLaughlin, Millar and Cooke, 1989:110–111).

On the other hand, this also illustrates how hard it is for even those unemployed people who know of the existence of in-work benefits, but who have been existing 'at the margins' or 'on the edge' because of the low levels of out-of-work benefit support, to wait for a 'mixed income package' to become realised. While claims for Family Credit or Housing Benefit are being processed, while tax codes are being processed, during attempts to build up clients or contracts in self-employment, while one waits for lump-sum payments due on completion of sub-contracted work, all the while, expenditure demands (most critically in respect of food and heating) have not been waiting. As another father, encouraged to apply for a labouring job at £80 gross a week by Jobcentre staff, expressed it:

> He says—you'll get FIS. I says—you have to wait three months and put in three months pay slips. And he says but you'll get it back and I says, but what do we eat in the meantime? Because I would have bus fares and everything, school dinners. I would have my rent out of it. He just didn't seem to understand the way life works (quoted in McLaughlin, Millar and Cooke, 1989:111).

Neat equations contrasting the total income which could be yielded by some particular job-and-benefit package compared with out-of-work benefit income mean very little unless it is assumed that individuals are prepared to go without food and heat, or see their children go without food and heat, for days, and more realistically, weeks. Paradoxically, in light of the concerns which have led to out-of-work benefit incomes being held down to tight subsistence levels, if out-of-work benefit incomes were higher (leaving individuals with a larger margin of weekly income after expenditure on necessities and preventing the erosion of savings), unemployed individuals and families would be better placed to move out of unemployment. At present unemployed people have virtually no room for manoeuvre, and whilst very low-paid jobs, own-account work, and so on, do not represent a cure for contemporary unemployment, at the same time, it is important to note that current low levels of social security provision largely preclude unemployed people taking a chance on such opportunities as there are, or, more accurately, do so if those concerned are not prepared to starve and freeze in their attempts to 'better' themselves. This is compounded by more stringent voluntary unemployment rules which have contributed to anxiety among unemployed people about taking chances on low-paid jobs. If they leave such jobs because they cannot manage financially on the wages and/or benefits available, they will be deemed to be voluntarily unemployed and face substantial penalties in subsequent out-of-work benefits for up to six months (Ritchie and Faulkner, 1989).

The fundamental issue here is the fact that income from the labour market can no longer be assumed (if it ever could be for unskilled working-class men and women) to provide an income which will maintain an earner plus dependents, even at subsistence levels. Rather than address this issue comprehensively—through minimum wage legislation, minimum income policies, radical tax and social security reform—government response has been weak: on the one hand, the development of Family Credit and Housing Benefit, and on the other, measures to hold down the levels of benefits available while out-of-work, both designed to force unemployed people to take jobs which pay below even their basic subsistence needs. This section has shown some of the reasons for the failure of this policy strategy, though obviously low levels of labour demand have also made much of this strategy a nonsense.

Social security and female dependency

The main determinant of labour supply attitudes and the principal characteristic of unemployed people's decision-making found in McLaughlin et al. (1989), Jordan et al. (1992) and Dawes (1992) was the potential earner's assessment of the minimum required to meet basic needs. There is little evidence of unemployed people setting a reservation wage directly in reference to the level of out-of-work income available to them. When unemployed people are estimating the amount of income or wages they would need from employment, out-of-work benefit levels provide one indicator of the amount of money required to meet basic household needs, but they are not the only indicator. Even among those who know of the existence of in-work benefits, in the absence of a substantial degree of transparency and the presence of a substantial degree of risk, the most usual strategy is to seek a job which will offer nearly a 'family wage' (that is, a family-based basic income), in order to reduce the extent of potential income risk (see also Jenkins and Millar, 1990 for a more abstract discussion of the same point). As a result it is common to find unemployed people applying for jobs which pay below their own estimates of basic income needs (that is, their reservation wages), but not by a large amount, despite the fact that the current system of in-work benefits, as far as tenants are concerned, means that a wage of as little as £31 gross a week (for 16 or more hours of work) would result in the same income as received when out of work for a married couple with one, two or three children (DSS, 1992). The level of wage sought instead varies with the number of people who are dependent on the potential earner for their basic needs. In addition to dependent children, however, the social security system, and employment policy more generally, generate a higher level of dependency on male potential earners by allowing for (and to some extent, creating) dependent adult women.

It is well known that the social security system presumes adult female dependency within marriage or cohabitation through aggregated benefit entitlements (Lister, 1992). As a result, wives' earnings from employment of less than 16 hours a week, over and above £5 a week during the first two years of unemployment and thereafter £15 a week, are deducted pound for pound from an unemployed couple's income support (and of course the majority of British mothers work part-time). Nationally, use of this minimal disregarded earnings provision is low (about 5 per cent of unemployed people on income support in 1989, for example). The net effect of male unemployment in a system of aggregated benefit entitlement with minimal provision for disregarded earnings is to discourage the female partners of registered unemployed men from taking up, or keeping on, part-time work (see Dilnot, 1992). Because of the assumption of adult female dependency in the social security system, the female partners of registered unemployed men (and indeed lone mothers) are 'free' to give up any previous labour market participation they may have had (this includes full-time as well as part-time work)—that is, there are no financial penalties imposed by the social security system in this situation.

Whilst this is not the sole explanation of why so few of the wives of unemployed men are in employment compared with the wives of employed men (this is also caused by the nature of the local labour markets faced by both partners, and by partners tending to share characteristics which leave them both disproportionately vulnerable to unemployment), nevertheless the assumption of female dependency in social security policy is part of a wider context of sex-segregated labour markets and other social policies (such as low levels of subsidised childcare services) which combine to concentrate paid work in 'work-rich' (two-earner) households. As Schmitt and Wadsworth note above, rising male registered unemployment and male economic inactivity and rising female employment have not counterbalanced each other. Rather, most of the rise in female employment has come from women married or cohabiting with employed men, and therefore also in households where both partners have skills and qualifications.

From the point of view of labour supply decision-making, this concentration of unemployment/inactivity in certain households is not only about whether wives combine some earnings with out-of-work benefit receipt but also about indirect effects on couples' labour supply in relation to other forms of work. Because wives are generally not employed when their husbands are unemployed, husbands generally attempt to find full-time jobs which will pay enough to keep the whole family (that is, dependent children and a dependent wife), precluding the possibility of lower-paid full-time or part-time jobs supplemented or complemented by wives' earnings. The latter would require wives to regain previously held jobs (hardly likely), or find new ones simultaneously with their husbands taking a job. This kind of dove-tailing is obviously difficult to achieve in practice. Adult female dependency therefore raises the wage (or income) level sought by unemployed men, determined as it is principally by the need to secure enough income to meet the basic needs of themselves and their dependents. Thus, wives' employment status affects husbands' labour supply.

Social security and 'atypical' employment

Implicit in the set of issues described above (that is, the assumption of female dependency, aggregated benefit entitlements and minimal levels of disregarded earnings provision), is the more general issue of the way the social security system addresses atypical forms of employment (see also Bradshaw, 1985 and McLaughlin, 1991). The term 'atypical' covers most forms of paid work which are not full-time (over 30 hours a week) and/or where a traditional employment contract does not exist. The extent of atypical forms of work is such that they constitute a highly significant part of the labour market. By 1986, permanent full-time 'traditional' jobs accounted for only about two-thirds of the work-force; the remaining third comprised a wide variety of other types of work (Hakim, 1989). Ignoring overlaps, about half of these other types of work were part-time, a third self-employed, and a fifth temporary. In 1988, a survey for the Department of Employment found that 25 per cent of vacancies in Great Britain were for part-time workers and another 15 per cent for temporary workers, giving a total of at least 40 per cent atypical vacancies. Recently (September 1990), 33 per cent of the workforce in employment were r(in part-time jobs or self-employed (Labour Market Data, *Employment Gazette*, Feb. 1991) to which must be added whatever proportion of full-time workers are on temporary contracts.

While the labour market is therefore increasingly 'flexible', the structure of contemporary social security is highly rigid. In relation to part-time work, the low level of disregarded earnings under income support constitute obvious disincentives, whilst those on invalidity benefit require medical and DSS permission to undertake small amounts of paid work, and then only if the work is deemed to be therapeutic. The newly introduced disability working allowance is intended to encourage paid work by disabled people but operates along the same lines as Family Credit, and thus requires disabled people to sign off income support or invalidity benefit. Although Family Credit and Disability Working Allowance have quite low work-hour thresholds—an attempt to bridge the gap between full-time and part-time employment (for example, Family Credit can now be claimed by those working 16 or more hours a week)—those working towards the lower ends of these thresholds would face a huge reliance on family credit (or disability working allowance) to bring their incomes up to subsistence levels. For example, for an unemployed couple with two children, if the husband finds a job of 16 or more hours a week, paying £65 gross a week, the couple's Family Credit entitlement would be £62, nearly equalling take-home pay of £63, and there would also be entitlements to Housing Benefit (of around £12 against an average rent of £30) if in rented accommodation, and Community Charge Benefit, resulting in the family income being heavily weighted towards benefits (DSS, 1992). The uncertainties of means-tested in-work benefits, and the problems of a transition period outlined above, mean that this is rarely viewed as a positive option, except by a minority of lone mothers (for some of whom this particular employment-benefit arrangement may have advantages, mainly because it minimises the amount of substitute childcare which has to be paid for, or called upon from relatives). The lack of an equal recognition of housing costs for owner-occupiers as compared with tenants may also be an obstacle to 'long' part-time work combined with in-work benefits.

The availability of unemployed men and women in respect of temporary, seasonal and casual work is similarly adversely affected by the structure and administration of the social security system. Skilled men, men in rural areas, and most women, all of whom might be able to access limited-duration (that is, temporary and casual) forms of paid work, face one of two options. Either such work is treated in the same way as small amounts of regular part-time work, and thus comes under the system of disregarded earnings in income support, or individuals sign off benefits completely, work for a short time, and then make a fresh claim. In the first case, since one's small weekly disregarded earnings entitlement cannot be 'rolled up', only a very small proportion of money earned from occasional jobs can be retained. There are also a number of very considerable problems with the second option. First, because such work is of short durations (and often low paid), in-work benefits can play no role from a practical point of view. Secondly, new claims for income support can, and frequently do, take several weeks to be processed. Thirdly, frequent signings-on and off are likely to be regarded as highly suspicious by social security and Employment Service staff who may instigate investigations as to whether, in each instance, subsequent unemployment is involuntary. Much the same problems, though probably even more acutely, apply to those on disability and long-term illness benefits. Each of these problems means that signing-off and signing-on again carries a high risk of being followed by a period with no income. The earnings offered by casual and temporary work are unlikely to be high enough to carry people through an 'incomeless' period, and the net return from such an exercise is therefore likely to be a loss, zero or very little gain indeed.

The limits of policy and costs of exclusion

The main constraint perceived by government as preventing the extension of provision for disregarded earnings is the danger of undermining incentives for full-time work—that is, that 'people' (by which seems to be meant men) might settle for part-time or irregular paid work in combination with out-of-work benefit receipt. The result has been that the concern not to undermine full-time work incentives has in fact undermined part-time and casual work incentives—in some local labour markets, the only incentives that have any practical meaning. Meanwhile, the tightening up of availability for work and involuntary unemployment rules and increased investigations of unemployed claimants during which benefit is suspended (all of which are also intended to maintain incentives to take paid work), have had adverse effects on unemployed people's abilities to gain temporary and casual work. Similarly, because it is now more difficult to obtain benefits when unemployed, disincentives towards trying out uncertain jobs or forms of own-account working have increased in the 1980s.

Whilst it would be wrong to argue that the solution to contemporary high levels of unemployment is the movement of registered unemployed people into atypical forms of work, at the same time these unintended effects of the social security system are a considerable impediment to anything approaching a rational and efficient labour market system, both through their effects on the registered unemployed and the 'hidden' unemployed (Metcalf 1992) and/or the economically inactive. No government to date has departed from the premise that the bulk of a working-age individual man's or family's income should come from paid regular full-time employment, and no government has been free of the incentives/disincentives conception of the relationship between social security provision and (full-time) employment. No government has faced up to the question of what 'full employment', and relatedly what effective 'family support', might be in a society and economy, indeed a world, which has seen fundamental and far-reaching changes since the Second World War. As a result, the issue of how or whether it may be efficient to permit, even encourage, combinations of part-time or temporary employment with a range of other economically and socially necessary and productive activities (such as training and education, caring for children, supporting frail elderly or disabled people, and voluntary work) has been completely absent in policy discussions of the labour market. This is not to say that individuals do not engage in precisely these combinations of activities—they do, but they do so at a considerable individual income cost. Only those with no dependents will be easily able to bear the income costs involved; those with dependents can engage in this type of activity only under conditions of severe poverty and insecurity, conditions which most are unwilling to inflict on their children.

The constraints imposed through the influence of neo-classical ideas of incentives and disincentives on social security provision for unemployed people (in terms of both the levels and the structure of benefit provision) has had, and continues to have, serious implications for labour-supply at the level of immediate individual decision-making. The result is that the social security system, far from alleviating poverty or facilitating paid work, contributes to more general processes of inefficiency, exclusion and inequality in contemporary society. An increasing polarisation of working-age households, between those where at least one and more usually two adults have employment and those where none have, has been noted as an important development in the 1980s (Pahl, 1984). There can be no doubt that the social security system has made a considerable contribution to this development. The preceding discussion has shown how these processes of exclusion affect currently registered unemployed people in relation to paid work, but they have almost certainly also affected movements out of registered unemployment into economic inactivity. Where the possibility of moving off unemployment into employment seems remote, and where barriers include not only low levels of demand, but also types of demand to which one perceives one's labour supply to be constrained, then the likelihood of a discouraged worker effect is considerable. Schmitt and Wadsworth's analysis suggests that this has indeed occurred. By 1987 the inflow into inactivity was five times greater than in 1977, while the outflow rate by 1989 was 40 per cent lower than in 1977; and a quarter of all movements by unskilled people off registered unemployment were into inactivity rather than employment. A considerable proportion of this movement into inactivity seems to have resulted from changes in the nature of demand for unskilled labour, away from the primary sector to the secondary sector, characterised by higher levels of casual, temporary, part-time and low-paid full-time jobs. Hence, changes in labour demand have been towards the kinds of employment which the preceding discussion has shown to be problematic in terms of income maintenance policies.

Increasing levels of long-term unemployment and economic inactivity, the systematic structuring of unemployment and inactivity along the lines of class, race and locality (Pissarides and Wadsworth, 1992), and (relatively) lower levels of out-of-work benefit provision, have combined to produce significantly high levels of exclusion, not only from the world of work but also from participation in social, community and political life generally. The impact of this on the mental health of unemployed people has recently been reviewed by Fryer (1992). Fryer argues that the principal adverse mental health effects of long-term unemployment are caused by the long-term material deprivation (and hence the social exclusion or marginality) they experience, rather than by the absence of integrative and supportive social relationships of employment (as was previously argued by the Jahoda school). Depression, anxiety and passivity are then largely the result of the restrictions imposed on unemployed people by the material context of unemployment, rather than being either the cause of (continued) unemployment or the effect of the absence of the discipline of work, structured time, etc. The effect of long-term material deprivation, marginality and social exclusion is to further disempower unemployed people, and restricts their proactivity in relation to employment, training, education, voluntary work etc., contributing to reduced outflows from registered unemployment to employment, and increased outflows from registered unemployment to economic inactivity.

For these reasons, low levels of out-of-work benefits are not efficient in terms of developing a high quality labour supply—the most commonly agreed objective for British employment policy. In addition, it is highly likely that the children of currently long-term unemployed people are affected by the social, economic and political exclusion experienced by their parents. However, the extent of adverse educational and social effects for the children of long-term unemployed people has not been mapped, not least because of the difficulties of disentangling the many factors which come together to affect children and young people's achievement levels. Notwithstanding some of the wilder speculations about the creation or existence of an underclass (Murray, 1989), contemporary high levels of social exclusion caused by the nexus of long-term and structured unemployment, material deprivation caused by the low levels of out-of-work benefit levels, and the increasing polarisation of households with work against those without (at least partly caused by the rigidity of the social security system in comparison with the labour market itself), cannot be favourable in terms of either efficiency or equality. The spiral of damaging effects on efficiency, formed by diverse but related processes of economic, social and political exclusion, once begun, requires pro-active, imaginative and creative intervention by government if it is to be reversed. Minimising benefits will not do the job.

7 TAXES AND BENEFITS, EQUALITY AND EFFICIENCY

Paul Johnson

'Pay the unemployed for not working and they will not look for a job.' 'Raise income tax and individuals have less incentive to work or aspire to a better paid job.' 'Increase maternity benefits and more young women will get pregnant.' Assertions like these have become the common currency of much debate not just about tax and social security policy, but about the performance of the economy as a whole. In the minds of many people—politicians, journalists, academics and voters—such assertions have taken on the guise of indisputable fact. The conclusion drawn is that if the end is an efficient, productive and competitive economy then one of the means must be the reduction of both welfare benefits and taxes.

A large part of the force of these arguments lies in their simplicity. 'Of course' people won't work so hard if they get less for it. 'Of course' the unemployed will try harder to find work if they have no benefits whilst unemployed. At the very best the benefits of social security and progressive taxes, in terms of the welfare of those affected, might outweigh their detrimental impact. But none of these statements is uncontroversial, even if they have become widely accepted. Higher taxes lower people's net income, so far from reducing their work effort they might increase it in order to restore their incomes. And the evidence on the impact of social security benefits is neither conclusive nor convincing. State provision of social security can itself be seen as a response to market failure. Neither the theory nor the evidence points to the conclusion that a redistributive tax and benefit system, taken as a whole, significantly reduces the efficiency of the economy.

The first thing we do in this chapter is very briefly describe the UK tax and benefit system as it affects individuals, its effect on inequality, and how this has changed since 1979. It is important to be clear about the distinctions between different sorts of taxes and benefits when it comes to the discussion of their impact on economic efficiency.

Although many of the arguments regarding taxes are similar to, and connected with, those associated with benefits, they are treated separately for the purposes of this paper—benefits are explored in section 3, taxes in section 4. Section 5 concludes the chapter.

The current system[1]

There are two direct taxes on individuals' incomes—income tax and National Insurance Contributions (NICs). Income tax is levied at a basic rate of 25 per cent, with a lower rate of 20 per cent covering the first £2,500 of taxable income, and a higher rate of 40 per cent paid by 1.7 million people. Many millions pay no income tax because of tax allowances. NICs are levied at a rate of 9 per cent on earnings between a floor and a ceiling.[2] Nothing is paid if earnings are below the floor but once earnings exceed this level a tax of 2 per cent is charged on earnings below the floor. In 1993–4, income tax raised £58 billion, NICs raised £39 billion.

Indirect taxes—VAT and excise duties—also affect individuals by raising the prices they face. VAT at 17.5 per cent on all goods except those that are zero-rated—food, books, children's clothes and (until 1994) domestic fuel. Excise duties are levied on petrol, motor vehicles, tobacco and alcoholic drinks. In 1993–4 VAT raised £17 billion, excise duties raised £31 billion.

There are many more social security benefits than there are taxes. This reflects the varied range of circumstances which they are supposed to cover—unemployment, sickness, old age, costs of children, high costs of housing—and the division between those benefits which are given to all people in a group or situation and those which are means-tested. Easily the most expensive benefit is the basic state pension costing nearly £27 billion in 1993–4 and paid irrespective of means. Means-tested Income Support is received by 5.3 million people at a cost of £13 billion. The next most expensive benefits are Invalidity Benefit and Child Benefit each costing £5.7 billion. Overall there is a fairly even split between, expenditure levels on National Insurance Benefits and other benefits. As one would expect the existence of taxes and benefits significantly reduces income inequality. Table 7.1 (from CSO, 1993) shows the original income, gross income, disposable income and post-tax income[3] of each of the five income quintiles—i.e. of the poorest 20 per cent of households, the next poorest 20 per cent and so on up to the richest 20 per cent.

Table 7.1 Effects of taxes and benefits on households by income
level, (£ per year)

	Poorest	2nd	Quintile 3rd	4th	Richest
Original income	1530	5330	12740	19930	35190
plus cash benefits	3580	3100	2040	1190	670
Gross income	5110	8490	14770	21120	35860
less direct taxes	830	1390	2770	4400	7930
Disposable income	4280	7100	12000	16720	27940
less indirect taxes	1200	1720	2630	3270	4070
Post-tax income	3080	5380	9370	13450	23860

Note: Income is measured by disposable income adjusted for family size.

Source: Central Statistical Office (1993)

Gross income is clearly very much more equally distributed than is
original income because benefits are paid mostly to those on lower
incomes. The ratio of the original income of the top quintile to that
of the bottom quintile is 23:1. The ratio of gross incomes is 7:1.
Because of their progressive bias direct taxes also have an equalising
effect and the ratio of top quintile to bottom quintile disposable
income is 6.5:1. Indirect taxes, however, widen the distribution again
to 7.7:1 as the poorest group loses 28 per cent of its disposable income
in indirect taxes against less than 15 per cent for the richest group. So
the tax system as a whole is regressive; in other words, it widens the
income distribution.

The overall effect of the tax and benefit system is substantially to
reduce inequality, and it is social security benefits which are responsible. Note, however, that original income cannot be taken to mean
income as it would be in the absence of any taxes and benefits. If the
tax and benefit system did not exist then original incomes would be
rather different as individuals behaved differently.

The tax and benefit system as a whole therefore remains redistributive. Within it of course some taxes and benefits (e.g. income tax and
Income Support) are more redistributive than others (like VAT and
Child Benefit). Nevertheless the tax and benefit system has not
prevented the well documented increase in inequality in the UK over
the 1980s (DSS, 1992; Jenkins, 1991; Giles and Webb, 1993 and
Johnson and Webb, 1993). Indeed there is much evidence that changes
to taxes and benefits, often justified as a means of increasing

economic efficiency, were largely instrumental in increasing inequality. Johnson and Webb (1993) find that of all the changes that contributed to rising inequality—including higher unemployment and a more unequal distribution of earnings—it was changes to taxes and benefits and in particular cuts in income tax rates, which had the biggest effect.

Since 1979, all income tax rates above 40 per cent have been abolished and the basic rate reduced from 33 per cent to 25 per cent by 1988. The stated aim was to improve economic efficiency. For similar reasons some benefits, especially those for the unemployed, have been made less generous or more difficult to claim (Atkinson and Micklewright, 1989). The overall effect of all the changes to taxes (direct and indirect) and benefits on different parts of the income distribution are set out in Table 7.2, drawn from Davis et al. (1992). Using a complete model of the tax and benefit system, and using information on a representative sample of the UK population, the authors compared the impact of the 1979 system with that of the 1992 system. The results are striking. The changes resulted on average in only small gains or even small losses for those right at the bottom of the income distribution. But for those at the top the gains were enormous. The big falls in income tax rates were of unequivocal benefit to those on high incomes. The effect of the multiplicity of changes to the benefits system was less clear benefiting some, including low income families with children, at the expense of others (details in Davis et al, 1992).

Social security benefits

Different social security benefits are paid for different purposes and in different ways. Therefore it is impossible to make generalisations about the whole system. Increasing benefits for the very disabled is unlikely to have any impact on economic efficiency. Increasing benefits to the able-bodied unemployed might. Benefits payable subject to a family means test (like Income Support) will have different effects to those paid to individuals, and largely irrespective of the incomes of other family members (like unemployment benefit). Paying high levels of means-tested benefits to 65 year olds will have more effect on incentives to save than would paying similar benefits only to those over the age of 80. It is important, then, to identify the areas in which efficiency considerations are important. Here I

Table 7.2 Distributional effects of tax and benefit changes by income level, 1979–92

Decile	Average gain/loss (£ per week)	% gaining	% losing
Poorest	-1	48	40
2	2	66	24
3	2	65	27
4	4	69	24
5	9	81	13
6	13	84	10
7	15	85	10
8	21	89	7
9	25	90	7
Richest	87	92	6
All	18	77	17

concentrate on those that may arise as a result of the payment of benefits to the unemployed. That is not to say that these are by any means the only ones. Provision of benefits for pensioners may cause some sort of economic inefficiency because incentives to save for retirement may be reduced by the promise of state support. There is a huge literature on this aspect of social security provision alone. On a macroeconomic level it is argued that generous spending on the welfare state diverts valuable resources away from productive investment but there is no obvious correlation between welfare spending and economic performance across countries.

In orthodox economic theory benefits allow an unemployed worker to choose to enjoy leisure rather than return to work. While this might maximise that individual's well being, it lowers social output below what it might have been in the absence of such benefits. A wedge is driven between individual utility-maximising outcomes and socially efficient outcomes. Incentive problems may be created not just for the unemployed person but also for their spouse if benefits depend on the income of the family. If one partner works then the other may lose all rights to benefits.

Incentive problems may be created by the action of the benefit system as it affects those in work as well as those out of work. In the presence of means-tested benefits available to those in work but on low incomes very high rates of benefit withdrawal may lead to reduced incentives to work more or seek slightly better paid work because the marginal increase in net income will be very low. In the worst instance a poverty trap may be created whereby net income actually falls as gross income increases. For those in work the poverty trap in its extreme form has been all but abolished since the Fowler benefit reforms of 1988. Nevertheless for those receiving Housing Benefit and Family Credit and paying income tax and NI, marginal withdrawal rates of well in excess of 90 per cent still exist.

The role of the state

Before going any further it is worth asking quite simply why we have a state run social security system. And in particular why, in most countries, does a large part of that system take the form of a social insurance system? The question is not as fatuous as it sounds. The real point is that in many cases state transfer systems exist because the private sector is unable to provide individuals with the sort of insurance against, for example, income loss due to unemployment, for which they would be willing to pay. In other words part of the rationale for state social security benefits is to correct market failure.

The reasons for this failure of the market system to provide insurance against unemployment are well known. The first is the problem of adverse selection. Those most likely to become unemployed would be the ones most willing to insure themselves against that eventuality. But insurance companies would not be able adequately to distinguish high risk from low risk individuals. Low risk individuals would be unwilling to pay the high premia necessary to cover their high risk counterparts. It can easily be shown that no equilibrium can exist in which both low and high risk individuals would participate. A second problem for an insurance contract is that of moral hazard. If individuals can affect their own employment status they may be more likely to become or remain unemployed if they are insured. The insurance company may not be able to tell whether continued unemployment is a result of inability to find work or unwillingness to try. Some groups are simply uninsurable because they have never worked previously—school leavers, for example. Finally, some risks are non-diversifiable. Because of the cyclical nature of economic activity there tend to be periods of relatively low unemployment followed by periods of very high unemployment. If everyone becomes unemployed together then insurance companies may be unable to cover the claims.

Perhaps the best indication of the failure of the unemployment insurance market is the fact that it does not exist.[4] Despite the fact that state benefits are paid at flat rate low levels it does not seem to be possible even for relatively low risk, well paid workers to buy unemployment insurance on the private market (Creedy and Disney, 1985 and Barr, 1992). Public provision of unemployment benefits then becomes inevitable if any income support for the unemployed is to be provided. This outcome can be justified in efficiency terms by information problems in insurance markets (Barr, 1992). All such provision also includes precautions against moral hazard, in particular through availability for work conditions or through penalties for those who made themselves voluntarily unemployed either through quitting a job or being sacked for misconduct. Adverse selection is overcome by making membership of the state insurance scheme compulsory.

Unemployment Benefits

The features of unemployment just noted, introduced in an attempt to counter problems of moral hazard, are in fact very important. Recall the original arguments about the incentive effects of unemployment benefits. They refer to workers being more willing to give up their jobs or less willing to look for or take jobs when they are unemployed. In fact, institutional arrangements make this sort of behaviour rather more difficult than the arguments suggest. The arrangements for Unemployment Benefit make the assumption of the model difficult to defend. The real world is different from that of economic theory. Atkinson and Micklewright (1991) draw particular attention to these and other features of benefits payable to the unemployed and argue that the institutional features of benefit payment are at least as important as its level in determining its impact on incentives to work. As Atkinson (1987) puts it:

> A second-year student can see that a rise in unemployment benefit may reduce the incentive to work (in the simplest neo-classical model), but to judge whether the effect is likely to be important in a particular situation, one has to study the way in which the benefit is administered, the constraints to which the unemployed are subject, the prevailing social norms, and the nature of the labour market. Superficial application of micro-

economic analysis, not taking account of such real world factors, has done a great deal to discredit economics.

So what of the empirical evidence? First, in the context of the UK system it is worth knowing something about the replacement ratios— i.e. income out of work as a proportion of income in work—facing the working population. Data on this is not ideal but the DSS estimates the numbers of full time workers (over 30 hours per week) with high replacement ratios (DSS (1993)). These are shown for 1985 and 1992–3 in Table 7.3. For the whole working population fewer than half a million in 1992–3 would, if unemployed, have been able to claim benefits worth more than 70 per cent of their net earnings. Almost none are shown as having replacement ratios greater than 100 per cent. However the figures shown should be treated with some caution. First, because they are only for those in work they may simply exclude those groups who would be as well off out of work if they react to those incentives by not working. Secondly, the figures are for income after housing costs. This means the effect of benefit payments for housing costs are not included. This is most important for people with mortgages. There is no benefit to cover the mortgage payments of people in work, but for those out of work interest payments can be covered in full by the Income Support system.

Otherwise the benefit system is designed such that for anybody in full time work income in employment is higher than that out of employment.[5] Benefit levels are low enough that anybody without children earning £2 an hour full time will be better off in work. For those with children, means-tested family credit ensures (subject to take-up of the benefit and understanding of the rules) they have some incentive to take work (Dilnot and Duncan, 1992). Where real problems do appear to exist is in the transition between unemployment and employment. If the level of income in employment is uncertain, because of the complexity of benefits for example, or the duration of employment is expected to be short, then the problems associated with the transition to employment might be considerable. But this is not a reflection of undue generosity in the benefit system, rather of a complex structure which could be simplified in the interests of both equality and efficiency.

There have been numerous attempts to determine the impact of benefits on labour supply (for comprehensive surveys Atkinson, 1987 and Atkinson and Micklewright, 1991). If there is a consensus then it is that the impact on the labour supply of prime age men is positive

Table 7.3 Replacement ratios for working population,
1985–93 (percentages)

Thousands of people affected	1985	1992-93
100% and above	60	5
90% and above	210	35
80% and above	730	160
70% and above	1870	445

Source: DSS (1993)

but relatively small. Lancaster and Nickell (1980), for example, report as 'a rather firmly established parameter' that the elasticity of duration of unemployment with respect to benefit level was about 0.6—a 10 per cent cut in unemployment benefits would lead to a 6 per cent cut in average unemployment duration. Narandrenathan et al. (1985) find a smaller elasticity of 0.3, based on cohort data. Atkinson et al. (1984) show that even this result may be sensitive to the way in which benefit systems are modelled and some studies have failed to find any effect.

If benefit levels do affect the work effort of men then the effects are small. Reducing inequality by increasing benefits for the unemployed in this way would not have a substantial impact on economic efficiency. Reasons for this clearly include social pressures and social norms, but the structure of the benefit system should not be ignored. Availability for work is generally necessary to receive benefits. Unemployment benefit is available only for a limited period.

There are two groups, however, for whom the impact of the benefit system has been shown to be rather stronger. These are women married to unemployed men, and lone parents. If both partners of a couple are out of work then they will be entitled to some combination of non-means-tested unemployment benefit and means-tested Income Support. (Because of the rules surrounding the receipt of UB, including contribution conditions and the fact that entitlement ends after a year, only a relatively small proportion of the unemployed actually receive it. At the end of 1992, of 2.7 million benefit claimants only around 650,000 received UB while nearly 1.8m received Income Support(IS)). If they are receiving IS then benefits are reduced pound for pound for anything earned by either partner (above

Table 7.4 Women's working hours by status of husband
(percentages)

Wife's hours	Husband employed	Husband unemployed on benefit	not on benefit
0-10	34	38	74
11-20	14	19	4
21-30	14	7	8
31-40	31	36	11
41+	7	0	2

Source: Family Expenditure Survey data (1991)

a small disregard); hence there is a little or no incentive for one to take a low paid or part time job. Once either partner works more than 16 hours per week, all entitlement to IS is lost. Even for those whose spouse is receiving UB, incentives to work part-time are reduced by the fact that the dependant's addition to UB (£27.55 per week in 1993) is withdrawn completely once the spouse's earnings exceed £27.55 per week. Hence the net benefit of taking part-time job paying 30 per week is just £2.45.

One would expect, then, that the wives of unemployed men would tend to be less likely to work than the wives of employed men, especially if their spouse is receiving Income Support. In particular one would expect them to be most unlikely to work part-time. Dilnot and Kell (1987) show that precisely the expected pattern is evident in cross-sectional data. Kell and Wright (1990) provide statistically robust evidence that benefit levels have a substantial effect on the work incentives of women married to unemployed men.

Up-to-date evidence is provided in Table 7.4 drawn from the 1991 Family Expenditure Survey (FES).[6] It shows the proportion of women working particular hours according to the employment and benefit status of their husband. Unemployed husbands have been divided according to receipt of Unemployment Benefit. Wives of husbands receiving UB look similar to wives of employed husbands except they are only half as likely to work 21–30 hours per week. This probably reflects the effect of withdrawing the dependant's additional income. Those with unemployed husbands not on UB, by contrast, look very different to their employed counterparts. More than twice as many don't work at all, or work less than ten hours per week, while only half as many work part-time and not many more than one third as many work full-time.

Similar results have been found for lone parents whose benefit payments out of work are large enough to make part-time or low paid work unattractive. This is especially true where significant childcare costs, would follow from taking a job. Labour force participation rates for lone mothers are low and have been falling. Compared with married mothers lone mothers are in fact almost equally likely to be working full-time (19 per cent of lone mothers, 20 per cent of married mothers) but only half as likely to work part-time (22 per cent of lone mothers 41 per cent of married mothers) (figures are from the General Household Survey, 1990). Walker (1990) has shown that the benefit system explains much of this discrepancy.

The structure of social security

The relationship between equity and efficiency has been illustrated so far by reference to benefits for the unemployed. There are clearly areas in which both inequities and inefficiencies are produced. But as Dilnot et al. (1984) stress the conflict between equity and efficiency is often greatly exaggerated. We operate things so badly at the moment that there is rarely any difficulty in pointing to reforms which would lead to gains in both. What is inefficient is usually also unfair, and vice versa. Thus a benefit system in which marginal rates of withdrawal do exceed 100 per cent is without question both inequitable and inefficient. Such rates were largely abolished in the UK by the 1988 reforms. But one could plausibly argue that marginal rates of benefit withdrawal in excess of 90 per cent, which still do exist, are also both inequitable and inefficient. Why then do such marginal rates exist? If one is to provide benefits to the poorest which are high enough to live on, it is not possible to provide benefits at this level to everyone. To do so would simply be too expensive. Then either the benefits have to be withdrawn quickly as non-benefit incomes increase, thereby imposing very high marginal rates on a relatively small group, or they can be withdrawn more slowly imposing slightly less high marginal rates on a much larger group.

One can think of most reform proposals in terms of this dilemma. The commonest proposals—for basic incomes or negative income taxes—would guarantee everyone a minimum income. Basic income schemes then tend to impose a high marginal tax rate of, say, 60 per cent or more on everyone. Under negative income tax schemes the marginal rate schedule tends to look more like the current one with very high withdrawal rates right at the bottom of the income distribution. In terms of overall structure the differences between such proposals tend to be in their administrative arrangements and withdrawal mechanisms which are intended to ensure the automaticity of benefit payments (for a discussion of the relationship between the various proposed reforms Dilnot and Webb, 1991). Such reforms would be most effective in reducing the inefficiencies of the benefit system itself. There is little reason to suppose they would have a significant effect on the performance of the economy.

The current system is inefficient with reference to its own objectives in so far as benefits, in particular means-tested benefits, do not reach those for whom they are intended—this is the problem of non-take-up. It results in greater inequity than otherwise—both across the population as a whole and between individuals with equal rights to the benefit. Any reform which reduced this problem would both reduce inequality and improve the efficiency of the benefit system (as opposed to that of the economy).

If the only objective of social security is to reduce poverty, and hence inequality, then its efficiency may also be determined with respect to this objective. If this were the case then one would expect all benefits to be income related and hence paid only to those on the very lowest incomes. Those on average incomes or above would not expect to receive any benefit. The majority of benefit expenditure however is on benefits like the retirement pension and child benefit that are not explicitly income related—this explains why even the richest 20 per cent of households receive an average of nearly £700 per year in state benefits (see Table 7.1).

But the choice between income related and universal benefits, if such a dichotomy can be stated in terms as bold as these,[7] does not appear to be fundamental to the effect of social security on the efficiency of the economy (except insofar as the one would use fewer resources than the other). Benefits paid to those out of work will have some incentive-reducing effects, if withdrawn once work is entered, whether they are means-tested or not. Benefits available to those in work are only likely to be affordable (at meaningful levels) if they are income related. Providing income related benefits to those in work may indeed be a way of improving incentives to take some work. Dilnot and Duncan (1992) show how Family Credit might play this role in the UK.

Table 7.5 Shares of total income tax liability by income level, 1976–93 (percentages)

	1976-77	*1981-82*	*1986-87*	*1990-91*	*1992-93*
Top 1 per cent	11	11	14	15	15
Top 5 per cent	25	25	29	32	32
Top 10 per cent	35	35	39	42	43
Next 40 per cent	45	46	43	43	43
Lower 50 per cent	20	19	16	15	14

Source: Central Statistical Office (1992)

Taxation

It is the traditional view of economists that any form of taxation which affects incentives, whether they be to save, to work or to spend, will create distortions and inefficiencies. In its most extreme form this would relate to any sort of tax the payment of which was in any way dependent upon individuals' behaviour. For if one's behaviour can affect the amount of tax one pays then one may alter that behaviour in order to minimise tax payments. Hence, it is argued, the least distortionary taxes are lump sum or poll taxes, for the payment of these is independent of status. Working more or less, consuming more or less will have no impact on tax liability. Poll taxes are of course extremely regressive and utterly impractical as recent experience has shown.

This view depends for its overall weight on the existence of a perfectly competitive non distortionary economy in the first place. Given that such an economy does not exist it is not easy to show that (distortionary) taxes as whole will lead to inefficiency in the economy as a whole. As the so called theory of the second best shows, if there is any failure in one market then improving the free market features in any other part of the economy need not improve the efficiency of the economy as a whole. If, however, we look within a partial equilibrium framework there are two main areas of contention regarding the impact of taxes on efficiency and equity. The first arises from the structure of direct taxes and their effect on labour supply and work incentives. The second relates to the choice between direct and indirect taxes. The two have become associated by the fact that those who believe high rates of direct tax are undesirable frequently also believe that shifting the tax burden from direct to indirect taxation is desirable.

Cutting rates of income tax has been one of the most important of the Conservative Party's policies since 1979. The top rate of income tax on earned income was cut from 83 per cent to 60 per cent in 1979 and to 40 per cent in 1988. The basic rate was cut from 33 per cent, reaching 25 per cent in 1988, where it remains. The following extract from Nigel Lawson's 1988 budget speech is typical of the reasoning behind those changes:

> Excessive rates of income tax destroy enterprise, encourage avoidance, and drive talent to more hospitable shores overseas. As a result, far from raising additional revenue, over time they actually raise less.

Similarly, the 1992 Conservative manifesto asserted that 'Lower taxes have encouraged more people to work harder'. It is worth noting that the number of people paying higher rates of income tax (i.e. rates above the basic rate) has increased substantially since the early 1980s and is likely to increase further. At the end of the 1970s there were around 750,000 higher rate payers. There was a big increase in 1981 when allowances and the basic rate limit were frozen in a period of high inflation. In the late 1980s high real earnings growth again increased the numbers very quickly. They have not fallen in the 1990s despite the recession as the basic rate limit has been frozen in three budgets out of four since 1990. There are currently around 1.7 million higher rate taxpayers and if the government policy of freezing the basic limit is continued, as seems likely, then this number is likely to rise fast, possibly by another half a million over the next four years or so (Davies et al., 1993).

Leaving aside the question of whether income tax rates for everybody, or the tax burden as a whole, have actually fallen since 1979,[8] the evidence as to the impact of income tax cuts is not overwhelmingly favourable to the views quoted. First, consider the simple question of what one would expect the likely consequences for work incentives of a tax cut to be. Two possible effects may be distinguished: the 'income' and 'substitution' effects. The argument that lower tax rates encourage people, to work harder depends on the substitution effect: the lower the marginal tax rate, the greater the financial return from working an extra hour and the more likely people are to exchange an hour of leisure for an additional hour of

Table 7.6 Effects of taxes on lawyers and accountants (percentages)

	Incentive effect	Disincentive effect
Break	10	13
Fields and Stanbury	11	19
Fiegehen and Reddaway	12	12

Source: Brown 1988

work. But the income effect works in the opposite direction and may offset the substitution effect. Lower tax rates mean that the same amount of work will produce more take home-pay. With a higher effective wage rate people may choose to work less hard and consume more leisure while maintaining their pre-tax-cut income level. There is no theoretical reason for supposing that the substitution effect will outweigh the income effect. Even if it does many, indeed most, people do not have a free choice over the number of hours they work—they are constrained by their employer. So it is important to be clear that there is no theoretical or *a priori* reason to believe that cuts in income tax rates will improve incentives or increase work effort.

We need to look at the evidence. One piece of evidence often appealed to by the defenders of tax cuts, and referred to in the quotation from Nigel Lawson, and in the Conservative manifesto, is that the proportion of tax paid by the richest taxpayers has risen despite higher rate tax cuts. The explicit implication is that the tax cuts have resulted in so much extra work effort and such reduced tax avoidance that tax revenues have actually increased as a result of the tax cuts. The figures are shown in Table 7.5. At first sight, they appear to confirm the suggestion that cutting high rates of tax increases the amounts of tax raised from the richest.

If one were looking for a result showing that increased equity and increased efficiency were not just compatible but inextricably linked one might be tempted to consider this as the perfect evidence—lower tax rates increasing the tax take from the rich. This is one manifestation of the famous Laffer curve. According to this increasing the rate of income tax increases the amount of government revenue up to a certain point but then as tax rates rise further the revenue falls back again. The idea behind this positive and then negative relationship between tax rate and revenue raised is an old one. For example, Adam Smith in his 'Wealth of Nations' states:

High taxes, sometimes by diminishing the consumption of the taxed commodities, and sometimes by encouraging smuggling, frequently offered a smaller revenue than might be drawn from more moderate taxes.

Tax rates at or close to 100 per cent will naturally not raise much money. It is rather more contentious to claim that tax rates at 60 per cent, or 40 per cent, raise less than would lower rates. Estimates for Britain by Hemming and Kay (1980) suggest that average tax rates of 80–82 per cent and marginal rates of 85–86 per cent would maximise revenues. Even Lindsey (1987) whose work on US data is frequently quoted as showing that US tax cuts in the 1980s raised revenues, stresses that the main effect could not have been through extra hours worked. In fact the figures shown in Table 7.6 are quite compatible with other explanations. They are likely simply to be a result of the widening income distribution. If the top earners earn more then they will pay more tax.

Brown (1988) quotes estimates of the effects of changes in tax rates on labour supply in the UK. As far as the basic rate of tax is concerned he dismisses the idea that any changes contemplated would have other than negligible effects on labour supply. Referring to the 1988 cut in the basic rate from 27 per cent to 25 per cent he states:

so far as I know, no one (including Nigel Lawson) wishes to argue that the basic rate tax cut will have any significant labour supply effects.

His own estimates suggest that a 4 per cent drop from 29 per cent to 25 per cent would have no effect on labour supply. Estimates from Blundell et al. (1989) suggest the effects would be to reduce mean weekly hours of work by about 20 minutes.

Rather more contentious are the effects of reducing higher rates of, tax on labour supply. The number of studies of this, especially in the British context, is rather limited. Brown quotes three studies for the UK: Break (1957), Fields and Stanbury (1971) and Fiegehen and Reddaway (1981). All three looked at the effects of high tax rates on lawyers and accountants—a group of workers likely to understand the tax system and for whom varying their amount of work would be likely to be relatively easy, at least by comparison with most other groups. Only Fields and Stanbury found a significantly higher proportion of respondents claiming that high tax rates had a disincentive effect, though this may have reflected differences in their interviewing procedure. The results of the three studies are presented in Table 7.6.

A more recent study of the effects of the 1988 top rate tax cuts on a sample of accountants by Brown and Sandford (1990) found that the effects of the tax changes on work effort were minimal. Possibly a more important problem associated with high rates of tax is that of tax avoidance and evasion. There is much evidence that very high marginal rates (for example the 83 per cent on earned income and the 98 per cent on unearned income in force prior to 1979) do encourage a very substantial amounts of avoidance and evasion. Even referring to the drop from a top rate of 60 per cent to one of 40 per cent in 1988 Brown and Sandford conclude that:

> While the effects of avoidance on accountants are not large, there is considerable internally consistent evidence that suggests that the cuts in the higher rates of income tax will have reduced avoidance by their clients and in particular are an important part of the explanation for a better quality of investment decision.

Such avoidance on any scale reduces both the efficiency of the tax system and of the economy by causing decisions to be made not for good economic reasons but because of the tax system. It also reduces the equity of the tax system by favouring the well advised. Such problems can undoubtedly be ameliorated by making particular sorts of avoidance more difficult but especially where capital gains tax is levied at a lower rate than the highest income tax rate (they are currently equal), they are unlikely to be resolved completely.

I have concentrated on the impact of high marginal tax rates on efficiency for this has been one of the major areas of contention. But it is most important to remember that the progressivity of a tax is not measured by the way in which *marginal* tax rates change, but by the way in which *average* tax rates change. A progressive system is one in which the average tax rate is continuously increasing. It is sufficient for this to be case that a tax free allowance exists at the bottom of the income tax schedule. Overall a tax system with a large tax free allowance and then a single positive marginal tax rate is likely to be at least as progressive as one with no tax allowance but a series of increasing marginal rates. Because of the effect of the tax free personal allowance the UK income tax system is in fact rather progressive. Of 17 OECD countries surveyed by the OECD (1990), the United Kingdom proved to have the most progressive income tax system on one measure, the second most progressive on another and the ninth most progressive on a third.[9] An income tax which is progressive and thereby has an inequality-reducing effect need not involve very high marginal rates.

If one is looking for ways to make a major improvement to the equity of the UK direct tax system, without substantially altering its efficiency then one is drawn away from income tax and towards National Insurance Contributions (NICs). NICs stop being payable at the NI upper earnings limit (UEL). Hence above this level they form a regressive tax. Indeed the overall marginal direct tax facing individuals falls from 35 per cent (25 per cent income tax + 10 per cent NI) to 25 per cent once the earnings exceed the UEL, and do not rise again to 40 per cent until the basic rate limit is reached more than £5,000 per year later. This introduces a certain regressivity into the direct tax system without any apparent gain in efficiency.

But one can also look at NI as a very good example of a tax which introduces both inequity and inefficiency. Being charged only according to the level of earned income it introduces incentives for employers to pay their employees in forms other than cash. This is true even for those employees earning above the UEL for, while employees' NI contributions stop at this point, those of employers do not. Hence decisions about how to receive and pay remuneration are influenced by the tax system, possibly causing some inefficiency and certainly causing some inequities.

Indirect taxes

Direct taxes are of course only one of the ways in which taxes can be raised. In the UK income tax and NICs accounted for 43 per cent of government tax receipts in 1992–3. Although there is no space here to consider all other forms of taxation, including corporate taxes, it is worth at least considering briefly indirect taxes, VAT and excise duties, which raise a further 30 per cent of government revenue. Unlike taxes like corporation tax they can be clearly allocated to individuals and hence it is easier to make some sense of the concept of equity with regard to them. Furthermore there has been a deliberate move from direct to indirect taxation since 1979, partly justified on the grounds that indirect taxes do not have the same disincentive effects as direct taxes. Thus, as higher and basic rates of income tax have fallen so the VAT rate has risen from a dual 8 per cent and 12.5 per cent rate first to 15 per cent and then to 17.5 per cent. The VAT base was widened with announcement of its extension to domestic fuel in the 1993 budget.

Excise duties have also increased faster than inflation. There is no question but that indirect taxes are less redistributive than our direct tax system. But some element of progressivity is introduced by the existence of an important group of zero rated goods, including food, on which the poor spend a disproportionately large part of their budget. As Baker (1992) shows the VAT system is mildly progressive with zero rated goods forming a higher proportion of the spending of low income households. But the progression is minimal by comparison with that in the income tax system and is overwhelmed by regressive duties on alcohol and tobacco.

Is levying indirect taxes any more efficient than levying direct taxes? In terms of effect on labour supply the answer, in principle, is no. If there is no saving, levying (say) a 30 per cent tax on income will have exactly the same effect as levying a flat 30 per cent tax on spending. Real income is reduced by the same amount in each case and so incentive effects are identical. Where different tax rates are levied on different forms of expenditure an additional inefficiency is, however, introduced, for in this case there will be a tax driven incentive to buy the non-taxed items rather than the taxed ones. I know, however, of no estimates even suggestive of the size or importance of any such allocative inefficiency.

In connection with saving, however, there is an important difference between taxes levied on income and those levied on expenditure. If a tax is levied when income is earned, and again on any interest derived from saving that income, then a disincentive to saving is introduced and there is an economically inefficient incentive favouring current consumption as opposed to saving for future consumption. This is not necessarily an argument in favour of indirect taxes as they are currently levied; the required result could be achieved by altering the taxation of saving to make it more like, for example, current taxation of private pensions. Here tax is levied only once the income is received (and presumably used for expenditure) in retirement.

The question remains as to what the structure of indirect taxation should be. Two arguments may be put for charging varying rates of VAT. The first is that one might want to encourage the consumption of some goods (e.g. books) or discourage the consumption of others (e.g. tobacco). The other argument is of a redistributive nature—goods which make up a high proportion of the spending of the poor should be treated leniently. For those interested in equity this may appear to be a strong argument, but in many ways it is not. The poor do spend a higher proportion of their income on food than do the rich. Nevertheless the rich spend far more on food in absolute terms. Hence the bulk of money 'spent' on not charging VAT on food, goes to the rich. A more equitable arrangement might be to charge the same rate of VAT on everything and use the money raised to increase benefits and/or income tax allowances. This would introduce greater equity and reduce any inefficiency that may be caused by charging different rates of VAT.

There are many other facets of indirect taxes which one might want to discuss, but which are just mentioned here in passing. In particular the ability to use them to achieve, for example, environmental ends. One of the Chancellor's stated goals in charging VAT on domestic fuel in the 1993 Budget was to reduce energy consumption. Extra duties on petrol would be another way of achieving environmental aims. Because such taxes may correct market failures which exist because of externalities—I do not bear the cost of the pollution I cause by driving or using heating—they may increase efficiency. Their direct distributional effects may be regressive—putting VAT on domestic fuel certainly is—but again an appropriate use of other tax and benefit policies can lead to an overall improvement in equity alongside the greater efficiency achieved (Johnson, McKay and Smith, 1990).

Conclusions

The tax and benefit system is the most direct tool available to the government for altering the degree of income inequality. Other policies, such as those designed to reduce unemployment, may have large effects but they are less direct and reliable. On the other hand the tax system particularly does not have limiting inequality as its entire raison d'être: its main function is to raise revenue for the whole range of government activity, including the payment of social security benefits.

Any tax and benefit system which was intended to produce complete equality of outcome, by paying very high benefits and taxing all income above the benefit level at 100 per cent would not be compatible with anything approaching an efficient economy. Indeed the result would not be equitable either as non-compliance would be near universal. Complete equality of outcome is not achievable (and not desirable either). But application of particular taxes and benefits can, and does, reduce inequality. The extent to which this reduction can be continued is undoubtedly limited at some point by the impact of generous benefits or very high tax rates on the efficiency of the economy through reduced work incentives. It is also limited by the incentives and opportunities for tax avoidance and evasion which themselves reduce the equity of the system. Very high benefits are also likely to be associated with very high marginal rates of benefit withdrawal for a large number of people. This in itself can be considered inequitable, as well as inefficient, if work incentives are affected.

Inequities clearly are imposed if somebody working 40 hours a week is left no better off than somebody not working. In this sense of inequity, policies which are likely to lead to great inefficiencies are also likely to lead to considerable inequities. The point at which redistributive policies do start eating into the efficiency of the economy or start themselves to cause inequities is not clear cut. What is clear is that neither cuts in direct tax rates from their current levels nor cuts in benefits for the unemployed are likely to have much positive impact on the functioning of the labour market or the economy.

Conversely, moderate increases and reforms could reduce inequality whilst not harming efficiency. Child care benefits could improve rather than reduce the labour market possibilities for lone parents. Increasing the non means tested elements of benefits for the unemployed could improve, not reduce, the incentives for their spouses to work. Similar effects could be achieved by increasing benefits for the low paid in work. Similar reforms of the tax system are less obvious in terms of both increasing equity and efficiency, though further reform of the NI system is clearly desirable on both criteria. Within bounds there need be no serious conflict between equality and efficiency in the design of a tax and benefit system. To a large extent the contention is over where those bounds are. Nobody seriously proposes tax rates of over 90 per cent. If implemented their effect would be serious.

Equally nobody seriously suggests that taxes should be purely lump sum. Similarly nobody suggests unemployment benefits at average earnings, but their complete abolition is at least as unthinkable. Given our current position, proposals to limit the inequality reducing aspects of our tax and benefit system in order to enhance economic efficiency seem misplaced.

8 INHERITANCE: SYMBOLS AND ILLUSIONS

Paul Ryan[1]

Inheritance has long been recognised to be an important cause of inequality. It produces extensive inequality in property income, and fosters unequal opportunities, distributing silver spoons and wooden spoons amongst the rising generation according to parental wealth. As such, inheritance might be required to contribute strongly to efficiency to be socially acceptable. Yet its claims to promote efficiency are notably weak; it may even be detrimental. This combination of powerful inegalitarian and weak efficiency effects has long been the heart of the case for the progressive taxation of inheritance, and the protracted history of estate taxation in England reflects such considerations.

The year 1979 represents a potential watershed, however, in this as in other areas of economic inequality. The long-term trend towards lower inequality in property incomes has since 1979 been reversed; public interest in inheritance has declined sharply; successive Budgets have quietly eroded the scope and intensity of inheritance taxation; and the movement of property between generations nowadays captures national attention only in the case of such eccentricities as the bequest of a fortune to a domestic animal. In the political economy of property, however, appearances are often deceptive. Considerable continuity is visible across the presumptive break of 1979, reflecting both the enfeebled state of inheritance taxation by that time and the subsequent decision to modify rather than eliminate it. The enduring sensitivity of inheritance taxation can be seen in the handling of tax reform in the 1980s as an incremental process with its major components judiciously downplayed and selectively justified. Efficiency issues have predominated in those justifications, with improved business performance as the central consideration.

Little evidence has however been presented in support of official claims. The main goal of this chapter is to review the arguments made in support of post-1979 tax reforms in the light of recent research findings. The role of inheritance in generating inequality is outlined in the next section, followed by a discussion of inheritance tax methods and outcomes. The arguments advanced by the Government since 1979 in favour of tax reform are then considered. Two particular efficiency implications of inheritance taxation—business performance and bequest-oriented saving—are analysed. The political function of such appeals to efficiency is discussed, before concluding with suggestions for reform.

Inheritance and inequality

'Inheritance and capital are no longer a privilege of the wealthy few', remarked Norman Lamont in his 1992 Budget speech.[2] A significant inheritance of property has not however become the birthright of the majority. Inheritance remains a major source of inequality, both of outcomes and of opportunities. This section considers both effects.

Inheritance, broadly construed, covers all routes along which members of one generation acquire personal advantages from its predecessors, including such human attributes as ability and skill as well as property. This paper concentrates on non-human wealth, but the role of the 'human' channels must also be recognised. The first human route involves innate traits such as ability, genetically transmitted between the generations to a significant, albeit controversial, extent. Little is known however about the heritability of the traits of most interest here, notably business acumen and motivation, though it is typically taken to be limited: 'it should not be assumed that the children of the successful entrepreneur will necessarily inherit his acumen and energy', as the Bolton Committee put it (Bolton Committee, 1971, p.226).[3]

The second channel is human wealth proper (knowledge, skills, etc.), which, though destroyed at death and therefore not directly transmissible between generations, is indirectly inherited to a considerable extent through the associated advantages of home, school and parental contacts. The rate at which occupational status is reproduced across generations has remained high (Goldthorpe and Payne, 1986; Erikson and Goldthorpe, 1992). Indeed, inheritance of human wealth must have become more important with the growth of human relative to non-human wealth; the human wealth of the US household sector is now more than four times its disposable wealth (Wolff, 1987).

The third channel, inheritance of private property, is the focus of this study. 'Inheritance' refers henceforth to all downstream capital transfers between generations, including lifetime (i.e. pre-death) gifts. Similarly, 'inheritance taxes' is used as shorthand for all duties and taxes imposed on such capital transfers. The focus of interest for wealth inequality is household marketable wealth, i.e., the net value of the personal sector's financial and physical assets, exclusive of pension rights. It amounted in 1988 to £1,429 billion, or three times as much as annual national income, and comprised two-thirds physical and one-third financial assets (Inland Revenue, 1993, Table 11.2; CSO, 1992, Table 2).

Inequality of property income

Inequality in property ownership—and, implicitly, in property income—declined markedly through the late-1970s, continuing a fall which antedates World War I. The share of the top five per cent of property owners fell by up to 29 percentage points between 1950 and 1979. Inequality of property ownership thereafter remained stable until the mid-1980s but since 1986 the trend has turned upwards (Figure 8.1).

The contribution of inheritance to inequality of property incomes depends on several factors. It falls with the extent of bequests outside the family, of multiple bequests within the family, of out-marriage amongst wealthy inheritors, of dissipation of legacies by inheritors, and with the size and progressiveness of the share taken by tax. The evidence for the UK suggests contradictory effects: large wealth leavers prefer to bequeath their assets to their offspring and other relatives (when no spouse survives), their children tend to marry each other, and the tax 'take' has not, during the last two decades at least, made much difference; but major wealth leavers tend to divide their assets amongst their children, who in turn tend to run down rather than build up the value of their legacies (Diamond Commission, 1977, ch.8; Atkinson, 1974; Harbury and Hitchens, 1979).[4]

Inheritances accounted in the 1970s for at least 25 per cent of personal wealth (Diamond Commission, 1977, chapter 9).[5] Two-thirds of inequality amongst top male wealth holders in a 1973 sample proved attributable to bequests from fathers alone. The contribution of inheritance to such inequality had increased, having accounted for less than one-third of inequality in a comparable 1934 sample (Harbury and Hitchens, 1979). It is less likely that inheritance

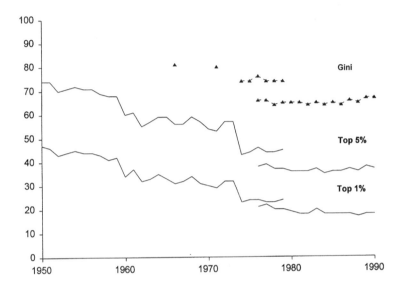

Figure 8.1 Inequality in ownership of marketable wealth, UK, 1950–90 (percentages)

Source: Inland Revenue Statistics; Atkinson and Harrison (1978)

Notes: Shares of top 1% and 5% of wealth holders in total wealth; Gini is coefficient of equality in wealth ownership, varying between 0 (zero inequality) and 100% (maximum inequality); revised definitions applied for 1976 on; Gini availability limited to two years before 1974

has been a major cause of the increase in inequality in property ownership since the mid-1980s, which is more plausibly associated with the increased equity and property prices and with accumulation out of rapidly rising top salaries. There is however every prospect that inheritance will remain important, as the new rich of the 1980s transmit their fortunes to their offspring.

Inequality of opportunity

Whatever the importance assigned to inequality of outcomes such as property income, inheritance must also be considered for how it generates inequality: by creating unequal opportunities. There is widespread support in modern Britain for the meritocratic principle of equal starting points in social and economic life (see Introduction). Fairly determined initial endowments are also central to the claim of a market economy to produce an optimal economic outcome (Meade, 1964; Johansson, 1991). Such views presumably informed John Major's 1990 presentation of a 'classless society', defined as an 'open society of opportunity', as a target for end-of-century Britain.[6] Inheritance differentiates the endowments with which individuals in a particular generation embark upon and continue their adult lives. Some get a lot, most get little or none. Further advantages follow for those who do well by inheritance. As borrowing is easier for those who can offer assets as collateral, heirs can use their inheritances to finance investment more easily than can others.

The contribution of inheritance to unequal opportunity might be thought a matter of less concern for non-human than for human wealth if only because of differences in timing. 'Most inheritances [of property] are received by individuals who are already in middle or old age' (Diamond Commission 1977, 188). Advantage accrues earlier along the human channels, whether by nature at conception and/or by nurture in early life. The force of the argument is however weakened by two considerations. First, many young people inherit considerable, if uncertain, amounts either as a result of early deaths or through lifetime gifts and accumulation trusts. Secondly, unequal opportunities are in any case a matter of social concern in the second as well as the first half of the life-cycle. There is unfortunately little detailed information on the extent to which inheritance causes inequality of opportunity; but its importance and its incompatibility with prevalent social values are both clear.

Taxation and inheritance

Wealth transfers at death have been taxed in England since 1694 and are currently taxed in nearly all advanced economies (Goody, 1987; OECD, 1988 and Pechman, 1987). In Britain such taxes have traditionally been levied progressively on the size of the estate. In the modern period the relevant taxes have been entitled Estate Duty (1894-1974), Capital Transfer Tax (CTT; 1974-86) and Inheritance Tax (IT; 1986-). The tax base has under all three included gifts made up to seven years before death, in order to prevent ready avoidance by

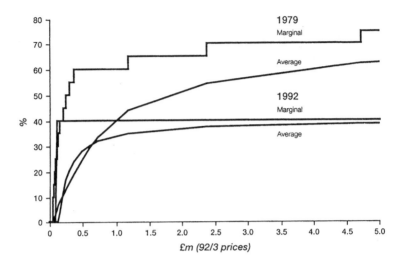

Figure 8.2 Marginal and average tax rates on wealth transfers at death (percentages), 1979 and 1992

Source: Inland Revenue Statistics

Notes: Rates of tax on value of estates notified for probate net of valuation relief

all but those who die suddenly.[7] Only under CTT, however, were all gifts made during the entire lifetime cumulated and taxed. The principle of taxing the estate rather than the individual bequest has prevailed throughout, despite widespread support for the latter.

Tax attributes in 1979

Redistributional intent is strongly suggested by the tax schedule left behind by the outgoing Labour Government in 1979. Marginal rates increased rapidly to 60 per cent as the size of the taxable estate rose to £375,000, and then more slowly to a maximum of 75 per cent on estates in excess of £470,000 (1992/3 prices; Figure 8.2). The redistributive potential of the tax is underlined by the high average rates implied by such a schedule, at 28 per cent on estates of half a million pounds and 60 per cent on those of four million pounds.

The redistributive ambitions of wealth taxation were the centre of a political battle royal during 1974–6, when a Labour Chancellor introduced CTT and promised an annual wealth tax, as part of an avowed intention to elicit 'howls of anguish from the 80,000 rich people', and when the Conservative Parliamentary Party fought in committee the protracted rearguard action which weakened CTT and aborted the wealth tax proposal (Sandford 1979). Considered in that context, the revenue yielded by inheritance taxation has proved remarkably low. During the 1970s it actually fell rapidly, attaining successive historic low points in relation to national income and personal wealth (Figure 8.3). CTT was expected to lead to a short-term reduction in tax receipts, given that it both exempted all transfers between spouses and reduced tax rates on transfers at death; but a longer-term rise in receipts was also anticipated, as the exempted spouses themselves died and as the taxation of cumulative lifetime gifts took hold. Such factors appear however to have been of secondary importance.[8] In any event, the 0.1 per cent of marketable wealth to which CTT revenue had fallen by 1978/9 represented an average tax on all intergenerational transfers of approximately 3 per cent, drastically below what might be expected from the tax schedule combined with the inequality of property ownership.[9]

The paradoxical combination of a highly redistributive schedule and low revenues reflects the narrowness of the tax base. Opportunities for tax avoidance had by the 1970s become abundant and widely exploited, relying primarily on the use of trusts to settle property on others. The property then passed out of the estate of the settlor and was applied to the interest of the beneficiaries according to the decisions of the trustees, a group chosen by and normally including the settlor. Although officially 'the object of [inheritance tax] provisions is to ensure that settled property is taxed no more or less heavily than unsettled property' (Whitestone and Stuart-Buttle, 1987, p.396), in practice settlement provides for the retention of at least partial control over one's property while taking much or all of it out of the category of a taxable transfer, reflecting the principle that a trust, unlike an individual, need not die and be taxed at death.[10]

Other forms of avoidance included lifetime gifts, temporarily drawn into the tax base by CTT in 1974; investment in exempt assets, including owner-farmed land, unquoted businesses and timber, which were eligible in 1979 for relief (discounts) of between 20 per cent of market value for unquoted company holdings and 50 per cent for owner-farmed land, when valued for inheritance tax purposes; and, finally, emigration. The rapid decline in the yield of inheritance

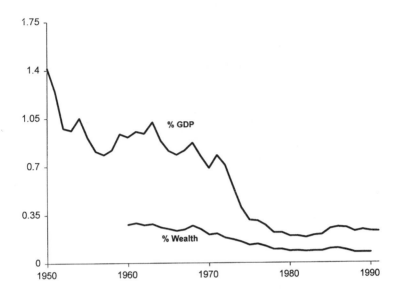

Figure 8.3 Inheritance taxes: revenues as percentages of GDP and
marketable wealth, UK, 1949–91

Source: Inland Revenue Statistics

taxation during the 1970s suggests a powerful growth of avoidance,
making increasingly apposite the traditional characterisation of inheritance taxes as 'voluntary'.

Tax changes since 1979

The manifest weaknesses of inheritance taxation when the Conserva-
tives took power in 1979 certainly lightened the task facing a
Government which had promised in its manifesto 'to deal with the
most damaging features of capital transfer and capital gains tax and
propose a simpler and less oppressive system of capital taxation in the
longer run'. The course chosen for inheritance taxation has however
not been the abolition sought by many of the Party's supporters, but
rather cumulative erosion.

Major alterations have been made in nine out of the fourteen
Budgets since 1980 (Table 8.1). The process was almost continuous

until 1988; thereafter only 1992 saw any major adjustment. The overall effect has been a marked reduction in the progressivity of the tax schedule for bequests at death (Table 8.2) and its abolition for lifetime gifts, combined with further expansion of the scope for avoidance. Only occasionally has a loophole been narrowed.[11]

The principal changes are the reduction of top marginal rates from 75 to 40 per cent; the re-exemption of gifts made more than seven years before death; the increase in the valuation relief allowed for various types of business-related assets, heritage property and charitable donations; and the exemption of offshore (Isle of Man and Channel Island) residents three years after they leave the mainland, bringing the benefits of emigration to a tax haven within reach of those unwilling to leave the country. Only the increase in the real value of the lower threshold has dampened the loss of progressivity amongst payers of the tax.

The effects of these changes show up to some extent in tax revenues. In 1980 the number of estates taxable at death fell and the average tax rate rose, in association with the rise in the threshold and the abolition of lower rates. The average rate of tax payable fell in 1988 in association with the cut in the top rate from 60 to 40 per cent (Table 8.2). On the other hand, none of the indicators in Table 8.2 alters to anything like the extent that might be expected from the changes to tax rules in Table 8.1. Business-related relief in particular remained small, at less than £150m yearly, and even declined in relation to estate values after 1981, suggesting that such assets have been largely and even increasingly transmitted outside the reach of the Exchequer, through settlements in particular.

The taxation of trusts has by contrast seen little action: reforms have been mooted and discarded (Venables, 1992).[12] Although the periodic ten year charge on the assets of discretionary trusts was eventually implemented in 1983, its implicit average tax rate has since averaged only 0.54 per cent per annum, and its yield had dwindled by 1991/2 to less than £1m (Table 8.3). Indeed, as the total value of discretionary trust assets implied by the data, assuming no trend in net trust formation during the period, is only £2 billion, only a small part of avoidance activity has become statistically visible.

Other types of settlement appear to have flourished outside the scope of official statistics. The elimination of taxation on lifetime gifts has made the accumulation and maintenance trust an effective channel for tax-free legacies to one's descendants. As tax is charged neither on the death of the donor, nor on the receipt of the benefit (at

Table 8.1 Major changes to inheritance taxation, on transfers at
death, annual Budgets, 1979–92

Year	Thresholds £000s		Marginal rates %		Other changes
	min	max	min	max	
1979	59	4720	10	75	(Emergency post-election Budget only)
1980	**99**	3990	30	75	Nominal exemption limit doubled
					Tax rates below 30% eliminated (income tax cuts)
1981	91	3640	30	75	Tax on lárge gifts cut to ²/₃ death rate
					Cumulation of gifts limited to 10 years
					Valuation of let land: 20% relief
1982	93	**4220**	30	75	(Over-)indexation of thresholds begun
1983	97	4280	30	75	Offshore domicile status after 3 years
					Minority holdings in unquoted companies and let land: 30% relief
					(Charitable gifts exemption limit ended)
1984	99	4390	30	**60**	Maximum tax rate cut to 60%
					Tax on all gifts cut to ¹/₂ death rate
					(Corporation Tax reform)
1985	98	4360	30	60	Land around historic buildings exempted
1986	100	4470	30	60	Tax on gifts abolished (end of CTT) except those within 7 years of death
					(Basic rate of income tax cut 1pt)
1987	**121**	4420	30	60	Four intermediate tax rates removed
1988	137		40		Maximum tax rate cut by ¹/₃
					(Income tax cut, 40% top rate)
1989	139		40		
1990	141		40		
1991	145		40		
1992	150		40		100% relief on holdings in unincorporated firms, unquoted firms (>25% stake), working farms; 50% relief on let land, holdings in unquoted (<25%) and quoted (controlled) firms

Notes: Figures in bold represent major changes; thresholds are reported in constant 1992/
93 prices, uprated on a FY basis by the GDP deflator; changes to other taxes are
reported in parentheses; thresholds refer to lower exemption limit and top rate
starting level.

Source: *Inland Revenue Statistics* (various years); *Financial Times*
(see note 2)

up to 25 years of age), nor periodically on the trust's assets, it follows
that 'once property is settled on these trusts there should be no [IT]

Table 8.2   Attributes of taxable estates at death, UK 1979–88

	Taxable estates		Average tax rate	Business relief	
	All		Inter-generation only		
	000s	£m	%	£m	%
1979-80	71.8	4661	15.6	140	3.0
1980-81	27.3	2995	19.8	114	3.8
1981-82	32.4	3256	19.2	135	4.2
1982-83	32.3	3166	16.9	126	4.0
1983-84	33.0	3443	16.8	104	3.0
1984-85	38.7	4253	17.8	136	3.2
1985-86	43.9	4876	19.2	143	2.9
1986-87	47.6	5136	18.4	132	2.6
1987-88	40.2	5215	19.4	134	2.6
1988-89	39.2	5141	16.9	135	2.6

Notes: All values in financial year 1992/93 prices (GDP deflator at market prices). Columns 1 and 2 show the number and real value of estates reported for probate whose net value exceeded CTT/IT threshold. Column 2 values are net of value of bequests to surviving spouse (eligible throughout for 100% relief). Column 3 shows tax payable as a percentage of taxable values of estates. Columns 4 and 5 show valuation relief on business assets (agricultural, business and unquoted share categories) in real values and as a percentage of column 2.

Source: *Inland Revenue Statistics* (1992), Table 10.5 (and previous years)

liability' (Whitehouse and Stuart-Buttle 1987, p.430).

Inadequate information on trust activity obscures the extent to which the tax avoidance industry expanded to exploit the changes of the 1980s. Innovation certainly appears to have been present. 'Inheritance trusts' were promoted by large insurers, in competition with the orthodox trusts offered by solicitors, until they were killed off in 1986 by the removal of tax relief on gifts in which the donor reserved an interest. A more durable innovation involved the purchase of insurance against premature death—i.e., within seven years—when making a lifetime gift, with proceeds of the policy payable into trust and therefore not taxable.[13]

Such changes are however of second-order importance. The broad stability of tax revenues and the declining importance of business reliefs suggest that for the avoidance industry it has been a case of 'business as usual', with most assets still transferred outside the reach of the tax system. The budgetary changes of the 1980s may have aborted the recovery in tax receipts which had been anticipated under

Table 8.3 Discretionary trusts subject to periodic charge, UK 1983–91

	Number of trusts	Gross asset value £m	Tax paid £m	Average tax rate %
1983-84	665	253	14.4	5.7
1984-85	581	395	22.5	5.7
1985-86	443	199	11.8	5.9
1986-87	462	281	16.2	5.8
1987-88	511	299	16.6	5.6
1988-89	204	113	4.3	3.8
1989-90	234	161	6.7	4.1
1990-91	139	64	2.5	3.9
1991-92	47	23	0.9	4.1
Nine year total	3286	1788	96.0	
Mean				5.4

Notes: All values in financial year 1992/93 prices. A periodic charge has been levied on the assets on every tenth anniversary of the trust's foundation since 1983/84; asset values in column two are not net of liabilities, relief and exemptions.

Source: Inland Revenue Statistics (1992), Table 10.9 (and previous years)

CTT once it had settled down. Their main effect, however, was simply to expand further an already extensive range of avoidance options. For most large property owners this amounted simply to the relaxation of a non-binding constraint. Nevertheless, the same tax changes have been elaborated with a skill and a caution which suggests that they are not simply unimportant, particularly when it comes to the emotive politics of property. The long-term decline of inheritance taxation has been consolidated and pressed further. More strikingly, the organised hypocrisy of the pre-1979 system, which combined the appearance of serious redistribution with the reality of little redistribution, has been largely destroyed.

The Government case for tax reform, 1979-92

The tax changes outlined above were invariably justified by the Chancellor of the Exchequer when outlining them in the annual

Budget speech. Successive Chancellors referred to the economic effects of inheritance taxes in ten speeches between 1979 and 1992. In the early years, the Chancellor typically turned towards the end to capital taxation as a whole, criticised it as damaging to economic efficiency and continued with a detailed tax-by-tax listing of defects and remedies in which CTT invariably came first. After 1984 attention to inheritance taxation became more irregular, in both presence and placing in the speech.

Amongst the arguments advanced in support of tax reform, efficiency considerations predominated and equity ones received almost no attention. A further imbalance appeared within the efficiency category, towards business performance.

Business performance

Nine Budget speeches referred to the need to encourage enterprise in general, and small, family or unquoted business in particular. Existing taxation of gifts and bequests was held to deter the formation, survival and growth of such businesses. Major pronouncements of the theme coincided with marked reductions in tax levels or progressivity. Thus Sir Geoffrey Howe described CTT in 1980, when doubling the tax threshold, as 'a particular burden on the small business, when it passes from one generation to another, whether on death or by lifetime transfer'.

The reduction of top rates from 75 to 60 per cent was accompanied by Nigel Lawson's statement that

> unnecessarily high rates of tax discourage enterprise and risk-taking. This is true of the capital taxes, just as it is of the corporation and income taxes. It is a matter of particular concern to those involved in running unquoted family businesses. The highest rates of capital transfer tax are far too high (1984).

The exemption of transfers made more than seven years before death was justified, similarly, by the assertion that

> capital transfer tax...has been a thorn in the side of those owning and running family businesses and as such has had a damaging effect on risk-taking and enterprise within a particularly important sector of the economy (1986);

and the reduction of the top rate to 40 per cent, by the statement that the flat rate of 40 per cent means that for the family business, enjoying 50 per cent business relief, the effective rate of tax can never exceed 20 per cent (1988).

Finally, a big increase in the reliefs offered to various types of business holding was introduced by Norman Lamont in 1992 as follows:

> I have one final change to announce which will be of substantial benefit, particularly to small businesses...I propose to take most family businesses out of inheritance taxation altogether.

As Lamont made no reference to the merits of family businesses or the deterrent effects of taxation, the argument was by then presumably taken for granted.

Other efficiency issues

The other efficiency implications of inheritance tax adverted to in Budget speeches fade into insignificance alongside business performance. Capital market efficiency cropped up twice: in 1982, when Howe attacked capital taxes in general as 'impeding the efficient working of capital markets', and in 1986, when Lawson criticised the taxation of lifetime gifts, which he was then abolishing, as, by 'deterring lifetime giving, [having] had the effect of locking in assets, particularly the ownership of family businesses, often to the detriment of the businesses involved.'

A striking area of neglect involves a major issue in the economics of inheritance: the bequest motive for saving. It was mentioned only twice, first at the outset in 1979 ('it is perfectly natural that people should want to build up capital of their own and pass it one to their children; this is particularly true of the small proprietor') and again in 1992, though with no particular relevance to the changes then in hand ('ordinary families want to be able to pass the wealth they have built up over their lives to their children without an excessive portion being taken by the state').

A fourth efficiency consideration involved the supply of rented farmland, which was said in both 1981 and 1983 to need the encouragement of valuation relief along the lines already applicable to owner-farmed land. The issue was again linked to the small business one:

> capital taxes can suffocate enterprise...I am concerned that the prospect of capital transfer tax may still discourage those who

are contemplating investing capital in small businesses. It may also be one of the factors reducing the number of farms available for letting (1983).

Finally, the international comparisons which featured in discussion of top rates of income tax were applied also to cuts in top tax rates on capital transfers. In 1984, existing UK rates were termed 'badly out of line with comparable rates abroad'; in 1988, the new top rate applied to family businesses was introduced as 'one of the lowest rates in the industrialised world'—though how either mattered for economic performance remained unclear.

Equity

The only explicit reference to equity came in the 1982 criticism of capital taxation as 'doing injustice to individuals and businesses alike', though the nature of the 'injustice' was not explained and the Chancellor reverted rapidly to the 'economic and social damage' produced by 'holding back business success and penalising personal endeavour'. The only indication that there might be an equity case *for* the taxation of capital transfers had occurred obliquely in 1980, when future cuts in tax rates were mooted—'there is of course a place for capital taxation, including in particular a charge on death'. The reasons for that 'place' remained tacit, however, and the implications of the ensuing tax reforms for inequality of opportunity were never explicitly mentioned.[14]

Efficiency: an assessment

The arguments reviewed in the preceding section must be set against the relevant evidence. Before doing so, it is worth considering the reason why, during the past two centuries, many prominent economists have advocated the taxation of inheritance. The weaker case holds that 'more intensive use of estate and gift taxation would add progressivity to tax systems with less impairment of economic incentives than [is the case for] many other taxes' (Pechman, 1987, p.857)—than, that is, for taxes on wealth accumulation, work effort or consumption as they occur, which are the main alternatives in personal taxation. To the extent that death is an involuntary event, which is removed in time and thought from decisions to save and invest, and which destroys the usefulness of property to the individual, taxing property at death redistributes wealth without damaging output and growth.[15]

The stronger form of the argument holds that inheritance reduces efficiency. The main channel involves ability. Inheritance selects individuals to run family businesses by birth rather than by talent, and birth and talent are seen as largely or wholly independent. Inheritance therefore reduces management quality relative to that under selection by talent. Keynes made the point with typical force in relation to inter-war British industry and politics:

> the hereditary principle in the transmission of wealth and the control of business is the reason why the leadership of the Capitalist cause is weak and stupid. It is too much dominated by third-generation men (Keynes, 1984, vol ix, p.299)[16]

A second route is the tendency of large bequests to undermine work incentives for those who receive them, particularly at a tender age. What might nowadays be termed the 'Hooray Henry' factor led a man as wealthy as Andrew Carnegie to support inheritance taxation and the application of large estates to charitable and public purposes (Pechman, 1987). The efficiency issues raised by inheritance taxation clearly range widely. Rather than rehearsing again the full range, this chapter concentrates on two aspects central to contemporary discussion: business performance, as emphasised in Budget speeches, and bequest-oriented saving, as emphasised in the economics literature. Economic knowledge has advanced in each area since the debate over inheritance last flourished in the 1970s.

Business performance

Although the capitalist market economy represents a historically extreme separation of inheritance from production (Goody, 1987), the two remain closely related in the sector variously described in Budget speeches as small, unquoted and family business. These three categories overlap heavily, exhibiting widespread family-based overlaps between ownership and management. A narrower definition is however appropriate: unquoted and unincorporated family-owned businesses, irrespective of size, here termed 'family business'. Quoted companies are excluded as their owners can more readily pay inheritance tax bills by liquidating assets without disrupting business continuity. Larger businesses are not however excluded, as family ownership or control is far from unusual outside small business.[17]

The potential for inheritance taxation to damage family business, and with it overall business performance, has impressed many, including an official enquiry into small firms, a major research study and an erstwhile ministerial sceptic (Bolton Committee, 1971; Hay and Morris, 1984 and Lever, 1984). There are indeed several potential advantages for family ownership over external ownership. The first concerns the principal-agent problem of ensuring that managers pursue the interests of owners rather than their own advantage in situations where the two conflict. Such goal divergence is endemic to quoted companies: 'people...look after their own money more diligently than other people's' (Bolton Committee, 1971, p.23). The principal-agent problem is difficult to resolve in quoted companies, incentive schemes notwithstanding (Morck, 1992). It is however absent in family firms where one or more owners manage the business; and restrained by family ties even when owners are numerous and some are rentiers. Evidence that small businesses suffer bankruptcy less often when managers have invested their own resources in the firm are consistent with this factor (Storey, 1993).

Second, amongst possible owner interests, family ownership can avoid the short-term perspectives prevalent elsewhere. The managers of widely-owned quoted companies, to the extent that they want to retain office, must maintain short-term profitability and share price if they are to stave off unwanted takeover bids. Long-term profitability suffers when it conflicts with quarterly results, to the detriment of research, training and strategic planning (Finegold and Soskice, 1988). By contrast, long-term perspectives are made possible in family firms by their insulation from hostile takeovers, and encouraged by the locking-in of assets associated with continuity of family ownership. Family business often scores highly in terms of finance and growth as well. Commitment to building the business is widely associated with both aversion to long-term debt and high rates of internal saving and growth, facilitated by low dividends and low salaries for owner-managers.

The case is not, however, at all one-sided. Family ownership shows defects too, first along the lines sketched above. Adverse outcomes are particularly likely in successor generations, when the energy and ability of the founder-owner have gone. There may be either no heirs, or none with appropriate interest and ability, to carry on the business. Hay and Morris (1984) found that management succession was unproblematic in only one-quarter of unquoted companies. Otherwise, management quality is expected to suffer relative to that in public companies, subject as the latter are to the market for corporate control.

Second, the benefits of family ownership in terms of goal harmonisation and long-term perspectives are permissive rather than mandatory. Given favourable product market conditions, owner-managers enjoy still more scope to become 'entrenched' and pursue their own goals than do the salaried managers of large quoted companies. Some owner-managers seek profitability and growth. Unproductive goals, such as social status, golf and patriarchy, are however also possible. Independence and family control feature widely in practice, in some cases to the detriment of performance. In particular, top positions are often reserved for family members even when they are not the best candidates. Similarly, as selling out is also widely associated with loss of face, it may be avoided even when it could improve performance (SBRC, 1992). Again, problems are particularly likely in successor generations, whose widespread interest in the quiet, settled 'way of life' of the family firm has often been noted. A quiet life may not be attainable anyway as, if more than one family member has an interest in the business, a weak boundary between family and business matters can turn the firm into an arena in which family conflicts are fought out in their full intensity.[18] In all such cases, business performance can easily suffer under family ownership.

A third drawback concerns finance. Lack of access to new equity and aversion to long-term debt imply heavy reliance on short-term bank lending and internal saving, which can constrain growth, particularly for capital-scarce small firms, as well as aggravating problems of liquidity and survival in recession, as in the early 1990s (SBRC, 1992). Finally, the varied types of tax relief available to owners of family businesses have created incentives to use such enterprises as tax shelters. Adverse effects follow, in that substandard productivity and profitability are made viable by tax concessions.

Family business therefore suffers from drawbacks as well as offering advantages. Evidence on the overall relative performance of the two types of business is clearly needed to resolve the issue. There is no lack of relevant evidence, including cases of decrepit, conservative family businesses run by inheritors and struggling wastefully to survive (Church, 1977). Against these must be set cases of failing public companies, as well as family businesses which retain their dynamism across the generations or which have recovered from decrepitude. The historical verdict that the failure of much British industry in this century has been encouraged by parochial amateurism amongst the owner-managers of numerous family firms speaks against the family business (Chandler, 1990 and Hannah, 1983).

On the other side stands the finding that during the 1970s unquoted UK companies generally outperformed quoted ones, in terms of productivity, profitability and growth (Hay and Morris, 1984). Similarly, Cosh and Hughes found owner-managed UK firms to be 'somewhat faster growing and more profitable' than manager-controlled ones (1989, p.45). Unfortunately, neither of the latter two studies examined the dispersion of performance *within* the family business category, where a decline with age relative to that of non-family business might be anticipated for the reasons outlined above. There is evidence consistent with that hypothesis. Heirs to business fortunes act as innovators in their own right less often than do non-owner managers (Shaw, 1993). Similarly the average performance of a sample of family firms declined absolutely with age. Within the initial generation, declining business performance was associated with widespread fatigue, inadequate delegation and overdue retirement amongst founders. Within successor generations, it was associated with inadequacy of numbers, interest, ability and external experience amongst heirs (Boswell, 1973).[19]

Both theory and evidence unfortunately remain open-ended concerning the implications of inheritance taxation for business performance. Family business does indeed appear to outperform its alternatives overall, but its advantages may well become negligible or negative with age, as successor generations take over from the founder generation. The latter issue is the key one for inheritance taxation and more evidence is badly needed on it, preferably from long-term longitudinal research into the performance of a set of young enterprises. More needs to be known also about the degree to which inheritance taxation actually forces the liquidation or sale of family businesses in the first place. In the light of these considerations, and in an era of declining family size and cohesion, it is less than convincing to expect the family business to play a major role in the productive regeneration of the British economy, let alone to accord it high priority in tax concessions.

Bequest motive for saving

The desire to accumulate property in order to bequeath it to the next generation has figured lately more in economics journals than in

Budget speeches. It suggests that inheritance taxation may damage economic efficiency by deterring saving. Those who wish to give to their heirs may save less when they anticipate that their bequests will be taxed, particularly at high rates. The aggregate savings rate is then lower and it falls still further if the revenue from inheritance taxation is devoted to current expenditure rather than investment. A shift from saving to consumption can indeed bring short-term benefits by raising demand and employment along Keynesian lines in a slump, but it would be less than welcome in the longer term, given contemporary interest in raising investment and growth (Deaton, 1992).

There is also a potential efficiency loss when the altruistic desires of donors are frustrated by the Exchequer (Bracewell-Milnes, 1989). The status of such losses is actually precarious,[20] but neither they nor those associated with aggregate savings can amount to much unless the bequest motive prevails in the first place. Property transfers between generations do not in themselves provide evidence for the bequest motive, as they may instead be the by-product of other motives or simply the lack of alternatives at death—as suggested by the quip that only those who dislike their offspring even more than the Inland Revenue elect to pay rather than to avoid inheritance taxes (Sandford, 1983).

Recent interest amongst economists in the bequest motive has been motivated not by inheritance taxation but by lifetime savings behaviour and debt finance.[21] An important bequest motive is suggested by low and even negative rates of dissaving amongst retired households, who might be expected to dissave more and enjoy higher consumption were they not interested in leaving bequests. It also features strongly in the declared intentions of the owners of family business, many of whom state a strong desire to keep it in the family (Bolton Committee, 1971; Hay and Morris, 1984). Economists who see the bequest motive as of only secondary importance cite the infrequency with which savers as a whole state a desire to bequeath. More telling is the tendency for retired couples without children to save no less during their working lives and dissave no more in retirement than do those with children, even though their interest in making bequests might be presumed much less.

Finally, there are alternative explanations for the widespread reluctance to run assets down before death. Prominent here is self-insurance against the potential costs associated with longevity, ill-health and medical care, to the extent that insurance markets and public welfare provide imperfect cover. There is also the independence, power and status derived from continuing possession of property. In that category one can distinguish the ultra-wealthy, whose ability to devise further forms of personal consumption is exhausted; the captain of industry and the landlord whose social standing depends on their wealth; and the parents who intend to avoid the fate of King Lear and keep their self-interested offspring loyal and attentive to the end.[22] Under all these alternatives to the bequest motive, legacies could be both large and involuntary, and their taxation at death unimportant for both savings behaviour and the welfare of savers. Such considerations caution against giving a prominent place to the bequest motive in personal savings behaviour in advanced economies. Even if 'bequest motives are a good deal more important than we used to think' (Deaton, 1992, p.217), particularly amongst top wealth holders and founders of family businesses, bequest-oriented saving appears to constitute for most savers a subsidiary impulse and, as such, a secondary consideration in the analysis of inheritance taxation.

Vested interests and special pleading

The efficiency benefits claimed by successive Chancellors since 1979 for the reduction of inheritance taxation are therefore tenuous, lacking appropriate research underpinning. The disparity between political claims and economic evidence points to the political uses of efficiency arguments. The absence of research support is itself revealing. The Thatcher Government disbanded early on a major potential source, the Diamond Commission, whose research had shed light on many distributional issues. Nor did the burgeoning pro-Conservative think tanks show any inclination to undertake the appropriate research. Conservative Chancellors used the interests of family business to defend tax changes which benefitted other types of wealth holder as well. Even had the case for helping family businesses justified increased valuation relief for their owners, that would not have warranted the associated benefits provided by the reforms to owners of *all* kinds of property—large as well as small, rentier as well as business, quoted public company as well as unquoted family business. Such was the case for the reductions in average tax rates on *all* estates in 1984, 1986 and 1988. Some measures even promised proportionately greater gains for the more wealthy, notably the 1981 cuts in marginal rates on lifetime transfers, the 1982 increase in top rate thresholds, the cuts in top rates in 1984 and 1988, the 1986 ending of taxation of lifetime gifts and the 1983 relaxation of offshore domiciliary restrictions.

The interests of small business provided in all these cases an effective camouflage for those of the large wealth owners and inheritors who constitute a powerful interest group within the Conservative Party. The interests of the small owner can be readily identified with a common, national interest in increasing output and employment, whereas those of rich inheritors are more immediately associated with privilege, inequity and waste. Small business thus acquires a political importance disproportionate to its economic role, important though the latter may be. An egregious instance of vested interests sheltering behind efficiency arguments involved granting valuation relief for let land, i.e., farmland which is rented out rather than owner-farmed. In 1979 CTT had granted 50 per cent valuation relief on owner-farmed land, reflecting the case for avoiding tax-enforced sale or breakup of such businesses at death. Whatever the merits of that argument (Sutherland, 1981), no such case could be made for assets which were readily marketable, including let land as well as listed shares.

The case made in 1981 for extending relief to let land relied instead on a proposed need to 'maintain a proper balance between owner-occupied and let land' by encouraging the entry of new tenant farmers. The main potential beneficiaries were clearly large landlords, owners of the most unequally held category of private wealth, whose interests had been conveniently advanced in the name of helping potential tenants find farms. It is difficult to imagine an intervention less targeted on its proclaimed objective, whatever the merits of the objective itself. The rate of relief on let land was nevertheless extended in 1983 and 1992 until it gave landlords the 50 per cent relief which had until 1979 been available only to owner-controlled enterprises.

The political abuse of efficiency issues can also be seen in matters of emphasis and omission. Within the series of criticisms levelled against capital taxes in the Budgets of the early 1980s, CTT invariably preceded Capital Gains Tax despite the latter's potentially stronger effects on saving and accumulation. Similarly, on the two occasions when the bequest motive was mentioned, any tendency to associate it with the dynastic interests of the wealthy was discouraged by linking it to two groups whose interests align more readily with the national interest, viz. small business and 'ordinary families'.

The most striking omission occurs on the equity side, where the issue of property rights might have been expected to surface. Following Locke, some social theorists take individual property rights to include a right to bequeath without being taxed.[23] Such a view is often congenial to those who benefit from inheritance. The closest approach made to the issue in Budget speeches was however the description of inheritance taxes as 'doing injustice to individuals'(1982), and even then the argument remained implicit. This remarkable omission reflects the political risks associated with invoking a right which benefits primarily a wealthy minority and which is readily countered by a right for all to equal opportunity. The utilitarian criterion of business performance faces none of these political pitfalls.

The weakness of the evidence supporting official arguments for tax reform is thus complemented by the special pleading visible in them. Inheritance provides an outstanding example of the political value to the beneficiaries of inequality of efficiency arguments which dress up the mutton of sectional advantage as the lamb of national interest.

Conclusions

The political economy of property and inheritance remains permeated by paradox and illusion. In the 1970s, the apparent high water mark of redistributive politics coincided with the most rapid ever decline in revenues from inheritance taxes. In the 1980s, the collapse of redistributive politics coincided with the greatest postwar stability in inheritance tax revenues; and Government cutbacks in inheritance taxation, conducted in the name of small and family business, coincided with declining importance for business-related relief. The real game of inheritance was played throughout behind closed doors, in the inaccessible arena of settlement trusts; the public game of inheritance taxation has remained largely symbolic.

The tax changes implemented since 1979 do at least get credit for reducing the hypocrisy of a tax regime which pretended to offer major redistribution but which delivered little in practice. Those changes have however been promoted with the help of a further hypocrisy, which has promoted the sectional interests of the wealthy behind unsupported, exaggerated or spurious claims about economic efficiency.

Inheritance taxation might well be considered for abolition were the alternative for it to linger on in its present form. Its redistributive contribution has become as low in appearance as in reality. The many tax officials and lawyers employed in its administration and avoidance might be found more productive employment. Before throwing in the towel, however, alternatives to abolition should be explored. The appeal of a tax which promises to reduce inequality significantly without imposing major efficiency costs is too great to be abandoned lightly even at this low point in its history. The complete rethink of goals and methods which failed to inform the abortive reforms of the 1970s might provide an appropriate first step. In such a reappraisal two issues should be prominent.

First, the legal treatment of settlements should be reconsidered with a view to separating their valid functions, such as protecting the interests of orphans, from their widespread orientation to tax avoidance. Statutory clearance of the thicket of settlement law appears essential, with abolition of the trust option examined as a last resort.

Second, the political visibility and appeal of inheritance taxation has to be increased. A contribution to both might be to link it clearly to the promotion of meritocratic norms, for example by explicitly devoting its proceeds to public education, whose funding has suffered badly relative to need. Using the proceeds of a tax on unequal opportunity in nonhuman wealth to reduce inequality of opportunity in human wealth might prove politically appealing.

9 THE MACROECONOMICS OF EQUALITY, STABILITY AND GROWTH

Dan Corry and Andrew Glyn[1]

This chapter looks at the macroeconomic relationships between inequality and economic performance. It examines whether economic performance is improved by inequality or whether the opposite is the case, by comparing both the post-war experience of the advanced countries as a whole and also the experience of different countries. Such comparisons are fraught with difficulties both as to the availability of data and the interpretation of causal relations. What is presented here is an impressionistic interpretation of the overall picture. The facts do not support those who argue that considerations of efficiency rule out egalitarian policies. In fact macroeconomic evidence tends to point in precisely the opposite direction; greater equality seems rather to be associated with better economic performance.

Post-war trends in equality and economic efficiency[2]

Growth since 1950 divides conveniently into two roughly equal periods. The twenty or so years before 1974 witnessed unprecedented economic growth, averaging nearly 5 per cent per year in the advanced countries and warranting the designation of the 'golden age'(see Maddison 1991, Marglin and Schor 1990). The UK's growth did not match that of most of Continental Europe and Japan, but was still rapid (3 per cent per annum 1950–73) by historical standards. Since 1973 growth rates have been much slower, averaging 2.5 per cent per year in the OECD and 1.7 per cent per year for the UK. These figures are for growth of total output (GDP); output per worker (labour productivity) is probably closer to the broad idea of economic efficiency but shows almost identical patterns (see Figure 9.1).

Whilst output and productivity growth are central indicators of

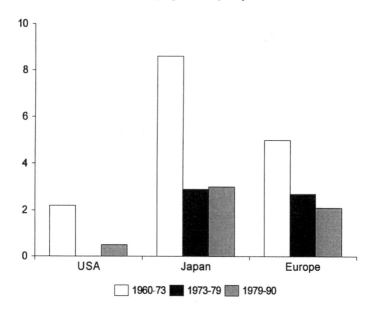

Figure 9.1 Labour productivity, 1960–90 (average annual percentage growth rate)

Source: OECD *Economic Outlook*, June 1992; business sector

economic performance, economic stability is also important. A high degree of economic instability (as manifested in severe slumps for example) results in insecurity, reducing the economic welfare implied by a given average level of output or rate of growth.[3] A comprehensive investigation of the size of cyclical fluctuations by Boltho (1989) showed that the economies of the advanced world were much more stable post-war than pre-war—such fluctuations (measured in a range of ways) were around one third as great over the period 1950–79 as for 1922–37.

During the 1950s and 1960s many advanced economies experienced no declines in output. Most countries did experience falls in GDP at some time between 1973 and 1989, but the typical decline was around 1–2 per cent (quite modest falls by inter-war standards). In the period 1973–9 (including the first OPEC oil shock) the absolute variability of output increased in the OECD countries as compared to 1960–73. The 1980s were less unstable; fluctuations were a little less than in the golden age, but in the context of much slower growth.[4]

There can be little doubt that economic inequality was sub-stantially lower during the golden age in the OECD countries than during the interwar period when growth was so much lower.

- Unemployment averaged 2.6 per cent per year in the advanced countries during 1950–73 as compared to 7.5 per cent during 1921–38.

- Government expenditure in 1950 was twice the share of GDP in the USA, Netherlands and France that it had been in 1929; in the UK the figures were 34 per cent of GDP as compared to 24 per cent (only Germany and Japan saw virtually no increase). Although not all of the increase was in welfare expenditure, in many countries such spending was greatly increased (in the UK spending on benefits, health, education and housing rose from 9 per cent of GDP in 1938 to 13.5 per cent in 1950).

- Overall comparisons of the distribution of household income as compared to pre-war show declines in the share of the top 5 per cent for all countries for which data is available; in the UK the share of the top 5 per cent in post-tax incomes fell by one quarter to 21 per cent between 1938 and 1947, whilst the share of the bottom 50 per cent crept up from 27 per cent to 30 per cent (Seers 1950). Redistribution was very similar in the USA but generally rather less in continental Europe.

- Between the 1920s and the early 1950s the share of personal wealth owned by the richest 1 per cent of the population fell from nearly 60 per cent in the UK to around 45 per cent and from about 37 per cent in the USA to around 25 per cent (Atkinson, Gordon and Harrison 1989, Woolf and Morley 1989).

Economic inequality also continued to decline during the golden age period. This conclusion is based on the following trends:

- Unemployment was sharply reduced in a number of European countries, above all Germany, where it was still high in 1950. Furthermore employment opportunities for women began to expand; the female labour force rose from 45.8 per cent of the female population of working age in 1960 to 49.4 per cent in 1974; in the UK the rise was from 46.1 per cent to 54.3 per cent.

- Welfare expenditure (on health, education and social transfers) rose very sharply in the OECD countries, from 12 per cent of

GDP in 1960 to 22 per cent in 1975; in the UK the rise was from 12.4 per cent to 19.6 per cent.

● Inequality of household income generally fell, quite strongly (USA, Japan, Sweden, France) or more modestly (UK, Germany, Netherlands).

It is clear that the period of unprecedented growth and stability coincided with a degree of inequality which, although disparities were still large, was probably lower than in the previous history of capitalism. Moreover, during this period of exceptional growth economic inequality was generally falling. All this is hardly consistent with the idea that greater equality is inconsistent with economic efficiency.

Inequality after 1973

The pattern of post-war growth breaks conveniently at 1973, after which the trend of output growth proceeded at little more than half the pace of the golden age. The pattern of inequality is less clear-cut. The broad picture is that the trend towards greater equality was reversed, but the timing differs markedly between indicators and countries. In the USA the 'U-turn' to rising inequality occurred in the late 1960s as the average unemployment rate rose and earnings inequalities widened sharply; these trends were amplified in the 1980s by cuts in top tax rates, cuts in social programmes and by very large capital gains. In many European countries, by contrast, the period between the two OPEC oil crises saw a continuation and even sharpening of egalitarian trends as governments struggled to contain unemployment, welfare expenditure grew rapidly, wage dispersion was reduced (especially between men and women) and earned income grew much faster than the capital value of shares. It was not until the 1980s that the increase in economic equality was typically halted or reversed as unemployment rose rapidly, poverty increased, welfare spending was contained, wage dispersion expanded, taxes for top incomes were cut and (later) stock exchanges boomed. The period between the oil crises is particularly important since sharply deteriorating economic performance coincided with a continuation of the sharp reductions in inequality characteristic of the late 1960s and early 1970s. This led many to accept the argument that greater equality itself was stifling incentives and thus contributing to the low growth. The rest of this section provides evidence for this reversal of the trend towards greater equality.

The employment position deteriorated after 1973, but with the important exception of the USA the rise in unemployment was considerably faster after 1979—the average unemployment rate for OECD outside USA rose by about 1.5 percentage points between 1968–73 and 1974–9, but by 3 percentage points between 1974–9 and 1980–90 (UK increases were 1.8 per cent and 5 per cent). To some extent this difference was due to deliberate policies in the inter-shock period to mitigate the impact of slower growth on jobs via employment maintenance policies (subsidising declining industries, etc.—see Rowthorn and Glyn 1990); these policies were widely abandoned after 1979 (the Temporary Employment Subsidy in the UK for example), to be replaced by government schemes to provide some kind of temporary work for the unemployed. Higher unemployment has strongly inegalitarian effects, especially because its incidence is so concentrated (see Chapter 7).

The 1980s saw a general increase in earnings inequality. The USA provides possibly the earliest example (starting around the late 1960s), probably the strongest increase in the 1980s (Davis 1993) and certainly the most studied case (Levy and Murnane 1992). A combination of factors involving the educational attainments of new entrants to the labour force, the increased demand for more skilled work but also greater inequality in the earnings of workers of a given qualification are all involved. Increases in earnings inequality in the 1980s seems to have occurred in most countries, with Germany being an important exception. Sweden provides the clearest example 'of strong declines in earnings inequality being reversed in the early 1980s. In the UK a century of virtual stability in the distribution of (male manual) earnings gave way after 1979 to sharply increased dispersion (see Chapter 6). One of the strongest equalising forces in the earnings distribution in the 1970s was the relative increase in women's pay; the ratio of female to male hourly earnings in manufacturing, for instance, rose by an average of 6 per cent in the OECD countries in the 1970s. In the 1980s this reduction in gender inequality of earnings virtually halted.

Finally the growth of government expenditure as a share of GDP was much slower after 1979. Between 1970 and 1979 the ratio of government expenditure to GDP excluding interest payments rose by 8.5 per cent in the OECD. In the next decade the rise was just 1.2 per cent. Over the 1980s the share of welfare expenditure in GDP (the category most relevant for income distribution but for which data is patchy) fell by at least 1 per cent of GDP in the UK, Germany and the

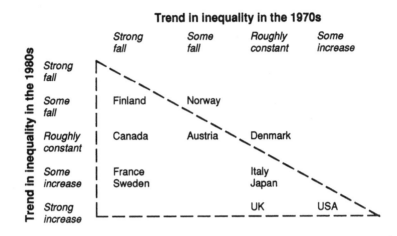

Figure 9.2 Income inequality in the 1970s and 1980s

Source: Atkinson (1993), Green et al. (1992), Gottshalk (1993), Rossi and Toniolo (1993), Smeeding and Coder (1993), Bauer and Mason (1992). Data refers to ratios of income of high and low income groups and/or Gini coefficients/Atkinson indices. Where possible data is for 1973–79 and then from 1979 until as late in the 1980s as possible.

Netherlands and appears to have declined markedly in Belgium, Sweden, Australia and New Zealand. In addition the financing of such spending became less progressive with cuts in the top rate of tax (averaging 17 percentage points for OECD as a whole with a 40 point cut in UK); this occurred at a time when the average direct tax burden was increasing for tax payers.

These factors—increased unemployment, greater earnings dispersion and restraint on welfare spending—all contributed to a reversal in the trend to greater equality. Not surprisingly, therefore, available data suggest the trend in overall household income distribution was usually less egalitarian (or more inegalitarian) in the 1980s than in the 1970s (nine countries are below the diagonal line in Figure 9.2), with the 1980s usually showing increased inequality. Currently data is not widely available beyond the mid 1980s; it is likely that more recent information will sharpen the picture of the turn towards inequality in the 1980s.

In 1967 the best off one fifth of US families received seven times the average income of the least well-off fifth; by 1989 the ratio was more than ten to one, with most of the rise taking place in the 1980s. In the UK between 1979 and 1989 there was a proportionately similar rise, concentrated particularly in the years after 1985. In Sweden, also, the ratio of the share of the top 20 per cent to the bottom 20 per cent rose from about four and a half in 1980 to five and half in 1988. Elsewhere the increases in inequality in the 1980s were apparently milder but they frequently still represented substantial changes in the trend, for example in France where inequality had previously been falling. There appear to be no cases where the trend was more egalitarian in the 1980s than in the 1970s.

The overall impression from this data, of a rather consistent trend away from increasing equality, is reinforced when capital gains are considered. A general boom in the stock market saw share prices rise by 8 per cent per year faster than wage earnings between 1979 and 1989 (having fallen by 13 per cent per year relative to earnings in the period 1973-9). This reflected the strong recovery of profitability in the 1980s, together with renewed confidence that the capitalist economies had been stabilised after the difficulties of the 1970s (see Glyn, 1992a). In sharp contrast to the increase in wealth, poverty (the proportion of people in households with incomes less than 50 per cent of the average) increased in nine out of twelve countries for the period 1979-85 with the UK having the second biggest increase.

It does seem clear, then, that the trend towards reduced inequality characteristic of the golden age was generally reversed, sometimes quite sharply, usually in the 1980s but earlier in the USA. Rising inequality did not, of itself, secure a marked improvement in economic performance in the 1980s—labour productivity growth showed no general tendency to accelerate in the 1980s, see Figure 9.1. As noted earlier there was only a moderate increase in the stability of output growth after 1979.

The links between economic growth, equality and stability are complex and susceptible to different interpretations. It may well be that it was rapid economic growth in the golden age which strengthened those social forces pressing for greater equality (above all the labour movement); conversely the slow-down in growth after 1973 weakened those forces through mass unemployment and encouraged the better off to attempt to offload the impact of slower growth onto the weaker sections of society. All that is being claimed here is that the broad patterns of post-war development, as shown in stylised form in Figure 9.3 below, do not support the notion that increasing equality necessarily has adverse effects on economic performance.

	Equality	Growth	Stability
Golden Age 1950-73	Increase as compared to pre-war; moderately increasing trend	Unprecedentedly fast	High
1973-79	Generally increasing (USA an exception)	Much slower	Some deterioration, though recessions still moderate
1979-93	Frequently decreasing; otherwise not increasing as fast as before	Generally no improvement on 1973-79	Some improvement on 1973-79

Figure 9.3 Patterns of equality, growth and stability

Cross national data:
Do more unequal countries perform better?

The evidence across countries is no more supportive than across time periods for the idea of a strong equality/efficiency trade off.

Equality and stability

There are good reasons for believing that equality may enhance economic stability. Policies to increase economic equality are frequently associated with higher levels of government spending; this tends to act as an automatic stabiliser, reducing the impact on production and employment of fluctuations in other elements of demand. Second, if the taxation to pay for the expenditure is progressive, this, together with the cyclical movements of the budget deficit, also acts to dampen fluctuations. Finally it may be expected that if the distribution of personal income is more equal, then consumption will show a steadier trend, as a greater proportion of income will be in the hands of those who will spend it consistently rather than those veering between bouts of saving and credit-financed consumption sprees. As J.K. Galbraith put it 'A reasonably equitable distribution of income is a stabilising economic influence it is macro-economically functional. The poor and the middle class spend their income; their support to aggregate income is stable and assured'.[5]

Figure 9.4 shows that the relationship between measured inequality

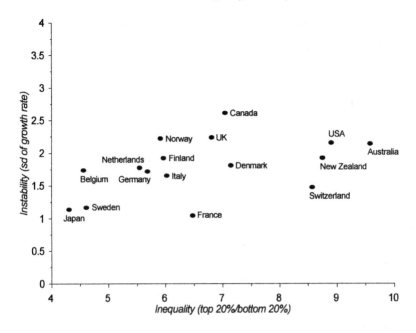

Figure 9.4 Inequality and instability, 1979–90

Source: World Bank; OECD

and economic stability in the 1980s was weak but if anything it suggests that the more egalitarian countries showed a more stable pattern of growth after 1979. The evidence, therefore, certainly does not suggest that egalitarian policies would hinder stability.

One indicator of economic performance adds the unemployment and inflation rates into a 'misery index'. It may be thought of as reflecting social stability and cohesion in the sense that a small value for the index suggests that low unemployment can be maintained whilst achieving low inflation, whilst a high value suggests that one has to be traded off at heavy cost in terms of the other. Again the relationship for the 1980s is far from strong (Figure 9.5) but if anything suggest that the more egalitarian countries performed better in this respect (the relatively low 'misery level' in inegalitarian Switzerland is partially a reflection of unemployment having been exported via repatriation of foreign workers).

One final consideration relates to the balance of payments. It would be expected that the consumption basket of the better off has a higher import content (foreign holidays, luxury consumer goods and so forth) than that of poor people. So a fall in inequality will tend to improve the balance of payments. Estimates by Borooah (1988) suggest that redistribution of income from the top 20 per cent to the bottom 40 per cent would have a significant effect in reducing the growth of imports and thus would relax the constraint on employment imposed by the balance of payments.

Inequality and growth

The relationship between inequality and growth has received more attention in the economics literature. The traditional argument is that inequality is required to generate the savings necessary to finance rapid growth and provide the incentive for enterprising behaviour. However, much productive investment is financed out of corporate savings, a high level of which does not necessarily imply extreme inequality of personal incomes. Further, much investment is in effect financed by the state running a budget surplus and does not require privately owned savings. Finally inequality may hinder the acquisition of education and training, and perpetuate the squandering of much of the labour force in low productivity jobs which will tend to inhibit growth.

There have been a number of studies aimed at discovering whether there is a strong relationship between inequality and growth. Alesina and Rodrick (1992) relate average growth rates for 65 countries over the period 1960–85 to income inequality at around the start of the period. After allowing for other influences such as the initial level of productivity, they found that the higher the share of top incomes (top 5 per cent or top 20 per cent) the significantly lower is growth, whilst higher shares for the poor and especially the middle income groups are associated with faster growth. They conclude that 'countries where income is more equally distributed also grow faster' (p.34). Persson and Tabellini (1992) reach essentially the same conclusion.

Such analysis has recently received the endorsement of the World Bank, often criticised for paying insufficient attention to inequality. Their *World Development Report 1991*, noted that 'there is no evidence that saving is positively related to income inequality or that income inequality leads to higher growth. If anything, it seems that inequality is associated with slower growth' (p.137). Whilst the World Bank's figures refer mainly to developing countries, the same relationship holds also for advanced countries (see Figure 0.1 in the

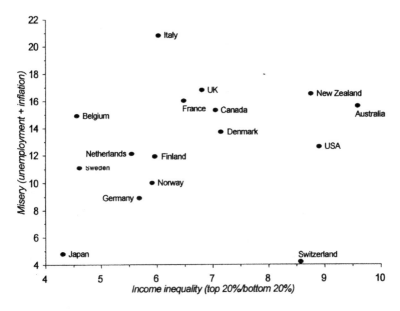

Figure 9.5 Inequality and misery index, 1979–90

Source: World Bank; OECD

Introduction). The economies with the most unequal income distribution at the beginning of the 1980s, like the USA and Switzerland, showed far slower productivity growth during the subsequent decade than did countries like Japan, Belgium and Sweden where incomes are apparently most evenly distributed. One supportive piece of evidence comes from a study by Garrison and Lee (1992) of the impact of taxation across 65 countries (45 low income and 18 industrial). They conclude that 'cross-country evidence provides no support for the supply side hypotheses that increases in tax rates adversely affect economic activity'.

Some policies may simultaneously worsen income distribution and raise the growth of productivity in a restricted sector of the economy. The 'Thatcher miracle' in UK manufacturing saw productivity growth accelerating from 1.1 per cent per year over the period 1973–9 to 4.2 per cent per year for 1979–89. This reflected a fierce process of rationalisation which itself had strong inegalitarian effects. The gainers were above all shareholders whose real dividends rose by 73 per cent; those who kept their jobs saw their real wages rise by about one quarter (see Glyn, 1992b). The main losers were the 2 million or so workers who lost their jobs and stayed unemployed or found worse-paid jobs in services. The striking feature of this process was that manufacturing output and investment rose hardly more than 1 per cent per year over the decade. The productivity growth was essentially a redistributive phenomenon, which did not provide a sufficient basis for a durable expansion.

Conclusions

The macroeconomic evidence reviewed in this section in no way supports the idea that greater equality leads to worse economic performance. The golden age of the 1950s and 1960s, when growth was at its fastest and economies were generally rather stable, coincided with unprecedentedly low, and generally decreasing inequality. The turn towards inequality in the 1980s did not produce generally improved economic performance. What is more countries with less inequality have tended to grow faster, and with generally no more instability. As repeatedly stressed the relationships are complex and such macroeconomic data can be no more than suggestive. But it is certainly not suggestive of a severely damaging equality/efficiency trade-off.

NOTES AND REFERENCES

Introduction

Andrew Glyn and David Miliband

1 We are grateful to the contributors to this volume, and to James Cornford, John Eatwell, Patricia Hewitt, Bob Sutcliffe, Richard Thomas and Philippe Van Parijs, for helpful comments on preliminary drafts of this chapter.

References

Atkinson, A. (1983) *The Economics of Inequality*, Oxford, Oxford University Press.
Bevins, A. (1992) 'Thatcher attacks all previous Tory governments' in the *Independent*, 4 September.
Blinder, A. (1990) *Paying for Productivity*, Washington, Brookings Institution.
CSJ (Commission on Social Justice) (1993) *The Justice Gap*, London, IPPR.
CSO (Central Statistical Office) (1993a) *Economic Trends* 1993, London, HMSO.
CSO (Central Statistical Office) (1993b) *Social Trends* 1993, London, HMSO.
Department of Employment (1992) *New Earnings Survey*, London, HMSO.
Davis, E., Dilnot, A., Flanders, S., Giles, C., Johnson, P., Ridge, M., Stark, G., Webb, S. and Whitehouse, E. (1992) 'Alternative proposals on tax and social security', *Commentary no.29*, Institute for Fiscal Studies, London.
Dobb, M. (1969) *Welfare Economics and the Economics of Socialism*, Cambridge, Cambridge University Press.
Gamble, A. (1993) *Party Programmes 1992*, unpublished paper.
Gilmour, I. (1992) *Dancing with Dogma*, London, Simon and Schuster.
Harberger, A. (1978) 'On the Use of Distributional Weights in Social Cost-Benefit Analysis', *Journal of Political Economy*, April.
Higgins, B. (1992) 'Equity and Efficiency in Development' in Donald J.

Savoice and Irving Breecher (eds), *Equity and Efficiency in Economic Development*, Intermediate Technology Publications.

Hirshman, A. (1991) *The Rhetoric of Reaction*, Cambridge, MA, Harvard.

Horgan, J. (1993) 'A Kinder War', *Scientific American*, July.

LeGrand, J. (1990) 'Equity versus Efficiency: The Elusive Trade-Of', *Ethics*, Vol.100.

Major, J. (1992a) 'The Threat to the Integrity of Britain', 5 April.

Major, J. (1992b) Election Rally, 7 April.

Marshall, G. and Swift, A. (1993) 'Social Class and Social Justice', in *British Journal of Sociology*, Vol.44, No.2.

Minogue, Kenneth (1989) *The Egalitarian Conceit*, London, Centre for Policy Studies.

Murray, Charles (1984) *Losing Ground: American social policy 1950–1980*, New York, Basic Books.

Murray, Charles (1989) 'Underclass', in *The Sunday Times Magazine*, 26 November.

Okun, A. (1975) *Equality and Efficiency: The Big Trade-Off*, Washington DC, Brookings Institution.

Oppenheim, Carey (1993) *Poverty: The facts*, London, CPAG.

SCPR (Social and Community Planning Research) (1992) *British Social Attitudes: The Cumulative Sourcebook*, Aldershot, Gower.

Sen, A. (1992) *Inequality Reexamined*, Oxford, Oxford University Press.

Snower, D. (1993) 'The future of the welfare state', *Economic Journal*, May.

Swift, A., Marshall, G. and Burgoyne, C. (1992) 'Which road to Social Justice?', *Sociology Review*, November 1992.

Townsend, P. (1979) *Poverty in the UK: A Survey of household resources and living standards*, London, Verso.

Van Parijs, P. (1992) 'The Second Marriage of Justice and Efficiency' in Van Parijs (ed.), *Arguing for Basic Income*, London, Verso.

Walzer, M. (1983) *Spheres of Justice*, New York, Basic Books.

1 Health, Redistribution and Growth

Richard Wilkinson

Atkinson, A.B. (1991) 'What is happening to the distribution of income in the UK?' Welfare State Programme working paper No.87, LSE.

Beale, N. and Nethercott, S. (1988) 'Job-loss and family morbidity: a study of factory closure', *Journal of the Royal College of General Practitioners*, No.35, pp.510–84.

CBI (1987) *Absence from work: a survey of absence and non-attendance*, London.

CSO (1992) *Regional Trends*, 27, HMSO.

Cohen, S., Tyrrell, D.A.J., and Smith, A.P. (1991) 'Psychological stress and susceptibility to the common cold', *New England Journal of Medicine*, 325, pp.606–12.

DOH (1990) *On the state of the public health for the year 1989*, HMSO.

DOH (1991) *On the state of the public health for the year 1990*, HMSO.

DOH (1992) *Health and Personal Social Service Statistics for England*, CSO, HMSO.

DSS (1992) *Households below average income 1979–1988/9*, HMSO.

Field, S. (1990) 'Trends in crime and their interpretation', *Home Office Research and Planning Unit Report*, HMSO.

Goldblatt, P. (1990) 'Mortality and alternative social classifications', in Goldblatt P. (ed.), *Longitudinal study 1971–81*, HMSO pp.163–92 (OPCS series LS, No.6.)

Gorman, T. and Fernandes, C. (1992) 'Reading in Recession', *National Foundation for Educational Research*, Slough.

Henke, D. (1993) 'Chronic sick leave ails Inland Revenue', *Guardian*, 27 May.

Henry, J.P. (1982) 'The relation of social to biological processes in disease', *Social Science and Medicine*, 16, pp.369–80.

House, J.S., Landis, K.R. and Umberson, D. (1988) 'Social relationships and health', *Science*, 241, pp.540–5.

Jenkins, S. (1991) 'Income inequality and living standards: changes in the 1970s and 1980s', *Fiscal Studies*, 12, pp.1–28.

Johnson, J.V. and Hall, E.M. (1988) 'Job strain, workplace social support, and cardiovascular disease', *American Journal of Public Health*, 78, pp.1336–42.

Kamen, L.P. and Seligman, M.E.P. (1987) 'Explanatory style and health', *Current Psychological Research and Reviews* 6(3), pp.207–18.

Lake, M.R. (1991) 'Surveying all the factors', *Language and Learning*, June, Vol.6.

Mackenbach, J.P., Bouvier-Colle, M.H. and Jougla, E. (1990) 'Avoidable mortality and health services: a review of aggregate studies', *J. Epidemiology and Community Health*, 44, pp.106–11.

Marmot, M.G. and Davey Smith, G. (1989) 'Why are the Japanese living longer?' *British Medical Journal*, 299, pp.1547–51.

Marmot, M.G., Shipley, M.J. and Rose, G. (1984) 'Inequalities in death—specific explanations of a general pattern?' *Lancet*, i, pp.1003–6.

Morris, J.N., Blane, D. and White, I. (1994) 'Wasting children: educational attainment, deprivation and mortality', *Journal of Epidemiology and Community Health* (forthcoming).

O'Higgins, M. and Jenkins, S.P. (1990) 'Poverty in the EC' in Teekens, R. and van Praag, B.M.F., *Analysing Poverty in the EC*, Luxemberg, Eurostat.

OPCS (1981) *1981 Census, Economic Activity Tables*, HMSO.

Piachaud, D. (1988) 'Poverty in Britain 1899 to 1983', *Journal of Social*

Policy, 17 (3), pp.335–49.

Pocock, S.J., Shaper, A.G., Cook, D.G., Phillips, A.N. and Walker, M. (1987) 'Social class differences in ischaemic heart disease in British men', *Lancet*, ii, pp.197–201.

Prins, R. and De Graaf, A. (1986) 'Comparisons of sickness absence in Belgian, German and Dutch firms', *British Journal of Industrial Medicine*, 43, pp.529–36.

Rickford, F. (1993) 'Children "dumped" in mental hospitals', *Independent on Sunday*, 4 April.

Ross, C.E. and Huber, J. (1985) 'Hardship and depression', *Journal of Health and Social Behaviour*, 26, pp.312–27.

Short, P. and McCleod, D. (1992) 'A necessary evil', radio broadcast presented by Philip Short and produced by Donald McCleod, BBC Radio 4.

Sterling, P. and Eyer, J. (1981) 'Biological basis of stress-related mortality', *Social science and medicine*, 15E, pp.3–42.

Townsend, P. and Davidson N. (1992) (eds), 'The Black Report' in *Inequalities in Health*, Harmondsworth, Penguin.

Vagero, D. and Lundberg, O. (1989) 'Health inequalities in Britain and Sweden', *Lancet*, ii, pp.35–6.

Whitehead, C. (1992) 'The health divide', *Inequalities in Health*, London, Penguin.

Wilkinson, R.G. (1990) 'Income and mortality: a *natural* experiment', *Sociology of Health and Illness*, 12, pp.391–412.

Wilkinson, R.G. (1986) 'Income and morality' in Wilkinson R.G. (ed.), *Class and Health: research and longitudinal data*, London, Tavistock, pp.88–114.

Wilkinson, R.G. (1989) 'Class mortality differentials, income distribution and trends in poverty 1921–1981', *Journal of Social Policy* 18 (3), pp.307–35.

Wilkinson, R.G. (1992) 'Social class differences in infant mortality', *British Medical Journal*, 305, pp.1227–8.

Wilkinson, R.G. (1992a) 'Income distribution and life expectancy', *British Medical Journal*, 304, pp.165–8.

Young, J. (1992) 'The rise in crime in England and Wales 1979–91', *Centre for Criminology*, Middlesex University.

2 Education: Opportunity, Equality and Efficiency

Tony Edwards and Geoff Whitty

1 The social-democratic middle ground which Joseph wished his Party to abandon had been occupied by Boyle and Crosland. Its neo-liberal replacement is evident in Stuart Sexton, *Our Schools—Future Policy*,

Warlingham, Institute of Economic Affairs Education Unit, 1992.

2 The CBI's even more ambitious target for the year 2000 is that 50 per cent should reach Level Three or its A level equivalent. GCSE is the General Certificate of Secondary Education which replaced the previous division between GCE O level and CSE candidates.

3 The effect of supply on demand is well illustrated in L.J. Paterson, 'The influence of opportunities on aspirations among prospective university entrants from Scottish schools 1970–1988', Statistics in Society (*Journal of the Royal Statistical Society*, Series A), Vol.155, No.1, 1992.

4 The scheme's origins and effects are evaluated in Tony Edwards, John Fitz and Geoff Whitty, *The State and Private Education*, Lewes, Falmer Press, 1989.

5 For an example of travestying the opposing position see Anthony Flew, 'Educational Services: independent competition or maintained monopoly', in David Green (ed.), *Empowering Parents: How to break the Schools' Monopoly*, London, Institute of Economic Affairs, 1991, p.44.

6 For exploration of a similar concept from several political perspectives, see D.G. Green (ed.), *Acceptable Inequalities*, London, Institute of Economic Affairs Health Unit, 1988.

7 International comparisons are reported in Central Statistical Office, *Social Trends*, 23, HMSO 1993, Table 2.2. The very large differences in provision between LEAs are reported in *Department of Education, Statistics of Education: Schools 1991*, DES 1992. The investment value of nursery education is outlined in K. Sylva and P. Moss, *Learning before School*, London, National Commission on Education, Briefing Paper 8, 1992.

8 The extent to which area characteristics reinforce the influence of home background is reported in C. Garner and Raudenbush, 'Neighbourhood effects on educational attainment: a multilevel analysis', *Sociology of Education*, Vol.64, No.4, 1991, pp.251–62.

9 Similar arguments about children's dependence on parents' 'consumer power' are presented in S. Gewirtz, S. Ball and R. Bowe, 'Parents, privilege and the educational marketplace', paper presented at the British Educational Association Annual Conference, 1992 and in the final chapter of G. Whitty, T. Edwards and S. Gewirtz, *Specialisation and Choice in Urban Education*, London, Routledge, 1993.

10 This argument is developed, in opposition to the concept of 'neutral' markets, in Raymond Plant, 'Citizenship and rights', in *Citizenship and Rights in Thatcher's Britain: Two Views*, London, Institute of Economic Affairs, 1990, pp.17–19.

11 For an earlier version of the argument which follows, see Tony Edwards and Geoff Whitty, 'Parental choice and educational reform in Britain and the United States', *British Journal of Educational Studies*, Vol.40, No.2, 1992, pp.101–17. The predictions are justified in greater detail in their

paper on 'Parental choice and educational diversity in England', given at the international conference on 'Theory and Practice in School: Autonomy and Choice', University of Tel-Aviv, June 1993.

12 This seems to be true so far of the first wave of grant-maintained schools; see D. Halpin, S. Power and J. Fitz, 'Grant-maintained schools: making a difference without being different', *British Journal of Educational Studies*, Vol.39, No.4, 1991, pp.409–24. The power of the traditional model of secondary education is explored in Geoff Whitty, Tony Edwards and Sharon Gewirtz, *Specialisation and Choice in Urban Education*, London, Routledge, 1993.

13 For detailed evidence of the effects of choice in Scotland see Michael Adler, J. Petch and A. Tweedie, *Parental Choice and Educational Policy*, Edinburgh, Edinburgh University Press 1989; D. Williams and F. Echols, 'Alert and inert clients: the Scottish experience of parental choice of schools', *Economics of Education Review*, Vol.11, No.4, 1992, pp.339–50.

References

Bates, Inge and Riseborough, George (eds) (1993) *Youth and Inequality*, Milton Keynes, Open University Press.

Brown, P. (1990) 'The "third wave"; education and the ideology of parentocracy', *British Journal of Sociology*, Vol.11, No.1, pp.65–85.

Burnhill, P., Garner, C. and McPherson, A. (1988) 'Social change, school attainment and entry to higher education 1976–1986', in David Raffe (ed.), *Education and the Youth Labour Market*, Lewes, Falmer Press.

Burnhill, P., Garner, C. and McPherson, A. (1990) 'Parental education, social class and entry to higher education', *Journal of the Royal Statistical Society (Series A)*, Vol.153, No.2, pp.233–48.

Commission on Social Justice (1993) *The Justice Gap*, London, Institute for Public Policy Research.

Confederation of British Industries (1991) *World Class Targets*, London.

Cox, C.B. and Boyson, Rhodes (eds) (1975) *The Fight for Education*, London, Dent.

Crosland, Anthony (1974) 'Comprehensive education', speech to the 1966 North of England Education Conference published in *Socialism Now and Other Essays*, London, Cape.

Davies, Lyn (1990) *Equality and Efficiency*, Lewes, Falmer Press.

Department of Education and Science (1992) *Statistical Bulletin 15/92*, table 11.

Department for Education (1993) *Statistical Bulletin 19/93*.

Finegold, David, Keep, Ewart, Miliband, David, Raffe, David, Spours, Ken and Young, Michael (1990) *A British Baccalaureat: Ending the Division between Education and Training*, London, Institute for Public Policy Research.

Finegold, David (1992) *Breaking Out of the Low-Skill Equilibrium*, London, National Commission on Education, Briefing Paper 5.

Gray, John, Jesson, David and Tranmer, Mark (1993) *Boosting post-16 Participation in Full-time Education: a Study of Some Key Factors*, Sheffield, Research Management Branch, Employment Department.

Gray, John, McPherson, Andrew and Raffe, David (1983) *Reconstructions of Secondary Education*, London, Routledge and Kegan Paul.

Gray, John, Jesson, David and Sime N. (1990) 'Estimating differences in the examination performances of secondary schools in six LEAs', *Oxford Review of Education*, Vol.16, pp.137–58.

Green, Andy and Steedman, Hilary (1993) *Educational Provision, Educational Attainment and the Needs of Industry*, London, National Institute of Economic and Social Research.

Halsey, A.H. (1986 and 1987) *Change in British Society (third edition)*, Oxford University Press.

Halsey, A.H., Heath, A. and Ridge, J. (1980) *Origins and Destinations: Family, Class and Education in Modern Britain*, Oxford, Clarendon Press.

Halsey, A.H. (1992) *Opening Wide the Doors of Higher Education*, London, National Commission on Education, Briefing Paper 6.

Heath, A. and Ridge, J. 'Schools, examinations and occupational attainment', in Purvis, J. and Hales, M. (eds), *Achievement and Inequality in Education*, London, Routledge and Kegan Paul.

Hillgate Group (1987) *The Reform of British Education*, London, Claridge Press.

HMSO (1992) *Households Below Average Income: A Statistical Analysis 1979–1989*, London.

Inner London Education Authority (1984) *Improving Secondary Education*, London, ILEA, 2.7.

Joseph, Keith (1976) *Stranded on the Middle Ground*, London, Centre for Policy Studies.

Kogan, Maurice (1971) *The Politics of Education: Conversations with Edward Boyle and Anthony Crosland*, Harmondsworth, Penguin Books.

Labour Party (1980) *Private Schools: A Discussion Document*, London, Labour Party.

Lord, Rodney (1984) *Value for Money in Education*, London, Chartered Institute of Public Finance Accountants.

McPherson, Andrew and Williams, Douglas (1992) 'School history and school effectiveness in Scotland', in Crouch, C. and Heath, A. (eds), *Social Research and Social Reform: Essays in Honour of A.H. Halsey*, Oxford University Press.

Modood, Tariq (1993) 'The number of ethnic minority students in British higher education: some grounds for optimism', *Oxford Review of Education*, Vol.19, No.2, pp.167–82.

Mortimore, Peter, Sammons, P., Stoll, L., Lewis, D. and Ecob, R. (1988) *School Matters: The Junior Years*, London, Open Books.

National Institute for Economic and Social Research (1989) *Productivity, Education and Training*, London, NIESR.

North, J. (ed.) (1987) *The GCSE: An Examination*, London, Claridge Press.

Hear, Anthony (1991) *Education and Democracy*, London, Claridge Press.

Office of Her Majesty's Chief Inspector (1992) Annual Report of the Chief Inspector for Schools.

Pilling, Doria (1990) *Escape from Disadvantage*, Lewes, Falmer Press.

Porter, M. (1990) *The Competitive Advantage of Nations*, London, Macmillan.

Postlethwaite, T.N. and Wiley, D.E. (1991) *Science Achievement in 23 Countries*, Oxford, Pergamon Press.

Prais, Sig and Wagner, K. (1987) 'Educating for productivity: comparisons of Japanese and English schooling and vocational preparation', *National Institute Economic Review*, no.119.

Reynolds, David and Cuttance, Peter (eds) (1992) *School Effectiveness: Research, Policy and Practice*, London, Cassell.

Sexton, Stuart (ed.) (1988) *GCSE: A Critical Analysis*, Warlingham, Institute of Economic Affairs Education Unit.

Smith, David and Tomlinson, Sally (1989) *The School Effect: A Study of Multi-Racial Comprehensives*, London, Policy Studies Institute.

Smithers, Alan and Robinson, Pamela (1991) *Beyond Compulsory Schooling: a Numerical Picture*, London, Council for Industry and Higher Education, executive summary.

Tomlinson, Sally (1991) 'Disadvantaging the disadvantaged: Bangladeshis and education in Tower Hamlets', *British Journal of Sociology of Education*, Vol.13, No.4, pp.437–46.

Wallberg, H.J. (1991) *Assessing National Education Systems*, Chicago, University of Illinois.

Williams, J.D. (1993) *Monitoring School Performance*, Lewes, Falmer Press.

3 Training: Inequality and Inefficiency

Francis Green

1 This statement assumes that any true opportunity costs to the citizens of acquiring the skills are small compared to the benefits.

2 In other words, it cannot be dismissed as down to individual choices.

3 The question referred to training from the current employer—hence the responses will be somewhat influenced by differences in the length of job tenure.

4 The disadvantages facing women have not been aided by the squeeze on the

budgets of TECs in recent years, which have led to the curtailment of courses for women returners (*Financial Times*, 31 March 1993).

5 A further aspect of inequality is noted by Clarke (1991): the disadvantages experienced by Asian and Afro-Caribbean youths in YTS schemes.

6 With full-time employees only, the differences among groups remain, but are less pronounced.

7 These estimates must be qualified in that in the 1987 GHS a large number of respondents who were trainees did not answer the question about non-payment of wages.

References

Booth, Alison (1991) 'Job-Related Formal Training: Who Receives It and What Is It Worth?', *Oxford Bulletin of Economics and Statistics*, 53, No.3 (August), pp.281–94.

CEDEFOP (1987a) *The Role of the Social Partners in Vocational Training and Further Training in the Federal Republic of Germany*, Berlin, CEDEFOP.

CEDEFOP (1987b) *The Role of Union and Management in Vocational Training in France*, Berlin, CEDEFOP.

Clarke, Karen (1991) *Women and Training: A Review of Recent Research and Policy*, Equal Opportunities Commission, Manchester.

Claydon, Tim and Green, Francis (1992) *The Effect of Unions on Training Provision*, Discussion Paper No.92/13, Department of Economics, University of Leicester.

Cockburn, C. (1987) *Two-Track Training: Sex Inequalities and the YTS*, London, Macmillan.

Department of Education and Science (1991) *Education and Training for the 21st Century*, London, HMSO.

Dolton, Peter J., Makepeace, Gerald H. and Treble, John G. (1992a) 'The Wage Effect of YTS: Evidence From YCS', mimeo, August 1992, University of Hull.

Dolton, Peter J., Makepeace, Gerald H. and Treble, John G. (1992) 'The Youth Training Scheme and the School to Work Transition', mimeo, October 1992, University of Hull.

Felstead, Alan and Green, Francis (1993) 'Cycles of Training? Evidence from the British Recession of the Early 1990s', paper presented to Centre for Economic Policy Conference *The Skills Gap and Economic Activity*, London, 19–20 April 1993.

Finegold, David (1993) 'Institutional Incentives and Skill Creation: Preconditions for a High-Skill Equilibrium', in Paul Ryan, ed. *International Comparisons of Vocational Education and Training for Intermediate Skills*, London, Falmer Press.

Finegold, David and Soskice, David (1988) 'The Failure of British Training:

Analysis and Prescription', *Oxford Review of Economic Policy*, 4(3), pp.21–53.

Furlong, Andy (1992) *Growing Up in a Classless Society?*, Edinburgh, Edinburgh University Press.

Green, Francis (1991) 'Sex Discrimination in Job-Related Training', *British Journal of Industrial Relations*, Vol.29, pp.295–304.

Green, Francis (1993) 'The Determinants of Training of Male and Female Employees in Britain', Oxford Bulletin of Economics and Statistics, Vol.55, No.1, February, pp.103–22.

Greenhalgh, Christine and Mavrotas, George (1993) 'Workforce Training in the Thatcher Era—Market Forces and Market Failures', *International Journal of Manpower*, forthcoming.

Greenhalgh, Christine and Stewart, Mark (1987) 'The Effects and Determinants of Training', *Oxford Bulletin of Economics and Statistics*, 49, pp.171–90.

Hawkins, Julia and Steedman, Hilary (1993) 'Mathematics in Vocational Youth Training for the Building Trades in Britain, France and Germany', paper presented to Centre for Economic Policy Conference *The Skills Gap and Economic Activity*, London, 19–20 April 1993.

Hutchinson, Gillian and Church, Andrew (1989), 'Wages, Unions, The Youth Training Scheme and the Young Workers' Scheme', *Scottish Journal of Political Economy*, 36(2), May, pp.160–82.

International Association for The Evaluation Of Educational Achievement (1988) *Science Achievement In Seventeen Countries*, Oxford, Pergamon Press.

Keep, Ewan and Mayhew, Ken (1993) 'UK Training Policy – Assumptions and Reality', paper presented to Centre for Economic Policy Conference *The Skills Gap and Economic Activity*, London, 19–20 April 1993.

Main, Brian G. and Shelly, Michael A. (1990) 'The Effectiveness of the Youth Training Scheme as a Manpower Policy', *Economica*, 57, pp.495–514.

Marsden, David and Ryan, Paul (1991) 'Initial Training, Labour Market Structure and Public Policy: Intermediate Skills in British and German Industry' in Paul Ryan (ed.) *International Comparisons of Vocational Education and Training for Intermediate Skills*, London, Falmer Press.

Mason, Geoff van Ark, Bart, and Wagner, Karin (1993) 'Productivity, Product Quality and Workforce Skills: Food Processing in Four European Countries', paper presented to Centre for Economic Policy Conference *The Skills Gap and Economic Activity*, London, 19–20 April 1993.

O'Higgins, Niall (1992) 'The Effectiveness of YTS in Britain: An Analysis of Sample Selection in the Determination of Employment and Earnings', paper presented at Oxford Economic Papers Conference 'Vocational Training in Britain and Europe post-1992: An Economic Perspective,' 7–8 September 1992.

OECD (1991) 'Enterprise-Related Training' in *OECD Employment Outlook 1991*, Paris, OECD.

Payne, Joan (1991) *Women, Training and the Skills Shortage. The Case for Public Investment*, London, Policy Studies Institute.

Prais, S.T. (1987) 'Educating for productivity: comparisons of Japanese and English schooling and vocational preparation', *National Institute Economic Review*, No.119, February, pp.40–56.

Ray, George F. (1990) 'International labour costs in manufacturing, 1960–88', *National Institute Economic Review*, No.132, May, pp.67–70.

Robitaille, David F. and Garde, Robert A. (eds) (1989) *The IEA Study of Mathematics II: Contexts and Outcomes of School Mathematics*, Oxford, Pergamon Press.

Ryan, Paul (1991) 'Introduction: Comparative Research on Vocational Education and Training' in Paul Ryan (ed.), *International Comparisons of Vocational Education and Training for Intermediate Skills*, London, Falmer Press.

Ryan, Paul (1993) 'Adult learning and work: finance, incentives and certification', in D. Hirsch and D. Wagner (eds), *What Makes Workers Learn?* Philadelphia, Hampton.

Stevens, Margaret (1993) 'Transferable Training and Market Failure', paper presented to Centre for Economic Policy Conference *The Skills Gap and Economic Activity*, London, 19–20 April 1993.

Streeck, Wolfgang (1989) 'Skills and the limits of neo-liberalism; the enterprise of the future as a place of learning', *Work, Employment and Society*, 1, pp.281–308.

Van Ark, Bart (1990a) 'Comparative levels of labour productivity in Dutch and British manufacturing', *National Institute Economic Review*, No.131, February, pp.71–85.

Van Ark, Bart (1990b) 'Manufacturing productivity levels in France and the United Kingdom', *National Institute Economic Review*, No.133, August, pp.62–77.

Whitfield, Keith and Bourlakis, Constantine (1991) 'An Empirical Analysis of YTS, Employment and Earnings', *Journal of Economic Studies*, 18(1), pp.42–56.

4 Crime, Inequality and Efficiency

John Hagan

Allan, Emilie (1985) *Crime and the Labour Market*, PhD dissertation, Pennsylvania State University.

Allan, Emilie and Steffensmeier, Darrell (1989) 'Youth, Underemployment, and Property Crime: Differential Effects of Job Availability and Job

Quality on Juvenile and Young Adult Arrest Rates', *American Sociological Review*, No.54, pp.107–23.

Blau, Judith and Blau, Peter (1982) 'The Cost of Inequality: Metropolitan Structure and Violent Crime', *American Sociological Review*, No.47, pp.114–28.

Bound, John and Freeman, Richard (1992) 'What Went Wrong? The Erosion of Relative Earnings and Employment Among Young Black Men in the 1980s', *Quarterly Journal of Economics*, pp.201–30.

Bureau of Justice Statistics (1985) 'The Prevalence of Imprisonment', US Department of Justice Special Report, Washington DC, US Government Printing Office.

Bursik, Robert and Grasmick, Harold (1993a) *Neighborhoods and Crime*, New York, Lexington Books.

Bursik, Robert and Grasmick, Harold (1993b) 'Economic Deprivation and Neighborhood Crime', *Law and Society Review* 27, forthcoming.

Centerwall, B. (1984) 'Race, Socioeconomic Status and Domestic Homicide, Atlanta, 1971–2', *American Journal of Public Health* 74, pp.813–15.

Chilton, Roland and J. Galvin (1985) 'Race, Crime and Criminal Justice', *Crime and Delinquency* 31, pp.3–14.

Chiricos, T.G. (1987) 'Rates of Crime and Unemployment: An Analysis of Aggregate Research Evidence', *Social Problems*, 34, pp.187–212.

Curry, G. David and Spergel, Irving (1988) 'Gang Homicide, Delinquency and Community', *Criminology*, 26, p.381.

Fagan, Jeffrey (1993) 'Drug Selling and Licit Income in Distressed Neighborhoods: The Economic Lives of Street-Level Drug Users and Dealers', in A. Harrell and G. Peterson (eds), *Drugs, Crime and Social Isolation*, Washington DC, Urban Institute Press.

Field, Simon (1990) 'Trends in Crime and Their Interpretation: A Study of Recorded Crime in Post-War England and Wales', *Home Office Research Study*, No.119, London, HMSO.

Fingerhut, L.A. and Kleinman, J.C. (1990) 'Firearm Mortality Among Children and Youth', Advance data from Vital and Health Statistics, No.178.

Freeman, Richard (1991) 'Crime and the Economic Status of Disadvantaged Young Men', Paper presented to the Conference on Urban Labor Markets and Labor Mobility, Warrenton, Virginia.

Ghodsian, M. and Power C. (1987) 'Alcohol Consumption Between the Ages of 16 and 23 in Britain: A Longitudinal Study', *British Journal of Addiction*, 82, pp.175–80.

Glueck, Sheldon and Glueck, Elenor (1950) *Unravelling Juvenile Delinquency*, Cambridge, MA, Harvard University Press.

Greenberg, David (1979) 'Delinquency and the Age Structure of Society', in S.I. Messinger and E. Bittner (eds), *Criminology Review. Yearbook*, Beverly Hills, CA, Sage.

Grogger, J. (1991) 'The Effect of Arrest on the Employment Outcomes of Young Men', Unpublished manuscript, University of California, Santa Barbara.

Hagan, John (1991a) *The Disreputable Pleasures: Crime and Deviance in Canada*, Toronto, McGraw-Hill Ryerson.

Hagan, John (1991b) 'Destiny and Drift: Subcultural Preferences, Status Attainments and the Risks and Rewards of Youth', *American Sociological Review*, 56, pp.567–82.

Hagan, John (1993) 'The Social Embeddedness in Crime and Unemployment', *Criminology*, forthcoming.

Hagan, John and Alberto Palloni (1990) 'The Social Reproduction of a Criminal Class in Working Class London, Circa 1950–80', *American Journal of Sociology*, 96, pp.265–99.

Hagedorn, John (1988) *People and Folks: Gangs, Crime and the Underclass in a Rustbelt City*, Chicago, Lake View Press.

Ianni, Francis (1972) *A Family Business* New York, Russell Sage.

Ianni, Francis (1974) *Black Mafia*, New York, Simon and Schuster.

Irwin, John (1991) 'The Persecution of Our New Pariah: The Convict', Paper presented at the American Society of Criminology Meetings, San Francisco.

Jencks, C. (1990) *Rethinking Social Policy: Race, Poverty and the Underclass*, Cambridge, MA, Harvard University Press.

Jessor, Richard, Donovan, John and Costa, Frances (1993) *Beyond Adolescence: Problem Behavior and Young Adult Development*, New York, Cambridge University Press.

Kasarda, J.P. (1989) 'Urban Industrial Transition and the Underclass', Annals of the American Academy of Political and Social Science, 501, pp.26–47.

Land, Kenneth, McCall, P. and Cohen, L. (1990) 'Structural Co-variates of Homicide Rates: Are There Any Invariances Across Time and Space?', *American Journal of Sociology*, 95, pp.922–63.

Langan, P. (1991) 'America's Soaring Prison Population', *Science*, 251: 1568–73.

Lowry, P., Hassig, S., Gunn, R. and Mathison, J. 'Homicide Victims in New Orleans: Recent Trends', *American Journal of Epidemiology*, 128, pp.1130–36.

Massey, Douglas (1990) 'American Apartheid: Segregation and the Making of the Underclass', *American Journal of Sociology* 96, pp.329–57.

Matsueda, Ross and Heimer, Karen (1987) 'Race, Family Structure and Delinquency: A Test of Differential Association and Social Control Theories', *American Sociological Review*, 52, pp.826–40.

Messner, Steven (1989) 'Economic Discrimination and Societal Homicide Rates: Further Evidence on the Cost of Inequality', *American Sociological Review*, 54, pp.597–611.

Messner, Steven and Sampson, Robert (1991) 'The Sex Ratio, Family Disruption, and Rates of Violent Crime: The Paradox of Demographic Structure', *Social Forces*, 69(3), pp.693–713.

Messner, Steven and Rosenfeld, Richard (1993) *Crime and the American Dream*, Belmont, CA, Wadsworth.

Moore, Joan (1991) 'Going Down to the Barrio: Homeboys and Homegirls in Change', Philadelphia, Temple University Press.

Munford, R.S., Kazew, R., Feldman, R. and Stivers, R. (1976) 'Homicide Trends in Atlanta', *American Journal of Public Health*, 14, pp.213–21.

National Academy of Sciences (1993) 'Losing Generations: Adolescents in High-Risk Settings', Washington, DC, National Academy Press.

Newcomb, M.D. and Bentler, P.M. (1988) 'Consequences of Adolescent Drug Use: Impact on the Lives of Young Adults', Newbury Park, Sage.

Newton, G.D. and Zimring, F.E. (1969) 'Firearms and Violence in American Life', Washington, DC, US Government Printing Office.

O'Hare, William, Pollard, Kevin, Mann, Taynai and Kent, Mary (1991) 'African Americans in the 1990s', *Population Bulletin*, 46:1.

Padilla, Felix (1992) *The Gang as an American Enterprise*, New Brunswick, New Jersey, Rutgers University Press.

Reiss, Albert and Roth, Jeffrey (eds) (1993) *Understanding and Preventing Violence*, Washington DC, National Academy of Sciences.

Reuter, P., MacCoun, R. and Murphy, P. (1990) *Money from Crime*, Report R–3894, Santa Monica, CA, Rand Corporation.

Revenga, Ana (1992) 'Exporting Jobs? The Impact of Import Competition on Employment and Wages in US Manufacturing', *Quarterly Journal of Economics*, pp.255–82.

Robins, Lee (1966) *Deviant Children Grown Up*, Baltimore, MD, Williams and Wilkins.

Robins, Lee (1987) 'Urban Black Violence: The Effect of Male Joblessness and Family Disruption', *American Journal of Sociology*, 93, pp.348–82.

Sampson, Robert and Byron Groves, W. (1989) 'Community Structure and Crime: Testing Social Disorganization Theory of Crime', *American Journal of Sociology*, 94, p.174.

Sampson, Robert and Laub, John (1990) 'Stability and Change in Crime and Deviance Over the Life Course: The Salience of Adult Social Bonds', *American Sociological Review*, 55, pp.609–27.

Sampson, Robert and Laub, John (1993) *Crime in the Making*, Cambridge, MA, Harvard University Press.

Sampson, Robert and Wilson, William (1993) 'Toward a Theory of Race, Crime and Urban Inequality', in John Hagan and Ruth Peterson (eds), *Crime and Inequality*, Stanford, CA, Stanford University Press.

Sanchez-Jankowski, Martin (1992) *Islands in the Stream*, Los Angeles, University of California Press.

Schwartz, Richard and Skolnick, Jerome (1964) 'Two Studies of Legal

Stigma', in Howard Becker (ed.), *The Other Side: Perspectives on Deviance*, New York, Free Press.

Simpson, Sally (1991) 'Caste, Class, and Violent Crime: Explaining Difference in Female Offending', *Criminology*, 291, pp.15–35.

Skogan, Wesley (1990) *Disorder and Decline: Crime and the Spiral of Decay in American Neighborhoods*, New York, Free Press.

Skogan, Wesley and Maxfield, M.G. (1981) *Coping With Crime: Individual and Neighborhood Reactions*, Beverly Hills, California, Sage.

Sullivan, Mercer (1989) *Getting Paid: Youth Crime and Work in the Inner City*, Ithaca, New York, Cornell University Press.

Taylor, Ralph and Covington, J. (1988) 'Neighborhood Changes in Ecology and Violence', *Criminology* 26, p.553.

Wacquant, L.D. and Wilson, W.J. (1989) 'The Costs of Racial and Class Exclusion in the Inner City', *Annals of the American Academy of Political and Social Science*, 501, pp.8–25.

Ward, David and Title, Charles (1993) 'Deterrence or Labelling: The Effects of Informal Sanctions', *Deviant Behavior*, 14, pp.43–64.

Williams, Terry (1989) *The Cocaine Kids*, New York, Addison-Wesley.

Willis, Paul (1977) *Learning to Labour*, London, Gower.

Wilson, William J. (1987) *The Truly Disadvantaged: The Inner City, the Underclass and Public Policy*, Chicago, University of Chicago Press.

Wilson, William J. (1991) 'Studying Inner-City Social Dislocations: The Challenge of Public Agenda Research.' *American Sociological Review*, 56, pp.1–14.

5 Low Pay, High Pay and Labour Market Efficiency

Paul Gregg, Stephen Machin and Alan Manning

1 There is also more recent literature on this: UK examples showing that profitable/productive employers pay more are Carruth and Oswald's (1989) aggregate study, Nickell and Wadhwani's (1990) firm-level study and Blanchflower et al.'s (1991) establishment-level analysis.

2 One can draw an interesting parallel with the (now outlawed) pre-entry closed shop arrangements that some (predominantly craft) trade unions were able to operate in the past.

3 The results suggested that a 10 per cent rise in shareholder returns (which is very big, of the order of £100 million for a company valued at £1,000 million) predicted a rise in compensation of a mere £227. This is in line with the US work which also finds very small effects (e.g. Jensen and Murphy, 1990).

References

Becker, Gary (1957) *Human Capital*, New York, Basic Books.

Blanchflower, David, Andrew Oswald and Anthony Garrett (1991) 'Insider power in wage determination', *Economica*, Vol.57, pp.143–70.

Brown, Charles, C.Gilroy and A.Kohen (1982) 'The effect of the minimum wage on employment and unemployment', *Journal of Economic Literature*, Vol.20, pp.487–528.

Card, David (1992a) 'Using regional variation in wages to measure the effects of the federal minimum wage', *Industrial and Labor Relations Review*, Vol.46, pp.22–37.

Card, David (1992b) 'Do minimum wages reduce employment? a case study of California, 1987–89', *Industrial and Labor Relations Review*, Vol.46, pp.38–54.

Card, David and Alan Krueger (1993) 'Minimum wages and employment: a case study of the fast food industry in New Jersey and Pennsylvania', *Princeton University Industrial Relations Section Discussion Paper No.315*, Princeton.

Card, David, Lawrence Katz and Alan Krueger (1993) Comment on David Neumark and William Wascher, 'Employment effects of minimum and subminimum wages: Panel data on state minimum wage laws', *Princeton University Industrial Relations Section Discussion paper No.316*, Princeton.

Carruth, Alan and Andrew Oswald (1989) *Pay Determination and Industrial Prosperity*, Oxford, University of Oxford Press.

Conyon, Martin (1993) 'Corporate governance in UK companies between 1988 and 1993', University of Oxford mimeo.

Conyon, Martin and Paul Gregg (1993) 'Pay at the top: a study of the sensitivity of chief executive remuneration to company specific shocks', NIESR mimeo.

Dickens, Richard, Stephen Machin and Alan Manning (1993) 'The Employment Effects of the Wages Councils', LSE mimeo.

Dickens, Richard, Paul Gregg, Stephen Machin, Alan Manning, and Jonathan Wadsworth (1993) 'Wages Councils: is there a case for abolition?', Paper prepared for conference on abolition of Wages Councils, January 1993, forthcoming *British Journal of Industrial Relations*.

Geroski, Paul and Paul Gregg (1993) 'Coping with the recession', NIESR mimeo.

Gibbons, Robert and Kevin Murphy (1992) 'Optimal incentive contracts in the presence of career concerns: theory and evidence', *Journal of Political Economy*, Vol.100, pp.468–505.

Gregg, Paul, Stephen Machin and Stefan Szymanski (1993) 'The disappearing relationship between directors' pay and corporate performance', *British Journal of Industrial Relations*, Vol.31, pp.1–10.

Jensen, Michael and Kevin Murphy (1990) 'Performance pay and top management incentives', *Journal of Political Economy*, Vol.98, pp.225–64.

Katz, Lawrence and Alan Krueger (1992) 'The effect of the minimum wage on the fast-food industry', *Industrial and Labor Relations Review*, Vol.46, pp.6–21.

Krueger, Alan and Lawrence Summers (1988) 'Efficiency wages and the inter-industry wage structure', *Econometrica*, Vol.56, pp.259–94.

Machin, Stephen and Alan Manning (1992) 'Minimum wages, wage dispersion, and employment: evidence from the UK Wages Councils', LSE Centre for Economic Performance Discussion Paper No.80, forthcoming *Industrial and Labor Relations Review*.

Machin, Stephen, Alan Manning, and Stephen Woodland (1993) 'Are workers paid their marginal product: evidence from a low-wage labour market', University College London Discussion Paper, No.93–09.

Main, Brian (1992) 'Top executive pay and company performance', University of Edinburgh mimeo.

Manning, Alan (1992) 'The Equal Pay Act as an experiment to test theories of the labour market', mimeo.

Mackay and Reid (1970) *Oxford Bulletin of Economics and Statistics*.

Mincer, Jacob (1974) *Schooling, Experience and Earnings*, New York.

Nickell, Stephen and Sushil Wadhwani (1990) 'Insider forces and wage determination', *Economic Journal*, No.100, pp.496–509.

Slichter, Sumner (1950) 'Notes on the structure of wages', *Review of Economics and Statistics*, No.32, pp.80–91.

6 Unemployment, Inequality and Inefficiency

6.1 The Rise in Economic Inactivity

John Schmitt and Jonathan Wadsworth

1 Thanks to Paul Gregg and the editors of this volume for several useful comments. LFS and GHS data made available by the ESRC Data Archive at Essex. The CEP is ESRC financed.

2 The population of working age is 18 million for men and 16.5 million for women.

3 Since the employment-population ratio, E/P, is the difference between the activity rate, L/P, where L is the labour force, and the unemployment-population ratio, U/P, then

$$E/P = (L/P) - (U/P) \qquad (1)$$

4 Using this relationship we can assess the relative importance of changes in the inactivity rate and unemployment in explaining the rise in joblessness.

5 The term 'intermediate' here captures the entire range of qualifications

below degree level.
6 For example given a male inactivity rate of 10.2 per cent in 1991, 52.8 per cent of whom were long-term sick, then this implies 5.4 per cent of the total population were sick. Comparing this figure with the equivalent for 1979 determines the proportions given in columns 4 and 8.
7 In addition, some 42,000 men were receiving the Lone Parent premium by 1991.
8 These numbers partly reflect the LFS definition of actively seeking work on which this study is based. If the numbers were calculated on the ILO/OECD definition of unemployment, which requires respondents to have sought work in the past 4 weeks (and not 1 week as in the LFS), then the numbers in column 4 would fall by around 20 to 25 per cent.
9 Long-term sickness benefit is not means tested, unlike Income Support, (IS), and currently pays around £30 a week more than the standard rate of IS, though the individual is then subject to claw back on Housing Benefit.
10 The change in the Standard Industrial Classification in 1981 precludes analysis of the employment structure prior to that date.
11 The KOS occupational coding on which the occupation categories are based classifies all manual manufacturing jobs as either skilled or semiskilled. Unskilled jobs are therefore either in construction or transportation.
12 The relevant ratios for graduates are 1.68 in 1977 and 2 in 1991 with differentials of 1.20 in 1977 and 1.24 in 1991 for intermediates.
13 Figure 6.1.2 takes no account of differences in experience or other characteristics of workers that could explain some of the differential. Schmitt (1993) shows that the adjusted earnings gap between graduates and the unqualified, grew by 7 percentage points between 1978 and 1988. For 16–30 year olds, the gap grew by 22 points.
14 The 1992 Labour Force Survey indicates that 32 per cent of new jobs filled by men were of a temporary nature and 11 per cent were part time.

References

Disney, Richard and Webb, Steven (1991) 'Why are there so many Long-Term Sick in Britain?', *Economic Journal*, Vol.101, March, pp.252–62.
Gregg, Paul and Machin, Stephen (1993) 'Is the Rise in UK Income Inequality Different?', in R. Barrell (ed.), *Is the British Labour Market Different?*, Cambridge University Press.
Juhn, Chinui, Murphy, Kevin and Topel, Robert (1991) 'Why has the Natural Rate of Unemployment Increased over Time?', *Brookings Papers on Economic Activity*, No.2, pp.75–142.
OECD (1992) 'Monitoring Labour Market Developments', *Employment Outlook*, June 1992.
Schmitt, John (1993) 'The Changing Structure of Male Earnings in Britain',

in Richard Freeman and Lawrence Katz (eds), *Changes and Differences in Wage Structures*, University of Chicago Press.

Schmitt, John and Wadsworth, Jonathan (1993) 'Job Search Activity and Changing Unemployment Benefit Entitlement: Pseudo-Panel Estimates for Britain', Centre for Economic Performance Discussion Paper, No.333.

Social Security Statistics (1992) Department of Social Security, HMSO, London.

White, Michael and Lakey, Jane (1992) *The Restart Effect*, Policy Studies Institute, London.

6.2 The Incidence and Cost of Unemployment

John Philpott

Brown, Colin (1990) 'Racial Inequality in the British Labour Market', Employment Institute, *Economic Report*, Vol.5, No.4, June 1990.

Daniel, W.W. (1990) *The Unemployed Flow*, Policy Studies Institute.

Dex, Shirley (1989) 'Women and Unemployment', Employment Institute, *Economic Report*, Vol.4, No.5, May 1989.

Erens, Bob and Hedges, B. (1990) *Survey of Incomes In and Out of Work*, HMSO.

Erens, Bob and Ghate, Deborah (1992) *New Clients: A Survey of New Clients to the Employment Service and their Response to the New Client Adviser Interview*, Social and Community Planning Research.

Giles, C. and Webb, Steven (1993) 'A Guide to Poverty Statistics', *Fiscal Studies*, Vol.14, No.2, May.

Layard, R., Nickell, S. and Jackman, R. (1991) *Unemployment: Macroeconomic Performance and the Labour Market*, Oxford University Press.

Layard, R. and Philpott, J. (1991) *Stopping Unemployment*, Employment Institute.

McCormick, Barry (1991) *Unemployment Structure and the Unemployment Puzzle*, Employment Institute.

Meadows, Pamela, Cooper, H. and Bartholomew, Richard (1988) *The London Labour Market*, Employment Department.

Meager, Nigel and Metcalf, Hilary (1987) *Recruitment of the Long-Term Unemployed*, Institute of Manpower Studies.

Piachaud, David (1991) 'Unemployment and Poverty', Campaign for Work, *Research Report*, Vol.3, No.3.

Platt, Steve and Kreitman, Neil (1984) 'Trends in Parasuicide and Unemployment among Men in Edinburgh 1962–82', *British Medical Journal*, 289.

Rowthorn, R. and Ward, T. (1979) 'How to Run a Company and Run Down an Economy: The Effects of Closing Down Steel Making in Corby',

Cambridge Journal of Economics, Vol.3, No.4.

Taylor, Philip (1991) 'Unemployent and Health', Campaign for Work, *Research Report*, Vol.3, No.6.

Trinder, Chris (1991) 'Older Workers and the Recession', Employment Institute *Economic Report*, Vol.6, No.2, May 1991.

Unemployment Unit (1992) *Working Brief*, October.

Wells, William (1992) 'Does the Structure of Employment Legislation Affect the Structure of Employment and Unemployment?', Paper Presented to Employment Department's European Labour Market Conference, 18–20 November.

6.3 Employment, Unemployment and Social Security

Eithne McLaughlin

1 Definitions of 'basic needs' (what they are and what level constitutes 'basic') may be indirectly and historically influenced by social security benefit levels, just as they may be influenced by the general standards of living current in one's community, or indeed nationwide standards, information on which is easily acquired through television, newspapers, etc. While further research is needed to understand how people arrive at their definitions of what constitute 'basic needs', it is clear that whatever influence social security benefit levels have, it is not of the type presumed by neoclassical labour supply theory.

References

Alcock, Pete (1987) *Poverty and State Support*, Harlow, Longman.

Atkinson, Tony (1981) 'Unemployment benefits and incentives' in J. Creedy (ed.), *The Economics of Unemployment in Great Britain*, London, Butterworth.

Atkinson, Tony, Gomulka, J. and Micklewright, John (1984) 'Unemployment benefit, duration and incentives in Britain: how robust is the evidence?' *Journal of Public Economics*, Vol.23, No.3, pp.3–26.

Atkinson, Tony and Micklewright, John (1988) *Turning the screw: benefits for the unemployed 1979–1988*, Discussion Paper TIDI/121, Suntory-Toyota International Centre for Economics and Related Disciplines.

Atkinson, John (1985) 'Flexibility and the Workforce', *Work and Society*, Vol.9, pp.2–4.

Baldwin, Sally and Cooke, K. (1982) *How Much is Enough? a review of supplementary benefit scale rates*, London, Family Policy Studies Centre.

Beenstock, M. and associates (1987) *Work, Welfare and Taxation*, London, Allen and Unwin.

Bradshaw, Jonathan (1985) 'Social Security Policy and Assumptions about Paid Work' in Rudolph Klein and Michael O'Higgins (eds), *The Future of Welfare*, Oxford, Blackwell.

Bradshaw, Jonathan and Deacon, Alan (1983) *Reserved for the Poor*, Oxford, Martin Robertson.

Brown, Joan (1990) *Victims or Villains? Social security benefits in unemployment*, York, Joseph Rowntree Foundation.

Dawes, Len (1992) 'Long-term Unemployment and Labour Market Flexibility', Unpublished report, The Employment Service, Sheffield.

Dept. of Social Security (1992) *Tax/Benefit Model Tables*, London, HMSO.

Dex, Shirley (1985) *The Sexual Division of Work*, Brighton, Harvester Wheatsheaf.

Dilnot, Andrew (1992) 'Social Security and the Labour Market' in Eithne McLaughlin (ed.), *Understanding Unemployment: new perspectives on active labour market policies*, London, Routledge.

Ditch, John (1987) 'The undeserving poor: unemployed people then and now', in Martin Loney, et al. (eds), *The State or the Market*, Milton Keynes, Open University Press.

Fryer, David (1992) 'Psychological or Material Deprivation?' in Eithne McLaughlin (ed.) *Understanding Unemployment: new perspectives on active labour market policies*, London, Routledge.

Hakim, Catherine (1989) 'Employment Rights: a comparison of part-time and full-time employees', *Industrial Law Journal*, Vol.18, no.2.

Heady, Patrick and Smyth, Martyn (1989) *Living Standards during Unemployment*, London, HMSO.

Jenkins, Stephen and Millar, Jane (1989) 'Income Risk and Income Maintenance: implications for incentives to work' in Andrew Dilnot and Ian Walker (eds), *The Economics of Social Security*, Oxford, Oxford University Press.

Jordan, Bill, James, Simon, Kay, Helen and Redley, Marcus (1992) *Trapped in Poverty? Labour-market decisions in low-income households*, London, Routledge.

IFF Research Ltd/Department of Employment (1992) *The London Labour Market*, London, Department of Employment.

Leather, Suzi (1992) *Your Food: whose choice?*, London, National Consumer Council.

Lister, Ruth (1992) *Women's Economic Dependency*, Manchester, Equal Opportunities Commission.

McLaughlin, Eithne, Millar, Jane and Cooke, Kenneth (1989) *Work and Welfare Benefits*, Aldershot, Avebury.

Metcalf, Hilary (1992) 'Hidden Unemployment and the Labour Market' in Eithne McLaughlin (ed.), *Understanding Unemployment: new perspectives on active labour market policies*, London, Routledge.

Millar, Jane, Cooke, Kenneth and McLaughlin, Eithne (1989) 'The Employment Lottery: Risk and social security benefits', *Policy and Politics*, Vol.17, No.1, pp.75–81.

Moylan, Sue, Millar, Jane and Davies, Robert (1984,) *For Richer, for Poorer: DHSS cohort study of the unemployed*, London, HMSO.

Murray, Charles (1989) 'Underclass' in the *Sunday Times Magazine*, 26 November.

National Childrens Home, *Poverty and Nutrition*, London, NCH.

Narendranathan, William et al. (1979) 'Determinants of the length of male unemployment spells: results from the DHSS cohort study of unemployed men', London School of Economics, Working Paper, No.500.

Novak, Tony (1988) *Poverty and the State*, Milton Keynes, Open University Press.

Pahl, Ray (1984) *Divisions of Labour*, Oxford, Oxford University Press.

Pissarides, Chris and Wadsworth, Jonathan (1992) 'Unemployment Risks' in Eithne McLaughlin (ed.), *Understanding Unemployment: new perspectives on active labour market policies*, London, Routledge.

Ritchie, Jane and Faulkner, Alison (1989) *Voluntary Unemployment— benefit sanctions*.

Smith, Lesley with McLaughlin, Eithne (1989) *Labour Market flexibility among the long-term unemployed*, Sheffield, Employment Service.

Stone, Deborah (1985) *The Disabled State*, London, Macmillan.

Thane, Pat (1978) 'Women and the Poor Law in Victorian and Edwardian England', *History Workshop*, Vol.6, pp.29–51.

7 Taxes and Benefits, Equality and Efficiency

Paul Johnson

1 It will, of course, not be possible to describe the whole tax and benefit system in any detail. For more information on the benefit system see, for example, Dilnot and Walker (1989), Barr (1992), Dilnot and Webb (1988). On the tax system, see Kay and King (1992), Hills (1988).

2 In 1993, the floor was £56 per week and the ceiling £420 pw.

3 Original income is just income from earnings and investments. Gross income is this plus social security benefits. Disposable income measures gross income less direct taxes whilst post-tax income also takes off indirect taxes.

4 Except in the case of mortgage insurance whereby it is possible to buy insurance to cover the cost of your mortgage if you become unemployed.

5 This does not take account of such costs as for child care or travel to work which may be necessary expenditures if a job is taken, and may make an important difference to the ratio of disposable incomes in and out of work.

6 Because one partner working 16 hours per week disqualifies both from IS it

238

is clearly not useful to compare those on UB with those on IS. Those not on UB would generally be entitled to IS if neither partner were working.
7 In fact the UK has no 'universal' benefits that go to every citizen.
8 In fact as a proportion of GDP taxes as a whole have not fallen since 1979 and are predicted to rise (HM Treasury, 1993).
9 The difference between the first two and the third relates to the way in which the measures were constructed. The first two are really measures of the structure of the tax system while the third is strongly influenced by the amount of tax raised.

References

Atkinson, A. (1987) 'Income maintenance and social insurance' in Auerbach, A. and Feldstein, M. (eds), *Handbook of Public Economics*, North-Holland.

Atkinson, A. and Micklewright, J. (1989) 'Turning the screw: benefits for the unemployed 1979-88', in Dilnot, A. and Walker, I. (eds), *The economics of social security*, Oxford University Press.

Atkinson, A. and Micklewright, J. (1991) 'Unemployment compensation and labor market transitions: a critical review', *Journal of Economic Literature*, Vol.29, No.4, pp.1679-727.

Baker, P. (1992) 'Value added taxation', in Davis, E. (ed.), *Tax reform for the fourth term*, Commentary no. 32, Institute for Fiscal Studies, London.

Barr, N. (1992) 'Economic theory and the welfare state: a survey and interpretation', *Journal of Economic Literature*, Vol.30, No.2, pp.741-803.

Blundell, R., et al. (1989) 'Labour supply specification and the evaluation of tax reforms' in *Journal of Public Economies*.

Break, G. (1957) 'Income taxes and incentives to work: an empirical study', *American Economic Review*.

Brown, C. (1988) 'Will the 1988 income tax cuts either increase work incentives or raise more revenue?', *Fiscal Studies*, Vol.9, No.4, pp.93-107.

Brown, C. and Sandford, C. (1990) 'Taxes and incentives. The effects of the 1988 cuts in the higher rates of income tax', Economic Study no.7, Institute for Public Policy Research, London.

Central Statistical Office (1993) 'The effects of taxes and benefits on household income, 1990', *Economic Trends*, no.471, HMSO, London.

Creedy, J. and Disney, R. (1985) *Social insurance in transition*, Clarendon Press, Oxford.

Davies, G., Davis, E., Dilnot, A., Walton, D. and Whitehouse, E. (1993) 'Tax options for 1993: the green budget', *Commentary no.33*, Institute for Fiscal Studies, London.

Davis, E., Dilnot, A., Flanders, S., Giles, C., Johnson, P., Ridge, M.,Stark, G., Webb, S. and Whitehouse, E. (1992) 'Alternative proposals on tax and social security', *Commentary no.29*, Institute for Fiscal Studies, London.

Department of Social Security (1992) 'Households below average income, a statistical analysis 1979-1988/89', HMSO, London.

Department of Social Security (1993) 'Departmental report. The government's expenditure plans 1993-94 to 1995-96', HMSO, London.

Dilnot, A. and Duncan, A. (1992) 'Lone mothers, family credit and paid work', *Fiscal Studies*, Vol.13, No.1, pp.1-21.

Dilnot, A., Kay, J. and Morris, N. (1984) *The reform of social security*, Clarendon Press, Oxford.

Dilnot, A. and Kell, M. (1987) 'Male unemployment and women's work', *Fiscal Studies*, Vol.8, No.3, pp.1-16.

Dilnot, A. and Walker, I. (1989) *The economics of social security*, Oxford University Press.

Dilnot, A. and Webb, S. (1988) 'The 1988 social security reforms', *Fiscal Studies*, Vol.9, No.3, pp.26-53.

Fiegehen, F. and Reddaway, W. (1981) *Companies, incentives and senior managers*, Oxford University Press.

Fields, D. and Stanbury, W. (1971) 'Income taxes and incentives to work: some additional empirical evidence', *American Economic Review*.

Giles, C. and Webb, S. (1993) 'A guide to poverty statistics', *Fiscal Studies*, Vol.14, No.2. pp.74-97.

Hemming, R. and Kay, J. (1980) 'The Laffer curve', *Fiscal Studies*, Vol.1, No.2, pp.83-90.

Hills, J. (1988) *Changing tax: How the tax system works and how to change it*, Child Poverty Action Group, London.

HM Treasury (1993) 'Financial statement and budget report 1993-94', HMSO, London.

Jenkins, S. (1991) 'Income inequality and living standards: changes in the 1970s and 1980s', *Fiscal Studies*, Vol.12, No.1, pp.1-28.

Johnson, P., McKay, S. and Smith, S. (1990) 'The distributional consequences of environmental taxes', Commentary no. 23, *Institute for Fiscal Studies*, London.

Johnson, P. and Webb, S. (1993) 'Explaining the growth in UK income inequality: 1979-1988', *Economic Journal*, Vol.103, No.417, pp.429-35.

Kay, J. and King, K. (1992) *The British tax system*, Oxford University Press.

Kell, M. and Wright, J. (1990) 'Benefits and the labour supply of women married to unemployed men', *Economic Journal*, 100 (supplement), pp.119-26.

Lancaster, T. and Nickell, S. (1980) 'The analysis of re-employment probabilities for the unemployed', *Journal of the Royal Statistical Society*, Part 2, Vol.143, pp.141-52.

Lindsey, L. (1987) 'Individual taxpayer response to tax cuts: 1982-1984', *Journal of Public Economics*, Vol.33, pp.173-206.

Minford, P. (1988) 'Outlook after the budget', *Fiscal Studies*, Vol.9, No.2, pp.30–7.

Narendranathan, W., Nickell, S. and Stern, J. (1985) 'Unemployment benefits revisited', *Economic Journal*, 378, pp.307–29.

OECD (1990) 'The personal income tax base: a comparative survey', OECD, Paris.

Walker, I. (1990) 'The effects of income support measures on the labour market behaviour of lone mothers', *Fiscal Studies*, Vol.11, No.2, pp.55–75.

8 Inheritance: Symbols and Illusions

Paul Ryan

1 I would like to thank the editors, other contributors, and Cedric Sandford, David Good, Alan Hughes, Geoff Meeks, Derek Morris and S.J. Prais for advice, assistance or comments on preliminary versions of this chapter.

2 Details of Budget speeches are taken from verbatim reports in the Financial Times (13 June 1979 to 17 March 1993).

3 Evidence suggesting a significant heritability of IQ-type abilities is reviewed by Polachek and Siebert (1993, pp.52–9).

4 Much of the evidence is dated but the main contours are unlikely to have altered since it was collected.

5 Recent US studies estimate the share at up to 80 per cent (Kotlikoff, 1988). Note that not all wealth is destined to be inherited: some is dissaved during retirement (see below).

6 In his first Prime Minister's Question Time (*Financial Times*, 30 November 1990).

7 Under Estate Duty the exemption period for gifts before death had been increased markedly, from one year in 1894 to seven years by 1968 (Sandford, 1983).

8 Although the Chancellor predicted revenue declines of £15 million and £25 million in 1974–75 and 1975–76 respectively (Hansard 1974, 277), tax receipts actually declined by £154 million and £76 million (at 1974–5 prices) in those years.

9 Assuming that property passes smoothly between generations on average once every thirty years. See also Atkinson (1974, chapter 7).

10 In the 1960s and 1970s the discretionary trust apparently led the field, relying on the further principle that when the interest of the beneficiaries remains indeterminate (within a determinate set of potential beneficiaries), the benefits which they actually secure do not constitute part of their taxable estates. The tax advantages of discretionary trusts had been

threatened by CTT. The 1975 Finance Act taxed the ending or transfer of any interest in trust and imposed a periodic (ten-yearly) charge on trust assets. These provisions had however been neutered at least temporarily by allowing a reduced rate of tax on disposals and delaying until 1980 (in the event 1983) the imposition of both the disposals tax and the periodic charge (HMT 1976).

11 The early stages of the saga were discussed by Sutherland (1981) and Sandford (1983).

12 The 1991 proposals to bring the tax treatment of trusts closer to that of individuals were subsequently quietly abandoned (*Financial Times*, 19 March 1993).

13 'CTT—bark but not bite—if you draw its teeth' and 'Queen could face king-sized life insurance policy', *Financial Times*, 3 September 1983 and 27 November 1992.

14 Equity also cropped up indirectly in references to the family home. The over-indexation of tax thresholds was justified in both 1987 and 1988 as helping many more people 'to inherit the family home free of tax' (1988), though the equity status of a benefit slanted to the offspring of middle-class wealth holders was not explained.

15 The main exception involved the concern, expressed by Smith and Ricardo, that tax proceeds would be used for current rather than capital expenditure, thereby lowering investment.

16 The modern argument which claims greater representativeness for the House of Lords than for the Commons, on the grounds that heredity is a more random selection criterion than is ambition, implicitly agrees with Keynes, while avoiding his concern with ability.

17 Unquoted companies are debarred from issuing shares to the public and, as such, are exempt from the financial disclosure regulations governing companies whose shares are quoted on the Stock Exchange (Hay and Morris 1984). Some of the attributes of unquoted companies are shared by family-controlled quoted ones (Cosh and Hughes 1989; SBRC 1992).

18 The many family owners and managers of the 168 year old C. and J. Clark shoe company have recently fought bitterly and long over its business strategy and independent status ('A squall over Street', *Financial Times*, 17 April 1993).

19 Boswell's work was however largely non-quantitative and his results potentially biased by the tendency for successful family firms to outgrow his size category.

20 Bracewell-Milnes' criticism of inheritance taxation as 'a particularly destructive tax' (1989 p.47) arises from the attributes of a tax which displaces gifts rather than consumption. Such a tax goes beyond simply redistributing welfare from the taxed to those on whom the proceeds are spent, which all redistributive taxes do, with normally second-order efficiency losses. It also destroys without equivalent gain elsewhere the

altruistic utility which the donor would have derived from making the gift. The validity of the argument requires however not only the predominance of the bequest motive but also that (i) giving be motivated by altruism rather than guilt, as otherwise the satisfaction derived from giving falls well short of that of consumption; (ii) the individual, not the household or family, be the appropriate unit for welfare assessment, as otherwise within-unit gifts which do not reduce its consumption will predominate. The argument also implies that reciprocal gifts can increase joint welfare without any increase in joint consumption, a possibility favoured by religious precept but rarely seen in practice. Finally, this criticism of inheritance taxes ignores public good problems. Were individuals willing to give more to the poor only were others to do the same, the taxation without which such an outcome could not be achieved would raise efficiency.

21 Interest in the bequest motive was stimulated initially by its implications for the 'Ricardian equivalence' proposition that the effects on economic activity of debt- and tax-financed public expenditure are the same (Abel, 1987); more recently, by interest in aggregate US savings behaviour. This discussion draws on contrasting surveys of the latter issue (Modigliani, 1988; Kotlikoff, 1988).

22 An observed tendency for retired parents' wealth to be positively associated with visiting by their children, but only when they have two or more children, is interpreted as evidence that parents use the prospect of inheritance to elicit services from their children, with the implicit threat to disinherit for nonperformance being least credible when there is only one child (Bernheim, Shleifer and Summers 1985).

23 Even proponents of an untrammelled right to bequeath are often reluctant to argue the case in detail. Nozick, in his justification of the right to transfer one's property as one sees fit, unobtrusively includes therein a right to bequeath, to the recognised detriment of equality of opportunity, without discussing the unappealing implications of allowing property rights to survive death intact. This lacuna is part of Nozick's wider neglect of how injustice in past acquisitions of 'holdings' is to be rectified (1974, pp.176, 235–8 esp.).

References

Abel, A.B. (1987) 'Ricadian equivalence theorem', in Eatwell, J., Milgate M. and Newman P. (eds), *The New Palgrave*, London, Macmillan.

Atkinson, A.B. (1974) *Unequal Shares: Wealth in Britain*, Harmondsworth, Penguin.

Atkinson, A.B. and Harrison A.J. (1978) *Distribution of Personal Wealth in Britain*, Cambridge, Cambridge University Press.

Bernheim, B.D., Shleiffer A. and Summers L.H. (1985) 'The strategic bequest motive', *Journal of Political Economy*, December, 93,6; 1045–76.

Bolton Committee of Inquiry on Small Firms (1971), *Report*, Cmnd 4811, London, HMSO.

Boswell, J. (1973) *The Rise and Decline of Small Firms*, London, George Allen and Unwin.

Bracewell-Milnes, B. (1989) *The Wealth of Giving*, Research Monograph 43, Institute for Economic Affairs, London.

Chandler, A.D. (1990) *Scale and Scope: the Dynamics of Industrial Capitalism*, Cambridge, MA, MIT.

Church, R. (1977) 'Family and failure: Archibald Kenrick and Sons Ltd 1900–50' in Supple B. (ed.), *Essays in British Business History*, Oxford, Oxford University Press.

Cosh, A. and Hughes A. (1989) *Ownership, management incentives and company performance. An empirical analysis for the UK, 1968–80, Discussion Paper*, School of Economics, LaTrobe University, Australia.

CSO (1992) Central Statistical Office, *Economic Trends Annual Supplement 1992*, London, HMSO.

Deaton, A. (1992) *Understanding Consumption*, Oxford, Oxford University Press.

Diamond Commission (1977) Royal Commission on the Distribution of Income and Wealth, *Third Report on the Standing Reference*, Report No.5, London, HMSO.

Erikson, R. and Goldthorpe J. (1992) *The Constant Flux: a Study of Class Mobility in Industrial Societies*, Oxford, Oxford University Press.

Finegold, D. and Soskice D. (1988) 'The failure of training in Britain: analysis and prescription', *Oxford Review of Economic Policy*, 4,3; pp.21–53.

Goldthorpe, J. and Payne, C. (1986) 'Trends in intergenerational class mobility in England and Wales, 1972–83' *Sociology*, February; 20,1; pp.1–24.

Goody, J. (1987) 'Inheritance' in Eatwell, J., Milgate, M. and Newman P. (eds), *The New Palgrave*, London, Macmillan.

Hannah, L. (1983) *The Rise of Corporate Economy*, 2nd edn, London, Methuen.

Hansard (1974) *Parliamentary Debates: House of Commons*, 5th Series, Vol.881, London, HMSO.

Harbury, C.D. and Hitchens D.M.W.N. (1979) *Inheritance and Wealth Inequality in Britain*, London, George Allen and Unwin.

HMT (1976) *Report of Commissioners of Her Majesty's Inland Revenue for the Year Ended 31 March 1975*, Cmnd 6302, London, HMSO.

Inland Revenue (1993) *Inland Revenue Statistics 1992*, London, HMSO.

Johansson, P.-O. (1991) *An Introduction to Welfare Economics*, Cambridge, Cambridge University Press.

Keynes, J.M. (1984) *The Collected Writings of John Maynard Keynes*, Vol.9, Essays in Persuasion, London, Macmillan.

Kotlikoff, L.J. (1988) 'Intergenerational transfers and savings', *Journal of Economic Perspectives*, Spring; 2,2, pp.41–58.

Lever, H. (1984) 'Introduction' to Hay, D.A. and Morris D.J. (1984) *Unquoted Companies: Their Contribution to the UK Economy*, London, Macmillan.

Meade, J. (1964) *Efficiency, Equality and the Ownership of Property*, London, George, Allen and Unwin.

Modigliani, F. (1988) 'The role of intergenerational transfers and life cycle saving in the accumulation of wealth', *Journal of Economic Perspectives*, Spring; 2,2; pp.15–40.

Morck, R.K. (1992) 'Corporate ownership and management', in Eatwell, J., Milgate, M. and Newman, P. (eds), *The New Palgrave Dictionary of Money and Finance*, London, Macmillan.

Nozick, R. (1974) *Anarchy, State and Utopia*, Oxford, Basil Blackwell.

OECD (1988) *Taxation of Net Wealth, Capital Transfers and Capital Gains of Individuals*, Paris, OECD.

Pechman, J. (1987) 'Inheritance taxes' in Eatwell, J., Milgate, M. and Newman, P. (eds), *The New Palgrave*, London, Macmillan.

Polachek, S.W. and Siebert, W.S. (1993) *The Economics of Earnings*, Cambridge, Cambridge University Press.

Sandford, C. (1979) 'The wealth tax debate' in Field, F. (ed.), *The Wealth Report*, London, Routledge and Kegan Paul.

Sandford, C. (1983) 'Capital taxes—present, past and future', *Lloyds Bank Review*, October, 150; pp.34–47.

SBRC (1992) *The State of British Enterprise*, Small Business Research Centre, University of Cambridge.

Shaw, C. (1993) 'Patterns of success: twentieth century entrepreneurs in the Dictionary of Business Biography', Discussion Paper 114, Centre for Economic Performance, LSE.

Storey, D. (1993) 'A review of research on the factors influencing the death of small firms', Discussion Paper, Warwick Business School.

Sutherland, A. (1981) 'Capital Transfer Tax: an obituary', *Fiscal Studies*, November; 2,3; pp.37–51.

Venables, R. (1992) 'The taxation of trust income—back to first principles', *Fiscal Studies*, Feb; 13,1; pp.106–115.

Whitehouse, C. and Stuart-Buttle (1987) *Revenue Law—Principles and Practice*, 5th edn, London, Butterworths.

Wolff, E.N. (1987) 'Pensions and social security in the US' in Wolff (ed.), *International Comparisons of the Distribution of Household Wealth*, Oxford, Oxford University Press.

9 The Macroeconomics of Equality, Stability and Growth

Dan Corry and Andrew Glyn

1 Our thanks to Andrea Boltho and Wendy Carlin for their very helpful comments.

2 The data for the period up to 1973 in this section are drawn primarily from Kuznets (1966) Maddison (1991), Sawyer (1982), Glyn (1992a), Mishel, and Frankel (1991) and the sources cited in Figure 9.2.

3 It has been argued that rapid growth may require instability in that it is through recessions that inefficient enterprises are driven out and that it is 'over-investment' in booms which keeps up a high rate of productivity growth (see Boltho 1991). On the other hand instability may undermine the long-term economic relations (between firms and suppliers, or workers and employers) which may support high productivity levels (see Womack et al., 1991, p.250) and may, through the uncertainty engendered, reduce the level of investment. The relationship between instability and growth is not pursued further here.

4 The median standard deviation of growth rates for OECD countries was 2.0 for 1960–73, 2.6 for 1973–79 and 1.9 for 1979–93 (the measure of absolute variability). Allowing for the slowdown in average growth rates the corresponding coefficients of variation are 0.4, 0.9, 0.8; assessed in this way relative variability was still much higher after 1979 than during the golden age. For the UK absolute variability was greater after 1979 than before 1973 (the standard deviations being 1.7, 2.9, 2.4). These figures are calculated from OECD *National Accounts 1960–91* Vol.1 and OECD *Economic Outlook*, December 1992.

5 'The Social Left Today' IPPR lecture, 24 November 1992. The *Financial Times* ingeniously stood this argument on its head just before the 1992 election saying that Labour's proposals to increase taxation of the better off would smother the recovery by reducing the credit-worthiness of those sections of the population in a position to borrow most and launch a consumer boom!

References

Alesina, A. and Rodrick, D. (1992) 'Distribution, Political conflict and Economic growth' in Cuckierman, A., Hercowitz, Z. and Leiderman, L. (eds), *Political Economy, Growth and Business Cycles*, Cambridge MA, MIT Press.

Atkinson, A. (1993) 'What is happening to the distribution of income in the UK' STICERD Discussion Paper No.87.

Atkinson, A., Gordon, J. and Harrison, A. (1989) 'Trends in the shares of top wealth owners in Britain, 1923–1981', *Oxford Bulletin of Economics and Statistics*, 51.2, pp.315–32.

Bauer, J. and Mason, A. (1992) 'The Distribution of Income and Wealth in Japan', *Review of Income and Wealth*, December.

Boltho, A. (1989) 'Did policy activism work' *European Economic Review*, Vol.3, 33, pp.1709–26.

Boltho, A. (1991) 'A century of Japanese Business Cycles' *Journal of the Japanese and International Economies*, Vol.5, pp.282–97.

Borooah, V. (1988) 'Income Distribution, Consumption Patterns and Economic Outcomes in the UK', *Contributions to Political Economy*, Vol.8.

Davis, S. (1993) 'Cross-country patterns of changes in relative wages', in *NBER Macroeconomics Annual* 1993.

Garrison, C. and Lee, F.-Y. (1992) 'Taxation, Aggregate Activity and Growth', *Economic Inquiry*, Vol.20, No.1.

Glyn, A. (1992a) 'The Costs of Stability: the advanced capitalist countries in the 1980s' *New Left Review*, September–October 1992.

Glyn, A. (1992b) 'The Productivity Miracle, Profits and Investment' in J.Michie (ed.), *The Economic Legacy 1979–92*, London, Academic Press.

Gottshalk, P. (1993) 'Changes in Inequality in Family Income' *American Economic Review*, May.

Green, F. and Henley, A. and Tsakalotos, E. (1992) 'Income Inequality in Corporatist and Liberal Economies: A Comparison of Trends within OECD Economies' University of Kent Studies in Economics 92/13.

Kuznets, S. (1966) *Modern Economic Growth*, New Haven, Yale University Press.

Levy, F. and Murnane, R. (1992) 'US Earnings Levels and Earnings Inequality', *Journal of Economic Literature*, 30, pp.1331–81.

Maddison, A. (1991) *Dynamic Forces in Capitalist Development*, Oxford, Oxford University Press.

Marglin S. and Schor, J. (1990) *The Golden Age of Capitalism*, Oxford, Oxford University Press.

Mishel, L., and Frankel, D. (1991) *The State of Working America*, New York, M.E. Sharpe.

OECD (1989) *Historical Statistics*, annual.

OECD (1989) *The Future of Social Protection*.

OECD (1989) *Economies in Transition*.

O'Higgins, M. and Jenkins, S. (1990) 'Poverty in the EEC' in Teekens R. and Von Praag, V. (eds), *Analysing Poverty in the European Community*, Brussels.

Persson, T. and Tabellini, G. (1992) 'Growth, Distribution and politics' in Cuckierman et al., op cit.

Rossi, N. and Toniolo, G. (1993) *Italy's economic performance 1945–92* mimeo.

Rowthorn, R. and Glyn, A. (1990) 'The diversity of unemployment experience since 1973' in Marglin and Schor (eds), op. cit.

Sawyer, M. (1982) 'Income Distribution and the Welfare State' in Boltho, A. (ed.), *The European Economy: Growth and Crisis Economies.*

Seers, D. (1950) *The Levelling of Incomes since 1938*, Oxford.

Smeeding, T. and Coder, J. (1993) 'Income Inequality in Rich Countries during the 1980s' Eastern Economics Association Conference.

Womack, J., Jones, D., Ross, D. and Carpenter, D. (1991) *The Machine that changed the World*, Harper Collins, New York.

Woolff, E. and Marley, M. (1989) 'Long-run trends in US Wealth Inequality' in Lipsey, R.E. and Tice, H.S. (eds), *The Measurement of Savings, Investment and Wealth*, pp.765–844, University of Chicago Press.